Mainstreaming Ethics in Higher Education

The Teacher: Between Knowledge Transmission

and Human Formation

Vol. 2

Mainstreaming Ethics in Higher Education

The Teacher: Between Knowledge Transmission and Human Formation

Vol. 2

Obiora Ike / Justus Mbae / Chidiebere Onyia / Herbert Makinda (Eds.)

Globethics.net Education Ethics No. 7

Globethics.net Education Ethics

Director: Prof. Dr Obiora F. Ike, Executive Director of Globethics.net in Geneva and Professor of Ethics at the Godfrey Okoye University Enugu/Nigeria.
Series Editors: Divya Singh, Director of Globethics.net Southern Africa. Chief Academic Officer at Stadio Holdings, South Africa.
Christoph Stückelberger, President and Founder of Globethics.net, Executive Director of Geneva Agape Foundation GAF, Professor of Ethics in Moscow/ Russia, Enugu/Nigeria, Beijing/China.

Globethics.net Education Ethics Series 7
Obiora Ike / Justus Mbae / Chidiebere Onyia / Herbert Makinda (Eds.),
Mainstreaming Ethics in Higher Education. The Teacher: Between Knowledge Transmission and Human Formation, Vol. 2
Geneva: Globethics.net, 2021
ISBN 978-2-88931-383-9 (online version)
ISBN 978-2-88931-384-6 (print version)

Managing Editor: Ignace Haaz
Assistant Editor: Nefti Bempong-Ahun

Globethics.net International Secretariat
150 route de Ferney
1211 Geneva 2, Switzerland
Website: *www.globethics.net/publications*
Email: *publications@globethics.net*

All web links in this text have been verified as of February 2021.

TABLE OF CONTENTS

PREFACE

Obiora F Ike/Justus Mbae/Chidiebere Onyia/Herbert Makinda

In the first volume of our book, titled *"Mainstreaming Ethics in Higher Education – Research Ethics in administration, Finance, Education, Environment and Law",* published under the Globethics.net Education Ethics series, the editors indicated that a second volume would follow. This project is part of the result of those efforts made by Globethics.net Geneva, to lead the integration of Ethics in Higher Education globally, through ensuring that a conference with training held in March 2018 at the Catholic University of East Africa (CUEA), Nairobi Kenya reached a global audience. The book captured the potential for sharing of knowledge, triggering interdisciplinary collaboration and research. It is our joy as editors to present the second volume of this project. Higher Education institutions and their universities play vital roles in contributing to a better world.

These interdisciplinary works on ethical reflection address the needs of teachers and professionals, and show the urgency of preparing the next generation of leadership at all levels, with persons grounded and founded in ethical integrity. The lack of Ethics has remained one of the biggest challenges for a world without corruption, which is the bane of many societies, political groups, technologies, businesses, economies, law and research.

Ethics permeates every sphere of life and every activity so that no aspect of human life is beyond or above ethics. Not even witchcraft! On November 2019, the University of Nigeria Nsukka (UNN) held a controversial two-day conference on witchcraft despite prayers, fasting, strong opposition from Christians and social media. Under immense pressure, the conference organizers were forced to change the theme of the conference from the original "*Witchcraft: Meaning, Factors and Practices", to a new theme on "Dimensions of human behaviours*". So, is ethics relevant to the practice of witchcraft? Certainly! Anything that has to do with human behaviour is a subject of ethical consideration. The issues dealt with in the second volume of *Mainstreaming Ethics in Higher Education* clearly demonstrate this fact.

The articles contained in this volume cover a wide variety of issues ranging from religion, ethics, education, commercial entrepreneurship, leadership, corruption, witchcraft and fundraising for climate change. All authors emphasise the importance of mainstreaming ethics in the teaching of higher education, as a way of preparing students and professionals to live their ethical lives in full. The authors also address down-to-earth issues concerning the nature of ethics. While some of the chapters focus on the understanding of ethics and its relationship with the various other aspects of life, others concentrate on the methods and strategies of effectively teaching ethics, and on ways of ensuring that this teaching is not just another theoretical acquisition among other. Teaching should be a formation that ensures the graduates of universities develop skills and attitudes that help them to live as ethical professionals, and models for the rest of society.

The teacher is crucial to the success of ethics education, and programs in schools and universities. Unlike certain schools, where designated teachers are charged with the responsibility of teaching values and ethics, every lecturer and every professor in the university, is by virtue of their position, both an academic and a moral educator. As such, he/she must be expected to play an important role in ensuring that the students are ethically formed to live the life of morals and virtue. In addition to the academic qualifications that these teachers may hold, it is necessary that they should also be ethical exemplars for emulation. They must be models to be emulated by their students. This is in recognition of the fact that teachers are always teaching, even when they may not be conscious that they are. The most effective method of teaching is not the saying, but the doing. Students learn more from what teachers do than what they say!

Teachers must also understand the basics of values and ethics, such as the skill of ethical decision-making, and they must be willing to teach these skills along with ethical attitudes to their students. All this has serious implications for the way in which teachers are trained, as well as how they are recruited, selected and hired.

A couple of chapters in this volume allude to traditional African roots, and the traditional methods of education. We suggest that we could take a leaf out of their book, and learn from the effective methods used by African society. While they do not make a direct reference to the African philosophy of Ubuntu, which served to guide our African values and world-view, these authors lead us to reflect on the role of African identity, culture and values that seem to be conveniently forgotten. Perhaps a future study could be devoted to the importance of understanding our African identity and cultural roots, and how that can help Africans to better understand their roots, and perhaps fit in better within the globalized world in which we live today.

The authors of this volume are quite clear that it is not enough to introduce the teaching of ethics in our universities. That is only the first step. The goal is not achieved by simply adding one more course or programme to an existing university curriculum. The success of mainstreaming ethics in our universities must be measured by the degree of commitment of our graduates (read new professionals and leaders), to change our currently corrupt, unethical and unsustainable society, into one that respects integrity and honesty, and so guarantees sustainability for the future. Africa urgently needs people who will help transform our society by living a more ethical life. This transformation that our society so desperately needs can only come around when our learners commit to doing the right thing, because it is the right thing to do, and not because it profits them to do so.

1

THE ROLE OF LIBRARIES IN PROMOTING ETHICAL USE OF INFORMATION

Sarah W. Kibugi, Francis G. Nganga and Benjamin O. Kemboi

Introduction

Information ethics provides an ethical framework for library professionals to carry out information related works such as acquiring, storing, processing, making available and using information. [1,2,3]

Ethics is a branch of philosophy that is concerned with human conduct, more specifically the behaviour of individuals in society. Ethics examines the rational justification for our moral judgments; it studies what is morally right or wrong, just or unjust (Kaddu 2007).

With increasing recognition of information as one of the most important ingredients of development, more recently the term 'information ethics' has drawn attention from various quarters. Chuang and Chen (1999) views information ethics as one aspect of a much larger philosophy, known as social ethics. According to Chuang and Chen (1999), information ethics 'deals with the moral conduct of

---

[1]Sarah W. Kibugi, Director of the Library and Learning Resource Service, Technical University of Kenya.

[2] Francis G. Nganga, Assistant Counselor, Student Support Services, Catholic Technical University of Kenya.

[3] Benjamin O. Kemboi, Library Assistant, Technical University of Kenya.

information-users based on their responsibility and their accountability'. Free moral agents, individuals, organizations, and societies ought to be responsible for the actions they take.

Despite the presence of qualified professionals in libraries, and also rigorous campaigns by the library to uphold ethical standards in all spheres of information works, the question of information ethics is not widely recognized. The unprecedented explosion of information in all branches of knowledge, and massive proliferation of ICT tools and techniques have raised fundamental questions about privacy, freedom of expression, right to information and accessibility, among other issues. As a result, library and information professionals are struggling to solve the problems related to ethical use of information.

Information Ethics

Information ethics has been hugely affected by globalisation, which is characterized by extensive use of information and communication technologies, an increasingly open society, greater sharing of information, but also greater conflict among individuals and societies in asserting their dominance over others. This has posed new questions to the information professionals of today, because they have to serve an increasingly diverse group of clientele (Richard Mason 1986).

Information ethics investigates the ethical issues arising from the life cycle of information, including the generation, gathering, organization, retrieval, distribution and use of information (Cappurro 2008). As an interdisciplinary field of study, it relates among others to the fields of computer science, library and information science, philosophy, communication science, journalism and mass media. The focus areas include the right to privacy, the right of access to information, the right to intellectual property and the quality of information. Furthermore, information ethics addresses the moral conduct of information-users, based on their responsibility and their accountability. Free moral agents, individuals, organizations, and societies ought to be responsible for the actions they take.

Problem Statement

The ethical concerns of the libraries have been with regard to the freedom of access and use of information However; libraries have been sported to have greater functions in promoting the ethical use of information. Libraries promote ethical use of information in terms of provision of information, privacy of information, security of users' information, censorship and help avoid plagiarism, which is a risk to copyrighted information. Information through the librarians as the custodian is able to determine the kind of trend to be followed, so as to realize better services that is trusted by the public and users.

Ethical Use of Information

Ethics provide a framework for conducting essential information functions, such as instituting information policies and developing strategies for information services. Ethical conduct of information professionals is;

- Affirmation of the critical value of services
- Affirmation of responsibility to themselves and society
- Affirmation of respect for others
- Affirmation of the need to improve society

Ethics is the field of study that is concerned with questions of value. Ethical judgments are concerned with distinguishing "good" or "bad" behaviour in a given situation. Ethics include the standards, values, morals, principles, etc., that we use as the basis for our decisions or actions. In ethical decision making, there is often no clear "right" or "wrong" answer. The categories of ethical concern include the following:

Privacy and confidentiality

Privacy is a fundamental human right and a cornerstone of a democratic society. It is rooted in the foundation of law, the secret ballot, doctor patient confidentiality, lawyer-client privilege, the notion of private property, and the value our society places on the autonomy of the individual. Unfortunately, the growth of electronic technologies has challenged the ability of countries to ensure the privacy rights of their citizens. Many countries are concerned about the protection of their citizens' personal information, have adopted privacy laws and fair information practices. So, the ethical challenge is how to create institutions and procedures that foster this virtue, as an individual and social one, without falling into Big Brother nightmares. In this regard, Mason (1986) warns that

> "...more than 60,000 state and local agencies, for provide information to the National Crime Information Centre and it is accessed by law officers nearly 400,000 times a day. Yet studies show that over 4% of the stolen vehicle entries, 6% of the warrant entries, and perhaps as much as one half of the local law enforcement criminal history records are in error. At risk is the safety of the law enforcement officers who access it, the effectiveness of the police in controlling crime, and the freedom of the citizens whose names appear in the files. This leads to a concern for accuracy".

Accuracy and safety

Safe and accurate information can increase quality of information, which in turn leads to better consequences for both individuals and organizations. In fact, lack of accurate and safe information (misinformation) results in wrong and inaccurate decisions, as well as low quality performance, and existence of it results in good outputs.

Intellectual property versus plagiarism

In 1999, McFarland indicates that technological developments ignore the social role of the creator and of the work itself, thus overlooking their ethically significant relationships with the rest of society. The balance is lost. One could conclude that he emphasizes on necessity as a more balanced view. In this respect, WIPO1 (2002) has published a report entitled "*Intellectual property on the Internet: A survey of issues*" addresses the far-reaching impact that digital technologies (the Internet in particular) have had on intellectual property (IP) and the international IP system.

Access and equity

The rapid growth of electronic technology as a means of accessing information has led to increased concern over differences in access to information for various social, economic and ethnic groups. Smith, M. M. (1993), describe the right of freedom of access to information as essential, because without it, it is impossible to establish sustainable development. Access to information is thus a "common good, which must be distributed equally and according to developmental needs of people". Confirming low accessibility and inequity, Baker (2003) concludes that

> "...in a world where globalization, technological evolution, and fierce competition have led to the creation of new elite- those who are information rich, the knowledge workers- the vast majority of the world's population stands to be left behind. The failure to develop a new form of "social contract", which takes into account the information needs of citizens in developing countries, will have disastrous results for humanity as a whole. So, it is recommended that technological tools are used to

facilitate equitable access to information until such time as the imbalances can be equalized, and everyone has instant universal access".

Conflict of interest

Ethics are especially questioned in situations where there is a conflict of interests. Librarians and information professionals will face many situations where there may be conflict of interests, and they must rely on their professional standards and the values of the organization.

Freelancing is an area that is very controversial in information centres. There may be instances when an employee of the organization approaches the information professional with the request to help them research information for a project that is unrelated to their work. This employee may offer to pay the professional for their time. Through word of mouth this could potentially lead to more freelance work, and quite a bit of extra income for the information professional. There is nothing unethical about agreeing to do research, and for someone to pay you outside of work. However, the information professional must make sure that "outside of work" is where this freelancing remains. The biggest problem that information professional will face with freelancing, is how to avoid having it interfere with their duties at work (Hauptman 1988). The information professional of course can't do this outside research while at work, but they must also make sure that this outside research isn't keeping them up late at night or causing stress that could interfere with their performance at work (Hauptman 1988). There is also the issue of using the employer's databases to perform research, even if the librarian has the intention of reimbursing the company. The only way this is acceptable is if the information professional has permission from their supervisor (Hauptman 1988).

Another ethical issue that may arise involves consulting users. The information professional will sometimes be asked for advice as well as information. For example, a corporate information professional could be asked their advice on what stock to buy. A medical librarian will sometimes be asked for medical advice or even a diagnosis from patients, etc. (Hauptman 1988). Information professionals must avoid giving medical or legal advice to patrons, because the patron could hold the librarian and the organization responsible. There is a thin line between guiding a user and giving out advice. It is not just poor ethical practice to give out advice, it is also against the law, and so the information professional and organization could be held liable (Hauptman 1988). Information professionals should never put themselves in situation where they could risk legal action (Mintz 1991). Once the information professional reaches the point where the information being given is beyond facts or instruction, it is necessary to recommend the patron contact someone that is trained to help them (Hauptman 1988).

Factors that Influence Information Ethics

While the primary concern of the library and information professionals is information ethics, they also have to uphold their professional ethics. This relates to the application of principles to actions and decisions taken by information professionals. In today's world, the areas which directly and indirectly influence information ethics are:

- *Globalisation:* One of the most important features of modern society is globalization, which is characterized by extensive use of information and communication technologies, an increasingly open society, greater sharing of information and also greater conflict among individuals and societies in asserting their dominance over others.
- *More emphasis on individualism:* People tend to be more individualistic these days; they frequently place more importance upon individual good rather than social good. As a result, there

has been an increased demand for individualized and customized services from the library and information centres.

- *Privacy and information security:* With the increasing amount of networks, the security of public and private data held in databases, web sites and other information repositories are always at risk. People have become more worried about their privacy and libraries, as preservers and providers of sensitive information have to deal with this concern.
- *Diversification of 'information works':* Unlike their predecessors, today's library and information professionals are burdened with greater and bigger responsibilities. In addition to being information providers, they now frequently have to assume the roles of educators, consultants, technology experts, translators and synthesizers, among others. They must achieve new skills and capabilities for successfully performing these duties.
- *Conflict between 'right to information' and 'ethical use of information':* Many countries around the world have laws ensuring people's right to receiving and using information. However, library and information professionals find themselves in tricky situations, where they have to strike a balance between 'restricted use of information' and 'right to information'.
- *Access to information:* The issue of universal access to information may create a dilemma for many libraries. Many public and professional declarations refer unequivocally to free and public access to information. For example, the British Library Association code of conduct states that any individual should be granted free and public access to information. However, there is the risk that too great an emphasis on providing a service free of charge may result in funding problems, which could endanger the survival of information centres. Similarly, providing a service at zero cost often results in

its devaluation, which also has as a consequence the undermining of the prestige and feasibility of the profession.

Challenges of Libraries in Promoting the Ethical use of Information

Recruitment, education, and retention of librarians

The need to find and retain quality leadership for libraries is a key issue for the future. Even as retirements seem to increase, fewer librarians are entering the profession as a whole, and even fewer librarians are entering the academic library field in particular. Ensuring education of new librarians and re-educating existing librarians with skills and knowledge to support new roles in a digital information age, especially roles involving teaching and library promotion, is a challenge for the profession as well as ethical information.

Creation of digital resources and their preservation

Methods to determine what should be digitized, to find resources to do the work and to develop appropriate bibliographic control mechanisms for digital materials offer complex challenges. In addition, librarians want to ensure that digital materials are preserved appropriately and that permanent access to those materials can be provided.

Impact of information technology on library services

Librarians are aware that an appropriate institutional balance needs to be maintained between traditional library materials and services, and those services (which sometimes overlap) represented by instructional and information technology departments.

Conclusion

Arguments have been made that sanctions need to be written into a new code of ethics to make sure librarians behave ethically. Lanier (1993) discusses how a code can be enforced when ethics is so subjective.

. It is self-evident that there are additional ethical and moral issues influenced by new information technologies, which should be addressed. Considering above issues, it can be concluded that only identifying such problems is not a solution, but rather providing global strategies and recommendations, which promote equity, justice, accessibility, privacy and accuracy.

References

Chuang, C. & Chen, J. C. (1999).Issues in information ethics and educational policies for the coming age. *Journal of Industrial Technology.* 15 (4), 2-6.

Hauptman,Robert. *Ethical Challenges in Librarianship.* Phoenix: Oryx Press, 1988.

Kaddu, S. B. (2007). Information ethics: A student's perspective. *Information Review of Information Ethics,* Vol. 7 (9/2007), 1-6.

Lanier, Gene D.(1993). *ALA's Committee on Professional Ethics: An Insider's View.* North Carolina Libraries, Vol. 51, No. 1, 9-10.

Mason, R. O., 1986. Four ethical issues of the information age. *MIS Quarterly*, 10(1): 5–12.

Mintz, Anne. (1991) "Ethics and the news librarian" *Special Libraries* v82 n1, 7(5) Available on Infotrac One File

Smith, Martha M. (1993). *Information Ethics: Freedom, Democracy, Responsibility*. North Carolina Libraries, Vol. 51, No. 1, 4-8.

2

TEACHING ETHICS IN HIGHER EDUCATION: WHICH APPROACH?

Crispin Ong'era Isaboke

Introduction

The need for ethical consciousness is becoming increasingly desirable in the world, and especially in Kenya, today more than ever before.[4] Every time corruption is mentioned, for example, in the transport sector where traffic officers solicit for bribes shamelessly, when people deliberately cheat on their taxes, or when banks are involved with insider trading (like it recently happened recently with Chase Bank), it raises questions on ethics. Is it due to lack of ethical knowledge that all these ills are so rampant in our society? Is it a lack of values or moral education that is the cause of all these? It calls to mind the Socratic question whether values can be taught; and whether knowledge is really virtue.

In 2015, the President of the Republic of Kenya, H.E. Uhuru Muigai Kenyatta, addressed the state and reiterated the need for Ethics be taught in all levels of learning (which I interpret to have meant that it be taught right form Primary One all the way to institutions of Higher Learning). The reasoning was that at the end of their training, students would not only have attained the necessary skills for the job market, but

---

[4] Crispin Ong'era Isaboke, Assistant Lecturer, Chuka University, Kenya.

will have also nurtured an ethical culture, which should in turn make them better and patriotic citizens. Therefore, should Kenyans be ethically conscious, they would act ethically, more or less with the same way as the Socratic thinking know virtue is to be virtuous. Whether or not that would be the best approach, institutions of learning are yet to heed that call.

Nevertheless, the following questions remain: does knowledge really (necessarily) translate into action? To what extent and in which ways can we teach ethics? And, what kind of approach should be employed to ensure that proper ethic is taught, and who, therefore, should be the teachers?

The aim of this chapter is to interrogate whether ethical teaching should be based on values (value education), or whether it should be founded on the reasoning that informs ethical judgments. Should the teaching be on what ethical values there are (that ought to be done), or on how to arrive at (good) ethical judgments, a reasoning that should always guide us in making ethical decisions? In other words, is it the values or the training of conscience that should be the point of focus?

Knowledge of Virtue vs. Being Virtuous

This part deals with the relationship between knowledge of the good (virtue) and doing the good thing (being virtuous). The basic question answered here is the question of whether having knowledge of virtue makes one a virtuous person. The section spells the domain of ethics as a discipline, and attempts to answer the question of whether ethics can be taught.

Knowledge of Virtue

In *Saturday Nation* of May 14, 2016, an article from the leading newspaper in Kenya, titled "Networks stifle probe on graft", revealed information from a strategy the document. With regard to the new team of commissioners at the Ethics and Anti-Corruption Commission chaired by Mr. Philip Kinisu,it "exposes the rot and the systematic failures at the Commission and proposes new ways of fighting corruption."[5] According to that revelation, the EACC is deeply infiltrated by criminal networks which have made it difficult to prosecute prominent people mentioned in graft scandals. Yet,

> "...efforts to get rid of the individuals working for corruption networks through fresh vetting have been blocked after a section of employees moved to court and obtained an injunction...."[6]

According to the report, the Commission chairman and his team wanted the agency's annual budget increased from sh. 2.5 billion to sh. 6 billion (an increase of 140%), to pave way for fresh restructuring. The reason for his claim was that the failure to adequately fund the commission had opened it up to infiltration by corruption cartels, making it difficult to fight the vice.

> "The commission is infiltrated with people sponsored to frustrate investigations...what ails the commission are vested interests...manifested in poor investigations and weak charge sheets. For this reason, charges preferred against suspects in most cases fail to stand the scrutiny of top lawyers hired by suspects."[7]

He further adds that new ways have to be devised, whereby success against corruption shall be defined by laying emphasis on changing the attitude of the people.

What clearly transpires from the above is the fact that it is implied that what is instrumental to the fight against corruption is enough

---

[5] Saturday Nation May 14, 2016.

[6] Ibid.

[7] Ibid.

funding to the agency that fights the vice. Lack of enough funding is seen to be the main cause of shoddy investigations and failure of cases against graft suspects to stand. But there is also raised concern to change people's perception. The latter concern is of more interest for this paper: how are attitudes changed?

Ethics, which is etymologically derived from the Greek word *ethos* or *ethikos*, meaning *character*; which translates to the Latin *mores*, meaning *customs* or *habits of a person*, is generally defined as the science of morals. It is that kind of knowledge that studies human conduct (*actus humanus*) from the aspect of their rightness or wrongness. In other words, what is it that makes a certain kind of conduct morally good and what is it that makes conduct morally evil? Are there acts that are good or bad in themselves? How do we determine the morality of an action? Is there a standard criterion by which we establish the moral worth of an act?

It must be borne in mind that ethics, as defined, is founded on both the fact that man is *free* by virtue of the possession of the faculty of free will, and has the natural desire for *happiness* as the *summum bonum* or his highest good. Both have a mutually necessary relationship, to the extent that the freedom of man is fully realized only when it directs man toward his last end; otherwise, it becomes an abuse of freedom to direct it toward other ends (away from the last end). Human action is purposive, and *ipso facto,* it finds meaning in that purpose alone.

It should not escape our minds, though, that action presupposes knowledge of both virtue and vice. One can only make a free choice of what he knows, not vice-versa. Joseph Nyasani, in his *Metaphysical Psychology: Rational Psychology* argues that the intellect "…is the capacity…of the mind whose task it is to understand, think and reason…. It also happens to be the faculty from which the will flows."[8]

---

[8] Joseph M. Nyasani, *Metaphysical Psychology: Rational Psychology* (Nairobi: Consolata Institute of Philosophy Press, 2013) p.27.

From the above quote, it is abundantly evident that will, which is a free act, proceeds from intellect. One cannot will what they do not know. It follows therefore that before free choice and action, knowledge of value is essential. In essence, it is an irrefutable fact that before decision and action or implementation, the important process of deliberation takes place. Within this process, one weighs the options of doing one action as against the other, and then eventually decides to perform one and forgo the other. All this is meant to show that knowledge is a necessary requirement for decision and action.

Socrates, one of the greatest Greek philosophers, clearly pointed out that knowledge of virtue is a *sine qua non* condition for being virtuous. That is to say, it is impossible to be a virtuous person if you have no idea of what virtue is. Put in another language, Socrates equated knowledge with virtue or wisdom:

> "...the close connection between virtue and knowledge is characteristic of Socrates and Plato."[9] According to Socrates, "no man sins wittingly and therefore only knowledge is needed to make all men perfectly virtuous."[10]

In his view, evil is a result of ignorance, not deliberate.

In spite of the fact that we may not agree with Socrates when he goes further to claim that knowledge necessarily leads to virtue, it would be defeatist of us to deny that one requires knowledge of virtue as a necessary condition, to be virtuous.

This, in essence, calls the question of ethical education: is it moral education that we need to make people virtuous/ moral, or is there more to virtuous life than education can provide? If moral education does not

---

[9] Bertrand Russell, *History of Western Philosophy.* London: Routledge, 1999) p. 109.

[10] *Ibid.*

end up in transforming individuals, do we need it any way, particularly in the education system? Is it not waste of time to take the precious time of learners to teach them what is not going to make any impact in their productive lives?

In his *Virtue Ethics,* Aristotle, another ancient philosopher of great repute, argues that it is the virtuous or good and wise person who is the criterion and standard of virtue or goodness. That is to say that we learn virtue from virtuous men and women by emulating them. In his view, "virtues are character traits it's good for a human being to have, good in the sense of contributing to their possessor's well-being or happiness."[11] In this understanding, virtues are habits that constitute a person and define them. In addition, he sees virtue as a means by which a person achieves happiness or flourishes. In essence, therefore, virtue must not be chosen for itself as an end, but as a means to the end; the purpose of human action is to achieve happiness (*eudaemonia*). On the contrary, a vice "makes it more difficult for its possessor to achieve happiness or a satisfactory state of well-being."[12] Be that what it may, vice is not necessarily evil, but a choice of pleasure for itself. Disconnect between our free act from the ultimate end is what makes action evil.

For the philosopher, you cannot ask a vicious person of what virtue is, because they will show you what they practice as virtue. It is the good man who knows best about goodness, for the man of good character judges every situation rightly; in every situation, what appears to him is good. In his view, we are pulled both by pleasure and by happiness. For this reason, some choose a life of searching for pleasures of the flesh and their low form of human life. Others know the good but are weak-willed and do not do it. He here recognizes the force of habit; it takes repeated acts of bravery to attain the habit of bravery; then it is

---

[11] Emmett Barcalow, *Moral Philosophy: Theories and Issues* (Thomson: Wadsworth, 2007) p. 118.

[12] *Ibid.*

easy and pleasurable to be brave. Moreover, it takes many acts of stealing to turn you into a habitual thief; there after it is easy to steal. To change from that to become an honest person again is a long and difficult process. Thus, training is necessary for building a virtuous habit.

Teaching Virtue

Men are potentially knowers and have the ability to exploit or actualize those intellective potentialities. They also have the ability to constitute themselves as good persons by consistently practicing virtue. In other words, being a good person is something that must be cultivated by acting rightly all the time. From the above, it therefore follows that virtue can be taught, and to the extent that knowledge is necessary for deliberation and choice of the course of action to take. Put in another language, it would be illogical to expect that people would act virtuously when they have no knowledge of virtue; even though that does not necessarily imply that knowing will lead to doing. It is obviously true (as against Socrates) that ignorance is not necessarily the reason why people commit evil. More often than not, man chooses his course of action, regardless of whether it is good or not, with full knowledge of the nature of the action. He does so deliberately, knowingly and wilfully. In any case, every human culture spontaneously operates in a framework of morality. There is no known culture that is devoid of ethics and values. Ethical training has been one of the core functions of culture through proverbs, sayings, rituals and various practices. All this underscores the importance of ethical education in society, hence, the need to extend the same to institutions of higher learning.

The point of moral or ethical education in that regard is to make what is implicit, through the moral obligation, explicit. To be clearer about how we operate in the moral sphere, this is imperative to us as rational beings.

Hence, ethical teaching link human freedom with man's last end. Moral education is necessary since knowledge is a pre-requisite for action: emphasis should be on the fact that human conduct has an end, such as happiness, the highest good, and that the only way this can be achieved is by leading a virtuous life. We are pulled by both pleasure (short-term) and happiness (lasting), and it is therefore necessary that learners be trained on the need to choose pleasure only if it can lead them to their ultimate end, happiness. It is for these reasons that it is very important to base ethical education on the moral obligation, whereby it is undeniable that good ought to be done and evil avoided.

Ethical Education: Toward the Moral Obligation

Having seen that knowledge of virtue is a pre-requisite for acting virtuously, and that virtue can be taught since man is potentially a knower; this part discusses ethical education in the light of the moral obligation. That is, all moral education must be an education that is directed toward the moral obligation. The reason for this is that we intend to form a person (the learner) who can reason correctly in moral issues; yet morality is founded on the fact that man has an obligation to (always) do good and avoid evil. This is a reality that resides in the very rational nature of man.

Moral Obligation

It is an obvious fact, that there is a moral obligation, which is the source of goodness, and which commands that good be done and evil avoided. This command has been known as the golden rule.. It is a dictate of reason that good should be done, not once, or twice, not many times; but always. That means that good has to be done as a duty of our rational nature.

Immanuel Kant, a German philosopher of the modern period, rightly observed that right is right and it must be done 'even if the heavens fall.'

In his understanding, there will be no circumstances that will change the morality of an act either from good to evil or from evil to good; and given that happiness is the *summum bonum* or the greatest good that is only attained through virtue, no compromise should be allowed with regard to acting in accordance to reason. Kant says:

> "there is one end, however, which may be assumed to be actually such to all rational beings…and, therefore, one purpose which they not merely may have, but which we may with certainty assume that they all actually have by a natural necessity, and this is happiness."[13]

He rightly observes, just like Aristotle had done, that happiness is the greatest good of man and that it is attained through virtue.

The intention of Kant was to find the one source of moral obligation that will be universal for all human beings. He observes, and rightly so, that the moral obligation is in rationality itself. In his monumental *Fundamental Principles of Metaphysic Morality*, he says, "it is impossible to think of anything in the world, or indeed even beyond, that could be considered good without qualification except a good will."[14] The only ultimate good, then, is a good will. This is the case for the reason that

"a good will is not good because of what it effects or accomplishes, because of its fitness to attain some proposed end, but only because of its volition, that is, it is good in itself and, regarded for itself, is to be valued incomparably higher than all that could merely be brought about

---

[13] Daniel Bonevac (ed.) *Today's Moral Issues: Classic and Contemporary Perspectives* (London: McGraw Hill, 2005) p. 33.

[14] Immanuel Kant, *Groundwork of the Metaphysics of Morals*, Mary Gregor Ed., (Cambridge: Cambridge University Press, 2008) p. 7.

by it in favour of some inclination and indeed, if you will, of the sum of all inclinations."[14]

Thus, a good will is a will which acts for the sake of duty and not one that acts in accordance with duty. He stresses on the idea of duty, where he purifies it from selfish motives and inclinations. Alternatively, we have an inclination to seek happiness but if actions are done for the sake of happiness, then, even though they are done in accordance with duty they are not done for the sake of duty, and therefore have no moral worth whatsoever. To obey the law simply for fear of being imprisoned then that has no moral worth whatsoever and is not done for the sake of duty. Thus, only those acts that are done for the sake of duty have moral worth. Kant sees duty as the necessity of acting of reverence of the law.

It is clearly evident that a moral obligation exists by virtue of which morally good acts are objectively so, if they conform to it; and morally bad acts are objectively so, if they do not conform to it. It is for these reasons that it is not only important but also necessary that moral education be founded upon, and be directed toward the moral obligation. What that means is that all such education must aim at making the learner understand that the moral obligation is natural and therefore objective, and that all human conduct must conform to it. In other words, our actions must always be good because only then do we act virtuously and constitutes us as rational beings. On the other hand, evil must be avoided by all means for the reason that it is against the moral obligation, and thus, against our rational nature. It goes without saying that the moral obligation connects the human act with man's last end, *happiness*; man naturally wants to be happy, therefore the calling to act rightly, that being the only way happiness can be attained.

The above raises the question of how we can determine virtuous action. Accordingly, to determine the moral worth of an act, three important aspects are considered and evaluated. These are: the act itself, the motive, and the circumstances.

Necessary Conditions for a Morally Good Act

In this section, we look at the guide to morally good acts. We deliberate on those necessary conditions for a morally good act and how they should be evaluated while making ethical judgments. Ethical judgments are judgments about morality, hence, the focus here is what one should consider in judging human act as good or evil. It would be important, though, to begin by making a distinction between *human acts* and *acts of man* before we can deal with the criterion of moral goodness.

Human Acts and Acts of Man

Before we can discuss the necessary conditions of a morally good act, a distinction between human acts and acts of man is imperative to make. A human act (*actus humanus)* is the act of which man is master, one that is consciously controlled and deliberately willed, so that the agent is held responsible for it. It is the kind of act that distinguishes man from animals and therefore is specifically human. They define man as rational free being, for example, stealing, murder, abortion, and helping. An act of man (*actus hominis)* refers to the act which a man happens to perform, but he is not master of it, for he has not consciously controlled it, has not deliberately willed it, and for it he is not held responsible. These are the acts that man shares with animals, for example, *sneezing*, *walking*, and *eating*. Such acts have no moral significance and do not constitute human conduct. Morality, therefore, deals not with acts of man but with free acts, human acts, commonly referred to as conduct. Ethics, as a branch of philosophy, deals with the study of moral values. It is "an examination of all human conduct…."[15]

---

[15] Austin Fagothey, *Right and Reason: Ethics in Theory and Practice Based on the Teachings of Aristotle and St. Thomas,* 2nd Ed. (Charlotte, North Carolina, 2000), p. 20.

Evidently, free choices or acts are the ones for which man is held responsible because he is in control of them. Chris Horner and Emrys Westacott, in their book, *Thinking Through Philosophy: An Introduction*, hold that "when I make certain choices, whether they are trivial or momentous, it usually seems to me that I could have chosen otherwise and am thus responsible for my decision."[16] In effect, this means that one is held accountable of their acts if they are able to do otherwise, for only then can we question them why they did them in the way they did. If one's action were to be of necessity, then it would not make sense to ask anyone to take responsibility. Such then are voluntary acts which man can opt to do or not. They differentiate man from animals and are contrasted to involuntary acts because they are specifically human. They are human acts, not acts of man. For Nyasani reiterates, "all human acts as opposed to acts of man are voluntary, deliberated and consciously undertaken. They take place as a result of some conscious and voluntarily willed decision and hence create unshakeable moral, legal and social responsibility for an individual."[17] In addition, "the person who will not accept responsibility does not understand the true scope and meaning of his freedom, is not fully in possession of it, or is perhaps afraid of it."[18] This also implies that freedom translates into choosing the right course of action, making freedom and responsibility two sides of the same coin. In other words, freedom is the moral necessity to do the good; the two cannot be separated.

In the understanding of Thomas Aquinas, a Mediaeval Philosopher, "…since those acts are properly called human which are voluntary, because the will is the rational appetite, which is proper to man, we must

---

[16] Chris Horner and Emrys Westacott, *Thinking Through Philosophy: An Introduction* (New York: Cambridge University Press, 2009), p. 7.

[17] Nyasani 31.

[18] Burke 24.

consider acts in so far as they are voluntary."[19] This gives the further implication that such acts are free and deliberate acts of the will. Human acts are acts that man does and is in control of while acts of man are those acts that man does but is not in control of. It therefore follows that human acts are a product of free choices while acts of man are not. In that regard, man cannot be held responsible for acts of man. For example, you cannot ask a person why they have fallen sick but we can ask them why they steal. In answering the question of what constitutes a morally good act, we must adhere to the necessary components.

Criterion of Moral Goodness

By criterion we mean a standard, a yardstick, something by which we can measure something. This section deals with the standard of moral goodness, or the criterion to judge the rightness or wrongness of human acts.

A morally good act must agree with right reason. Yet to agree with right reason means that one's act agrees with knowledge that one has: if one knows that an act is good, then he performs that act since he is also implicitly aware of the obligation to do good and avoid evil. If the act is evil, one must refrain from performing it for the same reason of the consciousness of moral obligation.

The learners in institutions of Higher Learning should, therefore, be taught on what to look for in an act (whatever it is) to see whether it is in agreement or disagreement with good reason. What must we look for in the act to see whether it is in agreement or disagreement with reason?

To answer, we must break down the human act into its elements. We now seek those elements which can be the sources of harmony or conflict between the act and the reason. We may consider the act itself in its own very nature as an act, or we may consider the circumstances in

---

[19] Summa Theolgiae I, I, q.6.

which it is performed.[20] Among the circumstances, we may single out one, the motive or intention of the agent, as of such importance as to be put in a class by itself. Two people may do the same thing but from different motives, or different things from the same motive, or the same thing from the same motive but in different circumstances. In each case the act can have a different morality because of a different combination of these three elements.

Hence, considering the act itself, that is before looking at the motive for it or the surrounding circumstances, it is morally imperative that it be good or indifferent. An act that is evil in itself (intrinsically) cannot acquire goodness from the motive or the circumstances, for then, it would go against the golden rule that the (good) end does not justify the (bad) means used to attain it. It would as well imply that good can be obtained from evil, which is absurd. It is ethically imperative that evil should never be chosen for itself as an end, or even a means to an end; evil should never be deliberately willed and freely chosen.

Alternatively, if we look at the motive of the act in question, we also affirm that one must have a good motive in performing the act. To do a good act with a bad motive would be evil, for the reason that good would not have been done because it is good but because of the bad motive attached. For example, one cannot distribute money to poor people, which is a good thing, with the motive of convincing them to vote for him as a member of parliament.

Furthermore, when it comes to circumstances, they must also be good or rather necessary in the sense that there must be no any other possible option but to act in that manner. Circumstances cannot be necessary where an alternative way of acting is possible.

---

[20] Fagothey, p. 35.

Conclusion

To conclude, therefore, we must agree that though moral or ethical education does not necessarily lead to acting virtuously, however, it is a *sine qua non* condition for acting so; for knowledge precedes deliberation (due to the free will), decision, and implementation or action. In order for one to make a decision and implement the same, they must first need to have knowledge of fact, i.e., whether an act is good or not. And on the understanding that man has the natural call to do good and avoid evil, people with good knowledge will always make informed decisions; even when they do evil, they will do so knowingly, and therefore, must take responsibility.

Besides, ethics in higher learning can be taught by encouraging learners to put into practice the knowledge they gain in theoretical learning so that they can constitute themselves as good persons and persons of integrity. They should learn that it is a good thing to be a good person and be a criterion of moral goodness. They should strive to make virtue a habit, as Aristotle says, by consistently doing the good. This part should therefore consist of persons who have lived a good life to serve as role models and examples to be emulated.

It is my strong believe that if ethics in Higher Institutions of Learning takes this perspective, it will surely go a long way in transforming our society to make it the perfect society that we always dream about in demanding for constitutional amendments or reviews.

To the question of who should teach, I find it imperative that the teachers of ethics in higher education must be good moral thinkers (of course philosophers); while people of good character shall also play part as role models. In other words, on the part of theory we need people who can teach learners on good and correct moral reasoning while we need good role models on the part of practice. But, if there be good moral thinkers who also internalize and practice what they teach and constitute themselves as good persons, those should be preferable.

References

Barcalow, Emmett. *Moral Philosophy: Theories and Issues* Thomson: Wadsworth, 2007.

Bonevac, Daniel (ed.). *Today's Moral Issues: Classic and Contemporary Perspectives.* London: McGraw Hill, 2005.

Fagothey, Austin. *Right and Reason: Ethics in Theory and Practice Based on the Teachings of Aristotle and St. Thomas,* 2nd Ed. Charlotte, North Carolina, 2000.

Horner, Chris and Emrys Westacott. *Thinking Through Philosophy: An Introduction.* New York: Cambridge University Press, 2009.

Kant, Immanuel. *Groundwork of the Metaphysics of Morals*, Mary Gregor ed. Cambridge: Cambridge University Press, 2008.

Nyasani, Joseph M. *Metaphysical Psychology: Rational Psychology* (Nairobi: Consolata Institute of Philosophy Press, 2013.

Russell, Bertrand. *History of Western Philosophy.* London: Routledge, 1999.

3

INFLUENCE OF SCHOOL HEADS' DELOCALISATION POLICY ON SCHOOLS' STABILITY: A CASE OF WEST POKOT COUNTY

Aggrey Asitiba Okutu

Introduction

Delocalisation is a policy adopted by Teachers Service Commission, aimed at ensuring that School heads work away from their homes- their County of birth. According to TSC, head teachers who work in their home area are influenced by local people, especially politicians making them to be subjective in most, if not all their leadership obligations (TSC, 2007).[21] Opinions are divided on whether this is a viable policy. Some schools, especially students have embraced it while others have violently opposed it, a fact that raises ethical concerns. Cases of students' unrests across the country, including West Pokot County have been blamed on this policy. This paper sought to interrogate this policy and make informed view on its viability by conducting a study. The study's objectives were: to find out how well the delocalization policy could be handled to ensure secondary schools' stability in West Pokot

---

[21] Okutu, Aggrey Asitiba is Lecturer of Educational Administration and Planning, Kisii University - Kenya

County; to investigate why delocalization policy was causing unrests in Secondary schools of West Pokot County and to suggest measures that could guarantee secondary schools' stability in West Pokot County in light of delocalization policy. The study employed a survey design and was grounded on organic system model. Its respondents included Principals, student leaders (class prefects) and TSC County Director. The study found out that TSC rolled out the exercise of delocalizing Principals without making wider consultations with stakeholders on how well the policy could be implemented. Cases of Principals' health and approaching retirement age of some of them were not considered. Some Principals resisted the transfers and incited students to protest their transfers, which resulted in disruption of learning and destruction of property. The study recommended that: TSC should allow consultations with key stakeholder like Teachers Unions, Heads Associations, Sponsors, among others prior to effecting transfers of Principals; Delocalization policy should be introduced progressively. Only new Principals to be deployed outside their counties; Principals who are just about to retire should not to be transferred away from their homes; Those Principals with health conditions that cannot allow them to move to other stations with conditions detrimental to their health should not be transferred; Principals should uphold professional ethics of their profession and stop inciting students as means of resisting transfers. They should employ professionally, ethically, morally and legally acceptable means to express their contrary views on delocalization policy, to the concerned authorities.

Background to the Study

Teachers Service Commission is one of the Commissions provided for in the Constitution of Kenya that became operational in August 2010. According to Article 237 (2) c and d, the functions of Teachers Service Commission includes: assigning teachers employed by the Commission for service in any public school or institution in the country and to transfer them from one school to another as the need arises (Republic of Kenya 2010). The Teachers Service Commission Act of 2012, article 11 echoes this position. More so, section 64 of the Code of Regulations for Teachers of 2015 reemphasizes the fact that the Teachers Service Commission may transfer a teacher from one institution to another based on: the need for equitable distribution and optimal utilization of teachers; availability of vacancy in the proposed station, the need for replacement; existing staffing norms which may be reviewed from time to time; medical grounds, as certified by registered medical practitioner; or such other grounds as the Commission may consider necessary (Kenya Gazette Supplement No. 167 2015). This of course applies to deployment of the heads of institutions – Principals of Secondary Schools.

The term 'Principal', according to TSC Act (2012), refers to the lead educator or administrator in a post – primary school level educational institution appointed by the Commission as such and responsible for the implementation of educational policy guidelines and professional practices. According to Meyer and Macmillan (2011), Principal turnover has the potential to impact seriously school morel and values as teachers attempt to adjust to new administrators and their possible shits in focus. This implies that transfer of a school Principal call for a serious consideration and planning prior to its execution, to avoid the negative impact it can cause to a school and its community as a whole.

In the recent past the Teachers Service Commission has come up with the massive transfer of school heads of both Primary and Secondary Schools under a new policy that TSC says is meant to ensure Head teachers work away from their County of origin. TSC realized that there were many underperforming schools that were being headed by head teachers who hailed from the school's localities. These heads continued to enjoy patronage from influential parties at the expense of quality education.[22] This policy, popularly known as delocalization policy is informed by the fact that some heads of these institutions had fallen prey to vested interests of local politicians and suppliers and had ended up compromising in their administrative and management obligations. This was made worse if a head teacher was working in his or her home area. TSC had therefore been forced to stamp its authority and exercise its mandate pertaining recruitment and deployment of teachers.

Apart from the delocalization policy aiming at ensuring quality institutional management, it is aimed at realizing national cohesion. According to Education Cabinet Secretary Amina Mohamed (2018), the deployment of heads of Secondary Schools to regions other than their place of birth was aimed at creating a national outlook in the mind set of school heads by appreciating the cultural diversity of Kenya. This, according to the Cabinet Secretary was in the best interest of the students and the educational sector as a whole. She observed that the policy will enable the school heads to effectively nurture learners who hail from different cultural environment into patriotic members of our family.

However, teachers have different opinion. Through their Trade Union – the Kenya National Union of Teachers (KNUT), the policy was a threat to teachers' families. According to KNUT National Women Representative – Ms Jacinta Ndegwa (2018), the policy was not in the interest of teachers since it was going to separate them from their families. She blamed ethnicity and tribalism being experienced in the country to politicians, arguing that transferring teachers into "unfamiliar territories will never be a panacea to the evils."

---

[22]Teachers Service Commission, *Policy in Identification, Selection, Appointment, Deployment and Training of Heads of Post Primary Institution* (Nairobi:, 2007), 6.

According to KNUT Secretary – Wilson Sossion (2018), delocalization policy contravened the constitution because public participation was not done on the new policy before its implementation. Session said that if the Government was sincere on issues of national cohesion and integration, it would have allowed the introduction of a subject of cohesion and integration in the schools' syllabus and made it examinable, instead of disrupting teachers' work by forcing them to go on transfers away from their families.

The Ministry of Education through the Teachers Service Commission and teachers through their Unions especially the Kenya National Union of Teachers (KNUT), have maintained hard line stance on this matter. The Teachers' Union has been threatening to resort to industrial action to force the TSC rescind its decision to implement the delocalization policy. But TSC has remained adamant and is going on with its delocalization process. According to the Standard Newspaper of 22nd August 2018, this year (2018) alone 600 head teachers have been transferred to new stations, a fact that has had some negative effects in some schools. In some schools, the new heads have been rejected by students. Students in other schools have gone on rampage to protest the removal of their Principals. In some cases students have destroyed schools' property to send their message of discontent. In West Pokot County at least six schools have been reported to have had disruptions due to student unrests, all blamed on transfers of Principals.

Statement of the Problem

Challenges facing institutional management include: external interference in appointment and deployment of heads of institutions; promotions based on non-professional considerations; protection of ineffective heads of institutions by influential personalities even when such heads deserve to be disciplined; localization of appointment and deployment of institutional heads to serve in their home districts or communities; rampant cases of mismanagement and misappropriation of institutional funds and property; and frequent absenteeism due to personal and other interests.[23] This is also echoed by the Sessional Paper number 14 of 2012, which states that the main challenge in deployment of institutional administrators is the stakeholders' interference based on faith, nepotism and vested interest. [24] In its endeavour to tackle these challenges, the Teachers Service Commission came up with delocalization policy. However, the policy has faced some resistance. It has led to disruptions in some Secondary schools across the country, whose head teachers have been transferred and received new ones. Early this year (2018), when the implementation of delocalization policy began, many parents and other stake-holders opposed it. According to Standard Digital of 17th April 2018, attacks against new Head Teachers were reported in Bungoma, Vihiga, Kisii, Siaya, West Pokot and Kisumu counties. In West- Pokot County some of the senior schools have experienced student unrests blamed on delocalization policy. Property has been destroyed in these schools, a fact that has disrupted learning. It has been alleged that some heads resisted transfers and incited students to go on rampage to protest against their transfers and reject the in-coming heads. This raises ethical questions. Is this policy viable? How well can the policy be implemented to guarantee the schools' stability?

Objectives of the Study

This study's objectives were to:

- Investigate why delocalization policy was causing unrests in Secondary schools of West Pokot County;

---

[23] *Teachers Service Commission*, 6

[24] Republic of Kenya, *Sessional Paper Number 14 A Policy Framework for Education and Training* (Nairobi: 2012). 69

- Find out how well the delocalization policy could be handled to ensure secondary schools' stability in West Pokot County;
- Suggest measures that could guarantee secondary schools' stability in light of delocalization policy.

Theoretical Framework

This study was grounded on organic model advanced by Tom Burns and G.M. Stalker in the late 1950s. Organic models lay emphasis on the interdependence of component parts of system as well as their differentiation.[25] An organic model describes forms, methods and patterns found in living systems such as the organization of cells, populations, communities and ecosystems. Organic organizations as opposed to mechanistic organizations are flexible and adaptive. Organic organization thrives on power of personalities and relationships, lack of rigid procedures and communication and can react quickly and easily to changes in the environment. It is therefore an adaptive form of organization. In this model, decisions arise from the needs felt by individuals in the group, who propose changes to the group, either by discussions or by changing behaviour or operations without discussions. The rest of the individuals in the group adapt to the changes as they need to. Organic organization is a fluid and flexible organization composed of multi-talented individuals who perform variety of tasks. This model also advocates for cooperation and constant adjustment from all the members.

The principles of organic model were perceived to be applicable to the current study. Principals of Secondary Schools were the main focus of this study. They were key individuals of an organization called School which is part of a given environment. As the saying goes, 'an

---

[25] Burns, T. & Stalker, G. M. *The Management of Innovation* (London, 1981).

institution stands or falls by its head'. This is because heads of institution play a critical role in the development and management of educational institutions.[26] Being flexible and adaptive to changes in an environment are some of key aspects of organic model that were adopted to guide the study. A Principal does not need to resist a transfer, which is an inevitable change that is bound to occur, according to laid down rules. Rather he should be flexible and move to another school – environment and get adapted to it. As members of an organization, stakeholders like students, teachers, local politicians, school sponsors among others are expected to be flexible and allow changes in headship of their respective schools. They need not to resist them. In most cases such resistance turns chaotic which is unethical. Some heads earmarked for transfers are said to incite students against their transfers which is also unethical.

Since organic organization thrives on the power of personalities and relationships, the role of a Principal in the School Organization is of great importance. His decisions are to be guided by professional ethics of which resistance to transfers over flimsy reasons is definitely not among them.

On the other hand, organic model advocates for cooperation and constant adjustment from its members. In this case it is prudent for Teachers Service Commission to cooperate and engage the concerned stakeholders – teachers on the new policy of delocalization and make adjustments accordingly, for it to succeed.

TSC's unilateral decision to delocalize Principals can also be justified, basing on principle of organic model. In this model, decisions arise from the needs felt by individuals in the group, who propose changes to the group, either by discussions or by changing behaviour or operations without discussions. The rest of the individuals in the group adapt to the changes as they need to. TSC is mandated by law to make

[26] Teachers Service Commission, 3.

decisions it deems fit regarding teacher transfers – including transfers of Principals. Principals have no otherwise, but adapt to changes made by their employer – The Teachers Service Commission.

Brief Literature Review

Policy Documents

The absence of a clear, transparent and documented policy on appointment and deployment of heads of institutions has created loopholes for personal interest at the expense of effective institutional management, which is critical for the realization of quality education.[6] In order to ensure high quality in management of educational institutions in the country, this policy document states that it is important to identify, select and train the right people to head institutions. In this regard the document has developed and documented clear and transparent criteria, which is also aimed at guaranteeing effective succession management. Despite this, the deployment of Principals is still a challenge, ten years since this policy document came into force.

According to Sessional Paper number 14 of 2012 (a policy framework on education and training), among the main challenges in teacher deployment are: stake-holders interference when carrying out teacher balancing and rationalization and resistance of transfers by teachers due to medical reasons including HIV/AIDS and other terminal diseases; alcohol and subsistence abuse; marriage grounds and insecurity. On deployment of Principals, the same Sessional Paper notes that the main challenge is stake-holders interference based on faith, nepotism and vested interest.

Misunderstanding and confusion exist over the role of Sponsors and the Ministry of Education with regard to ownership, management and appointment of heads and teachers of faith-based sponsored schools.

This situation has led to some sponsors asserting undue influence on the running of schools.[27]

Stake-holders Views

Stakeholders have suggested that the Teachers Service Commission should spare elderly teachers from the delocalization exercise. According to the Standard Digital of 30th June 2018, Chuka High School Principal – Florence Mutwiri is quoted as having said that it would be hard for elderly teachers to adapt to a new environment. "Age should be the determining factor in the delocalization exercise. Those in 40s and below can adapt to any situation. Let the government transfer them and spare those aged over 50," said Mutwiri. Mentally, she said, elderly teachers were not prepared for transfer because they have few years left for them to retire.

KNUT Executive Secretary for Meru South Branch Mr. Albert Mutani is quoted by the same source (Standard Digital of 30th June 2018) saying that delocalization exercise could lead to family breakdown, immorality and divorce. Mutani echoed sentiments of the Principal of Chuka High School, saying that transfers should only target teachers below 50 as "they are physically and mentally prepared to move from their mother counties."

The Secretary General of KNUT, Mr. Wilson Sossion who is also a nominated Member of Parliament has vehemently opposed the delocalization policy. On several occasions the Secretary General has blamed school unrests to massive transfer of Head Teachers under this policy. On 12th July 2018, Mr. Sossion was quoted by the Star Newspaper as having said that the delocalization of the School Heads was the cause of widespread unrests of students that was going on by

---

[27] Republic of Kenya, *Policy Framework for Education – Aligning Education and Training to the Constitution of Kenya 2010 and the Kenya Vision 2030 and Beyond* (2012), 54 – 55.

then. "We have seen destabilized management of schools which were performing well by having their management changed", Sossion said at parliament buildings in Nairobi. In the same newspaper (The Star Newspaper of 12th July 2018), the Senate's Education Committee members led by their Chairman – Mr. Christopher Lagat called upon the Ministry of Education and the Teachers Service Commission to halt the delocalization so as to help in stopping the arson in schools.

On the other hand, the Teachers Service Commission has insisted that the transfers were in line with the provisions of the Code of Regulations for Teachers (2015) and the Collective Bargaining Agreement (CBA), signed between TSC and Teachers' Unions (The Standard Digital 17/4/18). TSC also said that transfers were also meant to ensure that fresh ideas were infused into institutions after long stay of some Head Teachers (Standard Digital 12/4/18). On several occasions, Teachers Service Commission has reiterated that the delocalization exercise is meant to promote national integration and improve the quality of education.

Empirical Studies

A study conducted by Meyer and Macmillan found out that new Principals' actions are under close scrutiny by teachers as they attempt to understand the implications of the new Principal's administration. New Principals must not ignore this scrutiny, but recognize the implications of privileging one person or group; the shifts in power could create conflict among staff members, which is neither desirable nor easily managed. They also found out that unconscious actions, or inadvertent, unfortunate statement could lead to conclusions about the new Principal that are inaccurate, but which could flavour the individual's tenure. [28]

This study recommended that the attending to the underlying micro-politics of a school is key to whether a Principal is deemed successful or not. The findings of this study have a bearing to the current study in that the way teachers perceive the new Principal can lead to him or her being accepted or rejected. The new Principal's first impression to teachers is therefore very important. Those Principals who have a weakness of not portraying a desirable first impression to the teachers and students are bound to resist being transferred to new schools, especially those that are far from their homes.

A study conducted by Catherine Bartlett (2011) on, "Principal Succession: Trends and Impacts", had an objective of addressing the issue of planning for Principal succession and the need for transitional succession as new leaders acquire the positions. This study found out that Principals' succession is overwhelmingly unplanned for, which impacts negatively on school management.[9] There is often unmet need for specific guidance as new leaders emerge.

The study recommends that there was need for school system to have plans in place that can address smooth Principals' succession. It also recommends that new leaders (Principals) should receive support and collaboration with their District Officers.[29]

A study conducted by Maithia, Mulwa and Ngumbi (1999) on Secondary School Head Teachers' Attitudes Towards Teachers' Transfer Exercise in Nairobi County of Kenya, found out that, favourable working station conditions facilitated positive attitudes of

---

[28] Matthew, J., Meyer and Robert, B., Macmillan, "Principal Succession and Micro politics of Educators in Schools", *Canadian Journal of Educational Administration and Policy Issue* # 17 (2011): 1-26.

[29] Catherine Bartlett, "Principal Succession: Trends and Impact", (University of Huston 2011), 52.

Head Teachers towards teachers' Transfer exercise. It also found out that teachers' transfer exercise was considered beneficial if it considered the welfare of the school and the teacher and vice versa.

The study recommended that; there was need to motivate teachers so that they can readily accept transfers; replacement of transferred teachers need to be prompt; there has to be appropriate timing for transfers to avoid disrupting learning process; and there was need to have consultation with the parties concerned·

Chumba (2014) conducted a study entitled, "Principals' Mobility in Kenya: Causes and Effects on Teachers Efficacy". The purpose of this study was to investigate the effects of the Principals' mobility on Secondary Schools Effectiveness as perceived by teachers in North Rift Region. The study found that school location, school type, religious affiliation, security and mismanagement influenced the mobility of Principals. It also found out that change of headship in schools helped to boost teachers' morale and teamwork.

The recommendations of this study were: The Teachers Service Commission should develop a policy governing Principals transfers that incorporated a term limit of 6-5 years; Change of School Principals should be done periodically so as to create an open school climate which has a strong bearing on the learning environment and in the academic achievement of students. [30]

Recommendations of this study are in line with some of the reasons that prompted the Teachers Service Commission to come up with the delocalization policy which is the concern of the current study. The delocalization policy has generated a lot of controversies in schools yet from the above study, its intentions are healthy for teachers and the

---

[30] Chumba Sammy K, "Principals Mobility in Kenya: Causes and Its Effects on Teachers Efficacy", *International Journal of Education and Research* 2 (2014): 243 – 254.

school as a whole. The current study is designed to unravel causes for these controversies.

Barasa (2017) conducted a study on "Succession of Principals and its Influence on Secondary Schools' Performance in Trans Nzoia County, Kenya." The study aimed at investigating how the succession of Principals influenced the morale of the teaching staff, school's performance in co-curricular activities, schools' academic performance and students' discipline. The findings of this study were that: the succession of Principals in Trans Nzoia County was necessitated by poor students' academic performance, students' indiscipline and normal TSC transfers. Succession of Principals led to both co-curricular activities and academic improvement.

The study concluded that proper succession management strategies should be put in place to enable enhancement of these positive outcomes. Succession management policies should be properly put in place and supported to avoid any incidences of resistance to succession.[31]

This study has a bearing on current study for it recommends Principals should embrace transfers and stop resisting moving to new stations. Its recommendations are in line with TSC's views that transfer of Principals injects new ideas in schools, prompting their academic improvement.

Methods and Materials

Research Design and Research Sample

The study used descriptive survey design to collect data from respondents, analyse and present data. Respondents were purposively

---

[31] Jane Barasa, "Succession of Principals and its Influence on Secondary Schools' Performance in Trans Nzoia County, Kenya", (Masinde Muliro University of Science and Technology; 2017), 106.

sampled, while others were obtained through simple random sampling. Respondents included TSC County Director, Principals, Teachers and class prefects who represented the students. Questionnaires, interview schedules and document analysis guides were the main research instruments that were used to collect the necessary data for this study. In sampling teachers who participated in the study, stratified sampling technique was used to sample categories of secondary schools in the Sub-County. The study used 30% of the respondents as a sample (Principals, Teachers and Class Prefects), apart from the TSC County Director who was purposively sampled.

The Study Area

The study was conducted in West Pokot County. West Pokot County has four Sub-Counties, which are also Constituencies, under different names. They are as follows: West Pokot Sub- County (Kapenguria Constituency); North Pokot Sub-County (Kacheliba Constituency), Pokot Central Sub- County (Sigor Constituency) and South Pokot Sub-County (Pokot South Constituency).

Kapenguria town is the head-quarter of West-Pokot County. West Pokot County borders Turkana county to the North, Baringo county to the East, Elgeyo Marakwet county and Trans-Nzoia county to the South. To the west, it borders the Republic of Uganda.

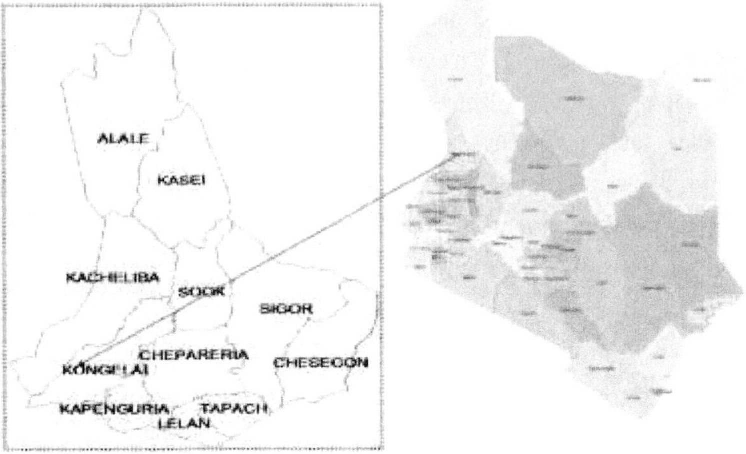

Figure 1: Map of West Pokot County

Table 1: Area, and Administrative Units by Sub-Counties

Sub-County	**Divisions**	**Area (Kms)**	**No of locations**	**No of sub-locations**
1) West Pokot	1) Kapenguria	335.6	9	28
	2) Sook	750.5	6	23
	3) Kongelai	736.4	4	16
2) South Pokot	1) Lelan	313.4	3	13
	2) Chepararia	495	4	15
	3) Tapach	205.2	3	9
3) Pokot central	1) Sigor	1582.8	8	30
	2) Chesegon	797.3	5	17
4) North Pokot	1) Kacheliba	925.4	5	18
	2) Alale	1571.5	5	18
	3) Kasei	1035.9	3	12
	4) Kiwawa	230.7	4	15
	5) Konyao	189.7	2	8
TOTAL	**13**	**9169.4**	**61**	**222**

Source: West Pokot County Statistics Office (2013), Kapenguria

West Pokot Sub- County was purposively sampled out of the four Sub- counties for the purpose of this study. This was due to the fact that most of school unrests that had been experienced in the recent past occurred in this Sub-County. More so, the Sub-County is comparatively accessible compared to other Sub-Counties, since it has the national government and County Government offices in Kapenguria town. The Sub-County has a total area of 1810.76 kilometres square with a total population of 131264 as per 2009 Population Census. The enrolments of children in schools is 105452 in primary level and 9897 in secondary schools level in the County (DNA1/12/2011).There are 121 public secondary schools in West Pokot County, of which 40 public secondary schools are found in West Pokot Sub-County. (Source: West Pokot TSC & CDE Office 2017).

Target Population/Sample

The study targeted one TSC County Director, all the principals, all teachers and all class prefects from all the 40 public secondary schools in West Pokot Sub-County. The researcher targeted a total population of 1 TSC County Director, 40 principals, 300 TSC teachers and 280 class prefects. This made a total population of 621 people. Concerning prefects, only 1 (one) class prefect per stream in the 40 public secondary schools was selected to participate in the study.

There are four categories of public secondary schools. Thus: National, Extra County, County and Sub-County schools. In West Pokot Sub-County, there are 2 National schools (1 boys' boarding school and 1 girls' boarding school). There are 2 Extra County schools (1 girls' boarding school, 1 boys' boarding school).The County schools are 16, three are girls' boarding schools, 2 are boys' boarding schools, 6 are mixed boarding schools and 5 are mixed day schools. There are 20 Sub-County schools in total. 1 is girls' boarding school; 2 are boys' boarding schools; 2 are mixed boarding schools; 11 are mixed day secondary schools and 4 are mixed day and boarding secondary schools.

In the whole Sub-County there are 300 TSC employed teachers.90 teachers are from the two National schools, 72 are from the two Extra County schools, 65 teachers from the16 County schools and 73 teachers from the 20 Sub-County schools. The total number of class prefects in all the 40 schools is 280.Each stream has one class prefect. The National schools have 7 streams per form while the Extra County schools have 5 streams per form. Out of 16 County schools 10 are double streamed each, while 6 are single streamed each. All the 20 Sub- County schools have single stream each (Source West Pokot TSC & CDE 2017 office).

The table below shows the target population for school categories, number of teachers and class prefects from all the schools in the area of study.

Table 2: Target population (Source: TSC & CDE office, 2018, West Pokot County)

School Category	No. of Principals	No. of TSC	No. of class Prefects	Boarding schools: Girls	Boarding schools: Boys	Boarding schools: Mixed	Day schools: Girls	Day schools: Boys	Day schools: Mixed	Mixed Day and Boarding	No. of Schools
National	2	90	56	1	1				-	-	2
Extra County	2	72	40	1	1	-	-	-	-	-	2
County	16	65	104	3	2	6	-	-	5	-	16
Sub-County	20	73	80	1	2	2	-	-	11	4	20
Target Popula	40	300	280	6	6	10			5	13	40

The sample of the study was 30% of target population (Mugenda and Mugenda 2009). Thus 12 schools were sampled to participate in the study. Therefore 12 principals; 90 teachers and 84 class prefects from the 12 public secondary schools that were sampled. The TCS County Director was purposively sampled. This gave a total sample of 187 respondents.

Table 3: Sample frame

Category	Target population	Sample size	% Sample Size
Principals	40	12	30
Teachers	300	90	30
Class prefects	280	84	30
TSC County Director	01	01	-
Total	621	187	

Figure 2: Pie Chart Showing Sample of Respective Respondents

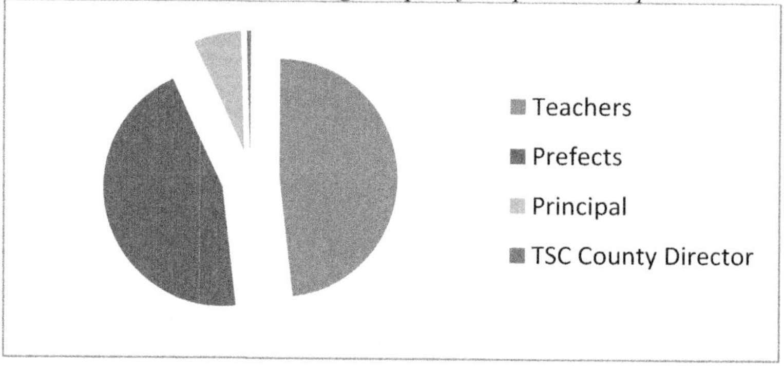

Teachers formed a bulk of respondents (90), followed by Prefects (84). Principals were 12. The least was the TSC County Director who was just one respondent.

Results and Discussions

Rate of Return of Questionnaires

Teachers and Prefects filled questionnaires while Principals and TSC County Director were interviewed by the researcher, guided by interview schedules. A total of 174 questionnaires were distributed to the sample group of the participants (Teachers and Prefects). A total of 54 out of 90 questionnaires for teachers were returned. This implies that 60% of questionnaires for teachers were returned, which was a good return rate. For prefects, 62 out of 84 dully filled questionnaires were returned, constituting 74% return rate. In total 116 questionnaires were retuned, constituting an overall 67% of returned questionnaires. Below is a table showing a summary of the questionnaires' return rate:

Table 4: Summary of Return Rate of Questionnaires Dispatched

Sub-Counties	Number Dispatched	Number Returned	Percentage Returned
Teachers	90	54	60%
Prefects	84	62	74%
Total	**174**	**116**	**67%**

The researcher was also able to interview 10 out of the 12 sampled principals and the TSC County Director. Due to unavoidable circumstances two Principals who had been selected did not participate in the study. They were not in their respective stations on two occasions the researcher visited them for an interview session.

Possible Causes of Recent Unrests in Schools

Five schools (about 42%) out of the sampled 12 schools had experienced unrests this year (2018). Respondents (teachers and class prefects) were requested to indicate possible causes of recent unrests in

Secondary Schools in West Pokot County. Their responses were as indicated in the table below:

Table 5: Possible Causes of School Unrests This Year 2018

Causes of Unrests	Teachers		Prefects	
	n = 90		n = 84	
	f	%	*f*	%
Transferred Principal	50	55.6	42	50
New Principal	23	25.6	21	25.0
Exam Fever	13	13.4	08	09.5
Bad Food	-	-	06	07.1
Strict School Rules	4	4.4	07	08.3
Totals	90	99%	84	99.9%

Key

n- Total number of respondents

f- Frequencies

From table 5 above, most respondents (Teachers - 55.5%, Students – 50%) attributed unrests to abrupt change of school Principals. This could be true because in all the schools that unrests were reported, had received new Principals from outside West Pokot County and old ones had been transferred to other Counties. A sizable number of respondents also indicated that unrests were caused due to the incoming Principal (Teachers – 25.5%, Students – 25%). The two scenarios of unrests due to outgoing and incoming Principal are related. This can be attributed to the fear of unknown. Both teachers and students could not understand the administrative styles of the incoming Principal. Since the administrative style of the incoming Principal could be unfavourable to them, they would rather maintain the status quo instead of risking then experience unfavourable situation brought in by the new Principal's way of administration.

Why Students Resorted to Riots in School

Respondents (Teachers and Class Prefects) were asked to indicate their views as to why the students decided to go on strike as a way of expressing their discontent. Their responses were as indicated in the table below:

Table 6: reasons for resorting to strikes

A: Reasons for resorting to strikes

AA: Incitement by the outgoing Principal

AB: Incitement by teachers

AC: Incitement by fellow student(s)

AD: Incitement by people from outside the school

AE: Individual students' own initiative

A	Responses												
	Prefects n = 84							**Teachers** n = 90					
	Yes		No		Not sure			Yes		No		Not sure	
	f	%	*f*	%	*f*	%		*f*	%	*f*	%	*f*	%
AA	45	53.6	0	35.7		10.7		0	1.1	0	6.7	0	22.2
AB	37	44.05	0	35.71	7	20.23		0	1.1	0	7.8	0	11.1
AC	10	11.9	2	73.8	2	14.3		1	8.9	4	5.6	5	5.6
AD	29	34.2	8	33.3	7	32.1		0	4.4	0	4.4	0	11.1
AE	40	47.6	3	39.3	1	13.1		0	7.8	5	6.7	5	5.6

*Key: n- Total number of respondents, **f**- Frequencies*

A big percentage of students (53.6%) indicated that there was incitement in one way or another from the outgoing Principals prompting students to go on strike, so that TSC could rescind its decision to have them transferred. 35.7% said that there was no incitement from the Principals, while only 10.7% were not sure whether the outgoing Principals had a hand in the strikes that were experienced in Secondary schools in West Pokot County this year (2018).

When asked whether teachers might have incited students to go on strike, many students (44.05%) said that teachers had a hand in students' strikes that were experienced in Secondary Schools in West Pokot County. 35.71% exonerated teachers from students' strikes. About 20% were not sure what might have prompted the students to resort to strikes to express their discontent pertaining to Principals' transfers in West Pokot County.

Students were also asked to indicate whether the incitement to go on strike came from fellow students. 73.8% exonerated their fellow students as being the inciters. Only 11.9% claimed that the incitement came from their fellow students. About 14% were not sure whether fellow students were instigators of the strikes.

Asked whether the incitement came from people from outside the school like parents, politicians, Schools' Sponsors, among others, responses were varied. Almost the same number of students gave different responses. 29 students (34.2%) agreed that incitement came from outside the schools, 28 students (33.3%) refuted this position, while 27 students (32.1%) were not sure. Thus, the responses were almost balanced.

Still, a sizable number of students - 40 (47.6%) claimed that the decision to go on strike was individual students' own initiative. Thus, transfer of Principals triggered unplanned strikes of students across the schools without any form of incitement from any given quarter. Out of 84 students, 33 (39.3%) said that strikes were actually properly planned and had ring-leaders. Only 11 students 13.1% were not sure how the strikes came about.

Over and above, students' responses indicated that outgoing Principals and teachers incited students to go on strikes to have Principals retained in their respective stations. This is unethical. A teacher worth his salt cannot incite students to commit an offence.

Through open ended segment of the questionnaire, students were requested to give reasons why they preferred striking instead of using other means to communicate their grievances. Reasons were varied. Common ones were: that strike was "a language that was well understood" by school's management, the Government and the public as a whole. They said that in most cases, strikes had bore good fruits to their course. Other forms of communication were hardly successful.

Teachers, on their side, exonerated themselves and their Principals from the blame of incitement of the students to go on strike. Only 10 teachers (11.1%) out of 90 teachers were of the view that teachers and Principals had a hand in students' strikes. A whooping 71 (78.9%) of teachers blamed students for having been sole instigators of strikes.

Teachers' views were also varied as to whether students had been incited by people from outside the schools. While 40 teachers (44.4%) felt that people from out the schools had a hand in students' strikes, the same number - 40 (44.4%) did not think so. Only 10 (11.1%) teachers were not sure whether outsiders had a role in students' strike.

Though teachers' views differed sharply with those of students as to whether teachers and Principals had a hand in students' strikes. The information given by the TSC County Director through an interview implicated some teachers and their Principals as having incited students. According to TSC County Director, investigations that were still ongoing had shown that some teachers and their Principals had played a role in one way or another in students' strikes in Secondary Schools in West Pokot County. "This was quite unprofessional", said the TSC County Director. The Director warned that if they were going to be found "culpable, then stern actions were going to be taken against them, which included dismissal by TSC and being arraigned before a court of law".

From interviews held with Principals, it emerged that most Principals were not against transfers per se. They were however against transfers that were done without any reference to those affected. They alleged that their employer – TSC never consulted them nor informed them in advance of the impending transfers. Others complained that age factor, individual Principals' health conditions, among other crucial factors were never put into considerations when the delocalization policy was being affected by TSC. One Principal said:

> "Apart from us being Principals, we are also human beings with families and responsibilities that we are handling at our homes. Some of our colleagues have health conditions that cannot allow them to relocate from their current environmental and climatic conditions to a county far from their current one which has completely different climatic conditions that are unfavourable to their health conditions. That will be tantamount to pronouncing a death sentence to such a Principal. It is quite inhumane."

Principals also denied vehemently that they had incited students to go on strike to protest the TSC's decision to have them transferred. They also refuted claims that they had instigated the rejection of new Principals who had been posted to replace them.

Interview schedules for TSC County Director and Principals had items that sought their views on how well the delocalization policy can be implemented. Many were of the opinion that the policy was to be implemented progressively and not at once. Thus, as new Principals are being deployed, they should be deployed in Counties away from their home counties. As old Principals exit through natural attrition, their replacement should be done according to delocalization policy.

Many principals were of the opinion that as TSC redeploys Principals, factors such as age, health conditions and Principal's other roles and responsibilities need to be put in consideration. There are some Principals who were remaining with few months- like six months to retire yet they were delocalized. "This is illogical", one Principal said.

Another Principal asked, "How can you transfer an old man to a school that is over 300 kilometres away from a school that was near his home, yet he is remaining with about five months to retire?" More so, there are some Principals who had some health conditions that could not allow them to be transferred but their pleas were not considered.

The researcher was informed that head teachers have an association (Kenya Secondary Schools Head Teachers Association – KESHA) that is recognized by the government. This association complements the Government's efforts of ensuring professionalism, quality management of institutions, among other issues. This association draws its leadership both at County and National levels from Principals across the country. These leaders are given mandate of representation based on where their working stations are located. For instance, delocalizing a County Heads Association Chairman oblivious of his position in Heads Association interferes with operations of the Heads Association in a given County. This, according to one Principal "can be interpreted as being punitive It can be seen in light of a calculated move to kill Heads Association." Therefore Principals felt that there was need for consultation prior to affecting the transfer of a head teacher.

Conclusion

Teachers Service Commission recently came up with delocalization policy to guide deployment of Secondary School Principals. According to this policy a Secondary School Principal is not supposed to head a school in his home County. The policy according to TSC had many advantages. It was meant to ensure that fresh ideas were infused into institutions after long stay of some Head Teachers in one station. It was meant to promote national integration. More so, Principals who worked in their home areas were prone to manipulations by local suppliers, of which some of them happen to be local politicians. This ends up lowering the quality of education being offered in these schools. Delocalization was therefore meant to improve the quality of education.

There was however some discontentment from stakeholders especially affected teachers (Principals). This was mainly on the way the exercise was conducted. There was no consultation. The policy was not introduced progressively. It was affected like a big bang, leading to sudden mass transfers of Principals, causing uproar. Health conditions of some Principals were not considered and those who were left with few months to retire were also forced to move to schools that were far from their homes.

In an attempt to resist these transfers, some Principals resorted to unorthodox, unethical and unprofessional means, key among them being incitement of students to go on strike. Students' unrests disrupted studies in some schools. Students destroyed schools' property and other students' property. The cost of disruption of studies and destroyed property was enormous. Ethically speaking, Principals who resorted to inciting their students to push through their case were not considerate. They were not mindful of other peoples' welfare, but their own. Their actions did not amount to a worthy course.

Recommendations

For delocalization policy to achieve its noble objectives, this study recommends that;

- It should be introduced progressively. Only new Principals to be deployed outside their counties;
- Principals who are just about to retire should not be transferred away from their homes;
- Those Principals with health conditions that cannot allow them to move to other stations with conditions detrimental to their health should not be transferred;

- TSC should allow consultations with key stakeholders like Teachers Unions, Heads Associations, Sponsors, among others prior to effecting transfers of Principals.
- Principals should uphold professional ethics of their profession and stop inciting students as means of resisting transfers. They should employ professionally, ethically, morally and legally acceptable means to express their contrary views on delocalisation policy, to the concerned authorities.

References

Ariko, Collins, Oliver & A. O. L. Othuon, *Minimizing Teacher Transfer Requests: A Case Suba District Secondary Schools, Kenya* International Journal of Education Administration and Policy Studies Vol. 4(2) (2012) pp. 61-69. http://www.academicorg/JEAPS

Barasa, J., "Succession of Principals and Its Influence on Secondary Schools Performance in Trans Nzoia County", PhD Diss. Masinde Muliro University of Science and Technology, 2017

Bartlett, C., Principal Succession: Trends and Impacts. PhD Diss. University of Huston, 2011

Beesley, A.,et. al, *Strategies for Recruitment and Retention of Secondary School Teachers in Central Region Rural Schools,* 2008

Chumba, Sammy, K., "Principals Mobility in Kenya: Causes and Its Effects on Teachers' *Efficacy"* International Journal of Education and Research Vol. 2 No. 6. (2014) Pp 243-254 www.ijern.com

Cooper, J. M, & A., Alvarado, *Preparation, Recruitment and Retention of Teachers* USA: UNESCO.

Donna L.P. & R., Longwell, "Teacher Recruitment: From Theory to Practice". MA Thiss, University of Wisconsin, Milwaukee

Fiske, B.E., *Decentralization of education; politics and consensus,* Washington D.C World bank, 1996

Gaynor, C., *Decentralization of education, teacher management,* Washington.D.C .World Bank, 1998.

Guarino, C.M., L., Santibanez, & A. G. Daley, *Teacher Recruitment and Retention; A Review of the Recent Empirical Literature*., 2006

Kenya National Bureau of Statistics, *.Kenya population and housing census* 2009, 2010.

Kenya News Agency, *Teachers Oppose Delocalization Policy.* Retrieved from https://knowledgebylanes.co.ke March 19, 2018

Kipsoi, E., & A., Sang, "Teacher Recruitment in Secondary Schools: Policy and Practice in Kenya" Med Thess. Moi University, 2008.

Linder, D. H., and C., D., Charles, *Recruiting and Retaining Teachers: What Matters Most and What Can Government do?* Stewart, HO 45778. 2011

Manyara. D., (*Teachers Service Commission Asked to Spare Elderly Tutors.* Retrieved From https://.www.standardmedia.co.ke June 30, 20`8

Meyer, M. J & B., R., Macmillan, *Principal Succession and the Micro-politics of Educators in Schools: Some Incidental Results from A Larger Study* Canadian Journal of Educational Administration and Policy Issue # 117, 2011

Monk,H.D, *Recruiting and Retaining High-Quality Teachers in Rural Areas*; Princeton University, 2009

Mulkeen, A. et. al, *Recruiting and retraining Secondary school teachers and principals in Sub –Saharan Africa*, The World Bank., 2007

Murimi, J., *Heads Transfers Cause Unrests* Retrieved from https://www.thestarpaper.co.ke July 12, 2018

Mutavi, L., *CS Amina Defends Delocalization of School Heads, Cites Diversity.* Retrieved from https://www.thestarpapers.co.ke May 28, 2018

Oduor. A., *Primary and Secondary Schools Targeted in Mass Transfer.* Retrieved from https://www.standardmedia.co.ke May 28, 2018

Onsomu, M. W, "Influence of Teachers' Transfer on Student Academic Performance in Public Secondary Schools in Kenya", Med Thess. University of Nairobi, Kenya, 2014

Republic of Kenya, *Constitution of Kenya, 2010*

Republic of Kenya, *Report of the task force no realignment of the education to New Constitution, 2012*

Republic of Kenya, *Sessional paper No 14 of 2012*

Republic of Kenya, *The Teachers Service Commission Act of 2012*. Nairobi, 2012

Republic of Kenya (2013), *The Basic education Act of 2013* Nairobi, 2013

Sang, A., "Teacher recruitment in Kenya: A study of urban secondary schools in Uasin Gishu District" Med Thess. Moi University, 2005

Tara, B., Demetra, K., and S., Loeb, *Effective Schools: Managing the Recruitment, Development and Retention of High- quality Teachers*, Calder Working Paper No.37, 2009

Teachers Service Commission, *TSC Operational manual on teacher management.* Nairobi: Jomo Kenyatta Foundations, 2002

Teachers Service Commission, *Policy on Teacher Recruitment and Selection* Nairobi: Government Printer, 2006

Teachers Service Commission, *TSC Code of Regulations for Teacher* Nairobi: Jomo Kenyatta Foundation, 2015

4

REBUILDING ETHICAL LEADERSHIP PRACTICES IN EAST AFRICAN UNIVERSITIES

Theonestina Katundano

Introduction

It is timely for East African universities to rethink the benefits of ethical leadership practices in terms of job satisfaction, job security, job performance, academic performance, management of universities utilities and the like (Cheteni and Shindika, 2017).[32] The above mentioned relevant principles are key to ethical leadership if put into practice by university management, teaching and nonteaching staff, and students as highlighted by Yukl, Mahsud, Hassan, and Prussia (2013). Faculty members are expected to be role models in academic freedom which requires full commitment in teaching, research and community service. It is through ethics that academic institutions can tap ethical standards to provide students with human values based on sound moral judgement when making decisions and choices that affect their lives. While ethical principles and values are critical in higher learning institutions, the paper also intends to look into challenges that interfere with ethical leadership practices and how to overcome them for quality purposes and academic excellence within East African Universities. The paper is written from reviewed related literature approach.

---

[32] Theonestina Katundano, PhD, Catholic University of Eastern Africa.

The world today more than ever before is in dire need of guiding principles and ideas that adhere ethical leadership. As pointed out by scholars, ethical leadership has been increasingly promoted as a means through which leaders tap into employees' positive attitudes towards everyday work, including job satisfaction, good work performance, excellent academic performance and the like (Judge and Kammeyer-Mueller, 2012; Kacmar et al., 2011; Neubert et al., 2009). The same applies to African public and private universities that seek success and academic excellence in the academic sphere. It is through ethics that academic institutions can tap ethical standards to provide students with human values based on sound moral judgement when making decisions and choices that affect their lives.

Some of the human values that are crucially important in spicing the ethical dimension include a sense of caring, sharing, compassion, showing respect for life and for each other. Not only that but also showing integrity or being honesty and justice to fellow human beings should not be overlooked in academic institutions. While these human values are important to any leader, commitment and accountability cannot be left out when discussing about ethical leadership in East African universities both private and public universities.

It is within this leadership cadre whereby teaching and non-teaching staff are encouraged to be animators of similar human values and beyond. They need to be role models to themselves, students and to the society around them and beyond. For this to happen, the employer or university administration should employ a better understanding of the effect of ethical leadership on job satisfaction, good conduct or job performance, commitment, as well as reflecting on challenges that are ailing our academic institutions. The paper intends to focus on the latter as part of reviving and rebuilding ethical leadership in East African private and public universities. This is because of employee mobility from public to private universities and vice-versa especially when searching for green pastures for academic gain and job security. In the course of employee movement, there are could be either shaping or damaging ethical leadership within higher learning institutions depending on strengthens and weaknesses of each individual.

Concept of Ethical Leadership

From the wider perspective of ethical leadership theory, there is no short cut of discussing ethical leadership without looking first at ethics. When defining ethical leadership, there would be different responses from various educators and leadership fathers. However, Merriam Webster Dictionary (2003), defines ethics as in plural in form but singular or plural in construction: is the discipline dealing with what is good and bad and with moral duty and obligation. Ethics then, takes into consideration the discipline dealing with good conduct while ethical leadership carries various definitions such as "good character and the right values or being a person of strong character" as pointed out by Freeman and Stewart (2006, p.2).

Another notable definition of ethical leadership is, "the demonstration of normatively appropriate conduct through personal actions and interpersonal relationships, and the promotion of such conduct to followers through two-way communication, reinforcement, and decision-making" take place (Brown, Treviño, & Harrison, 2005, p.120). Without open communication in any higher learning institutions, misunderstandings are inevitable to occur among university community. University community that include stake holders such as teaching and non-teaching staff, students, parents, university board members, university council, and the like.

On a similar note, Heifetz (2006) attributes that one of the responsibilities of an ethical leader is to provide directives to followers especially in times of conflicts and turmoil in the work place. Involvement of university management board members in making decisions paves the way to conflict management in case of any issues related to misunderstandings. In confirmation, Archbishop Desmond Tutu in his speech to the Leaders in Dubai also points out, "The important characteristic of good leadership is integrity and ethical uprightness. He emphasized that ethics and morality must be at the centre of all business undertakings as it should be in all aspects of life," (Tutu, 2009). The following section discusses ethical leadership principles namely job satisfaction, employee performance or good conduct, management of utilities, and academic performance in higher education institutions specifically in public and private universities in East Africa.

Job Satisfaction and Employee Performance

Job satisfaction and employee performance in private universities refer to various contributors at work place. Some of them include for employees to feel as sense of belonging and connectivity within the institution. Ethical leaders are expected to treat their employees with respect and accept them as they are. Most importantly is when employees come to work daily and feel respected by senior management. Such a feeling in itself creates a bond between employees and university leadership. At the end of it all, the role of educational leaders is to create an atmosphere whereby non-teaching and teaching staff feel appreciated for their efforts and contributions to the university community.

The same expression is narrated by Brown and Mitchell, 2010, about leaders who practice human values are expected to carry high standards of ethical behaviours which are exemplified through personal conduct with open communication of sincerity and kindness. Bailey (1965), Collins (2001), Cooper and Wright (1992), Denhardt (1993), Gibon (2002) and Schubert (1960) also reiterated that ethical leadership is about putting others' interest ahead of the self-interest. Such attributes create an atmosphere of employee satisfaction and performance in East African higher learning institutions.

While pay and its benefits are of great importance on the job, it does not overtake a sense of belonging, connectivity or being respected by employer within higher learning institutions. However, it also contributes to job satisfaction to employees in one way or another after one feels respected and appreciated. Contrary to this culture within a university set up, both academic and non-academic staffs develop a habit of just reporting to work but not performing duties with commitment as expected. Eventually, the university ends up losing quality staff and students to other universities with high standards of ethical leadership and a sense of caring. As argued by Yukl, 2013, leaders especially in top management should be on the forefront to play a key role of influencing employee attitudes towards work as well as paying them on time and with what they deserve.

Job security is another ethical principle senior management has to provide to its employees. When employees feel insecure in their job, the level of work performance and morale go down. In a survey, by Wang, Lu, and Siu, (2015), reported that employees ranked job security as the greatest contributing factor to job satisfaction. However, there could be instances whereby employees might feel insecure because of stress and low level of work performance. Researchers Wang, et. al (2015) argue that this is a call to [universities] to revisit policies and procedures about organizational justice to be put in place so that employees feel treated fairly. On the same note, Brown, Treviño, (2006a) highlight that being fair includes evaluating staff performance, employing new academic and non-academic staff, following promotion procedures, and the like, by making balanced decisions without favouritism. In this case, university management must make sure that staff medical cover is available, teaching facilities are secured, maintained and to the standard, security is provided across the university campus and the like.

Academic Performance

It is imperatively important for university management to own and encourage ethical standards in its day today practices. When senior administration cling to high ethical standards within the university environment this in itself enhances trust in teaching and non-teaching staff as well as to students. In the long run, it also spells out into neighbouring communities and beyond (Jones, and Hughes, 2011).

On the same note, Jones and Hughes (2011) point out that, "This in turn builds support for the school and establishes an environment that is conducive to success" (p. 50). Ethical leadership then should permeate in academic departments within faculties, to yield expected academic results which include the following activities; Commitment to quality teaching, research and community service, availability of qualified academic staff for teaching and supervision of students, designing, moderating, giving and invigilating semester examinations and releasing examination results on time. Not only that but also equipping the university classrooms with projectors, smartboards, computer labs, science labs and the like would promote practical and quality teaching and learning and attract more students to the university.

The maximization of academic performance cannot occur in a vacuum. It should be two sided. It requires university leadership to equip itself with essential values which are built in self-giving for the benefit of the students and lecturers within their discipline of specialization and the like. Whitaker (2003) echoes on the same, by suggesting effective leadership to be on the forefront in building trust among its faculties and to maintain solid moral foundation within the university in general. Some factors that indicate the building of trust in academic performance is when the university management works closely with its employees through delegation of power, working as a team, recognizing and acknowledging each one's contribution at work regardless of tribal background or ethnicity, religion, geographical location, clan, skin colour, age difference and gender.

Hawley and Rollie (2002) and Sergiovanni (1992) depict by saying that a leader must be a role model of the [university] community's values through showing good examples to faculty members and students with proper support.

Challenges to Ethical Leadership Based on Demotivation

The following section discusses challenges to ethical leadership based on some different forms of demotivation that continue to affect higher learning institutions in East Africa. There is no way demotivation can be presented without defining the concept of motivation because it has been the core of many studies as presented by Shaban, Al-Zubai, Ali & Alqotaish (2017) recently:

Bucharan and Huczynski (2004) define motivation as

> "the cognitive decision making process through which goal directed behaviour is initiated, energized, directed and maintained., … Osabiya (2015) defines motivation as the driving force within individuals by which they attempt to achieve specific goal in order to fulfil some needs or expectations"(pg. 2).

Motivation is easily mentioned in the work place and especially in higher education institutions. However, when it comes to putting it into practice, motivation becomes a problem. The challenge sprouts from a lack of understanding of what it requires to be an ethical leader in academic institutions and how to motivate academic and non-academic employees as well as students. Leave alone monetary gain, but some of the causes that demotivate the university community include the following:

Lack of Understanding

Sometimes, there are could be a lack of understanding on the side of university management on how to energize employees, when to recognize and acknowledge their contribution and achievement. A few mentioned causes of demotivation continue to creep in and affect retention of qualified teaching staff and quality productivity. Achievement is gained when the job well done is significantly recognized by the leader or heads of various functions.

Lack of Training Opportunities to Employees

Employees are always eager to improve their working skills and abilities at work place. As reported out by Sirota, Mischkind, and Meltzer, (2006) in their research findings that about 85 percent of the companies they surveyed, indicated that employees' morale declines sharply after their first six months of taking on new jobs. To avoid such boredom, the senior management is expected to motivate its workers with opportunities of improving work skills and abilities through seminars, training sessions, workshops and good working environment. As observed by Drucker, (2002) that for lecturers to be able to believe in themselves academically, it important for them to consistently gain knowledge to keep themselves updated as knowledge workers throughout their lives.

Most academic institutions are losing out on the training aspect because of financial corruption. Funds allocated for such activities like seminars, workshops, training sessions cannot be traced in some universities because they have been syphoned by the few greed individuals. The quality of performance for academic staff and non-academic staff is affected because of lack of stewardship by the entrusted parties.

The malpractice affects employees' economic gain by not being paid on time or sometimes receiving half of the salary. Consequently, lecturers end up employing unethical behaviour of bargaining students' grades with students' tips for financial security. Such unethical behaviour are frequently reported in Kenyan Public Universities whereby conflict of interest takes over based on ethnic favouritism when it comes to examination time as indicated by Ongong'a and Akaranga, (2013) in their conducted study at Kenyatta University and University of Nairobi.

Lack of Open Communication

"Communication is the process of sharing information, ideas with others at a particular time and place" (Mallet-Hamer, 2005, p. 1). As emphasized by Encarta (2005), communication is a vital part of personal life and it is also important in business, education and in higher learning institutions and in other situations where we encounter with other people. Open communication is key in maintaining team work in university environment but poor communication demoralizes not only lecturers but also students and non-academic staff. It builds the culture of distrust, confusion among university community. "Employees like all people need outlets or channels where they can express their ideas, concerns, thoughts" for example in regular meetings with fellow lecturers, senior management and the like (Mallet-Hamer, 2005, p. 9). Contrary to this, employees develop unethical behaviour such as work slow-down, tardiness, absenteeism, and apathy within university campus (Brennan, 1974). Students also develop anxiety and stress when there are cases of missing examination marks every semester and no proper action is taken at registry and responsible parties. These are clear signs of lack of open communication to university community which affects employees' morale as well as students in particular.

Lack of Active Listening

Not only the above but also lack of active listening by senior management to the employees and university community in general tends to paralyze the academic institution. Employees cannot voice up their concerns freely about the financial security, job security and satisfaction because of communication gap (Allesandra and Hunsaker, 1993). A lack of a listening ear to the university community about what they perceive not going right, it impacts students' academic performance negatively. Students are not awarded marks based on how they perform academically but on how much they can afford to tip the lecturer as observed by Ongong'a and Akaranga, (2013). The same applies to teaching staff that have no alternative but to look for alternative ways of financial survival either being part-timer at other academic institutions or seeking bribes from students during examination time. Lack of active listening by responsible leader in higher learning institutions, creates roadblocks that stand in the way of achieving excellent academic performance, personal and professional goals in life (Fowler and Manktelow, 2005).

How to Overcome Challenges

In curbing causes of demotivation it is recommended that senior management employs ethical leadership principles and human values by putting them into practice. It is not enough to frame ethical values and hang them by the entrance of administration buildings or on notice boards, but living ethical practices is what motivates employees to contribute willingly to higher learning institutions. Employees as human resources in the academic institution should feel acknowledged, respected, accepted, listened, and appreciated. Observation is also made by Ongong'a and Akaranga, (2013) that, "After all, the universities are founded to pay respect to human values and to be run on those beliefs and traditions that the society holds most sacred." (p. 15). To emphasize on the same, "the founders of universities believed that it should be a symbol of the spirit of its community, the guardian of its morals and formulator of its hope" (Radda, 2009, p. 4). Echoed by Ferrell and Ferrell (2001), a similar idea is that leaders have to also employ ethical values by playing a "key role in transmitting and diffusing values, norms, and code of ethics" (p. 64). Consequently, the leader is expected to build on ethical moral practices to keep the level of motivation high through training of academic and non-academic staff for career development and improvement. This is part and parcel of in-service programmes within higher learning institutions.

Not only that but also maintaining good relationship allows space for treating employees as fellow human beings instead of viewing them as working objects. The development of team work as well as maintaining channels of open communication with colleagues and students minimize the level of mistrust. Likewise, Men (2014) emphasize ethical leadership communication as a tool for employee encouragement and positive motivation within an organization. Once employees are engaged, they feel trusted and cared for instead of being invisible at place of work. Ethical leadership requires then, university management to develop team work spirit and a sense of belonging to maintain employee retention, academic success and quality assurance within higher learning institutions.

Conclusion

Based on the discussion raised in this paper, it is vital to revisit and rebuild ethical leadership practices if leaders and administrators are to lead higher learning institutions ethically (Saat et al, 2004). East African

Universities have to revive decision making practices, the way knowledge is being disseminated to students, how teaching, non-teaching staff and other stake holders are handled on daily basis. In the course of rebuilding ethical leadership, internalization of moral values such as honesty, fairness, accountability, commitment, kindness, altruism are key in guiding leadership behaviour on daily basis along with open communication (Walumbwa, et al. 2008). Emphasized by Yukl (2010), these are vital ethical core values that act as cornerstone in laying the foundation for ethical leadership and transparent organizational communication. Without employing the core ethical values with commitment and caring heart, ethical leadership will be hard to achieve in East African public and private universities. It is about time to remind university leadership and stake holders to rebuild ethical leadership practices for fostering academic excellence, attracting students who are immediate customers, employee retention, and for quality assurance purposes in higher learning institutions.

References

Allessandra, T. & Hunsaker, P. (1993). *Communication at Work.* Fireside, Simon & Schuster, New York, NY.

Bailey, S. K. (1965). *"The Relationship Between Ethics and Public Service."* In Public Administration and Democracy: Essays in Honour of Paul Appleby, edited by Martin, R. C. Syarcuse, N. Y.: Syracuse University Press.

Brown, M. E. & Mitchell, M. S. (2010). Ethical and Unethical Leadership: Exploring New Avenues for Future Research. *Business Ethics Quarterly, 20(4)* 583-616.

Buchanan, *D. and* Huczynski, A. *(*2004). *Organizational Behaviour: An Introductory Text (Instructor's Manual).* Financial Times/Prentice Hall.

Cheteni, P. & Shindika, E. S. (2017). Ethical Leadership in South Africa and Botswana. DOI: 10.1590/1807-7692bar2017160077. Article available in BAR - *Brazilian Administration Review 14(2);* available at https://www.researchgate.net/.../319088991_Ethical_Leadership_in_South_Africa_and_Botswana

Collins (2001), J. (2001). *Good to Great.* New York: Harper Collins.

Cooper, T. L. and Wright, N. D. (1992). *Exemplary Public Administrator: Character and Leadership in Government.* San Francisco: Jossey-Bass.

Denhardt, R. B. (1993). *The Pursuit of Significance: Strategies for Managerial Success in Public Organizations.* Prospect Heights, ILL: Waveland Press.

Ethics. (2003) In Merriam-Webster's dictionary (11th ed.). Springfield, MA: Merriam-Webster, Inc.

Fowler, *K. &* Manktelow, J. (*2005*). http://www.mindtools com. Retrieved on 20th March, 2007.

Freeman, R. E. & Stewart, L. (2006). *Developing Ethical Leadership. A Bridge Paper of Business Roundtable Institute for Corporate Ethics,* www.corporate-ethics.org.

Frost, M. (2016), Global, at https://www.universityworldnews.com/post.php?story=20160923111709132 Retrieved on January 25, 2019.

Gibon, P. H. (2002). *A Call to Heroism.* New York: Atlantic Monthly Press.

Hassan, S., Mahsud, R., Yukl, G. & Prussia, G. E. (2013). "Ethical and Empowering Leadership and Leader Effectiveness." *Journal of Managerial Psychology,* (28)*2*, 133-146, available at: https://doi.org/10.1108/02683941311300252

Hawley, W. D. & Rollie, D. L. (2002). *The Keys to Effective Schools: Educational Reform as Continuous Improvement.* Thousand Oaks, CA: Corwin Press, Incorporated.

Heifetz, R. (2006). Educational Leadership: Beyond a Focus on Instruction. *Phi Delta Kappan* 87(7), 512-513.

Heifetz, R. A. & Linsky, M. (2006). *Leadership on the Line: Staying Alive Through the Dangers of Leading.* Princeton, N.J.: Recording for the Blind & Dyslexic.

Jones, D. & Hughes, C. (2011). Public School Leadership, Ethics, and Student Achievement. Walden University. The Richard W. Riley College of Education and Leadership Publications. *National Forum of Educational Administration and Supervision Journal, 27(2)* 50-73.

Judge, T.A., Kammeyer-Mueller, J. D. (*2012*). Job Attitudes. *Annual Review of Psychology*, (63) 341-367, available at https://doi.org/10.1146/annurev-psych-120710-100511

Kacmar, K. M., Bachrach, D. G., Harris, K. J., & Zivnuska, S. (2011). Fostering good citizenship through ethical leadership: Exploring the moderating role of gender and organizational politics. *Journal of Applied Psychology, 96(3),* 633-642. http://dx.doi.org/10.1037/a0021872

Men, L. R. (2014). *Does Ethical Leadership Communication Engage Employees? Institute for Public Relations,* also available at https://instituteforpr.org/ethical-leadership-communication-engage-employees/ Retrieved on May 21st, 2019

Men, L. R. (2011). Exploring the impact of employee empowerment on organization-employee relationship. *Public Relations Review, 37, 435-437.*

Men, L. R., Stacks, D. W. (2014). The effects of authentic leadership on strategic internal communication and employee-organization relationships. *Journal of Public Relations Research, 26, 301-324.*

Neubert, M. J.; Carlson, D. S.; Kacmar, K. M.; Roberts, J. A., & Chonko, L. B. (2009). The Virtuous Influence of Ethical Leadership Behavior: Evidence from the Field. *Journal of Business Ethics,* (90)2, pp 157–170.

Ongong'a, J. J. & Akaranga, S. I. (2013). Work Ethics for Lecturers: An Example of Nairobi and Kenyatta Universities. *International Journal of Arts and Commerce, 2 (8); ISSN 1929-7106 www.ijac.org.uk*

Osabiya, J. B. (2015). The Effect of Employees' Motivation on Organizational Performance. *Journal of Public Administration and Policy, 7(4), 62-75,* DOI: 10.5897/JPAPR2014.0300 http://www.academicjournals. org/JPAPR Article Number: 721D2F153302 ISSN 2141-2480

Radda, S. I. (2009). *Unethical Practices in the Nigeria's University System: Pattern, Causes and Solutions* –Annual BEN –Africa Conference, 3-5 August, Accra.

Saat, M. M. et al (2004). *Lecturers and Student' Perceptions on Ethics in Academic and Lecturers-Students Interaction.* Universiti Teknologi Malaysia.

Schubert, G. A. (1960). *The Public Interest: A Critique of the Theory of a Political Concept.* Glencoe, ILL: Free Press.

Shaban, O. S., Al-Zubai, Z., Ali, N., & Alqotaish, A. (2017). The Effects of Low Morale and Motivation on Employees' Productivity & Competitiveness in Jordanian Industrial Companies. *International Business Research, 10 (7).* Published by Canadian Center of Science and Education. https://doi.org/10.5539/ibr.v10n7pl

Sergiovanni, T. J. (1992). Moral Leadership: Getting to the Heart of School Improvement. Sage *Journals Publication, (76) 547, 121-121*, https://journals.sagepub.com/doi/10.1177/019263659207654719#

Sirota, D., Mischkind, L. A. & Meltzer, M. I. (2006). "Stop Demotivating Your Employees!" *Harvard Management Update,* (11)1, available at https://hbswk.hbs.edu/ archive/why-your-employees-are-losing-motivation Retrieved on April 17, 2019.

Tutu, D. (2009). Tutu Calls for Integrity and Ethics in Leaders in Dubai Business Forum, https://www.thenational.ae/uae/tutu-calls-for-integrity-and-ethics-in-leaders-1.546309

Walumbwa, F. O., Avolio, B. J., Gardner, W. L., Wernsing, T. S., Peterson, S. J. (2008). Authentic Leadership: Development and Validation of a Theory-Based Measure. *Journal of Management, 34, 89-126.*

Wang, H.J., Lu, C.Q., & Siu, O.L. (2015). Job Insecurity and Job Performance: The Moderating Role of Organizational Justice and the Mediating Role of Work Engagement. *Journal of Applied Psychology,* available at https://www.ioatwork.com/when-does-job-security-affect-job-performance/ Retrieved on April 17, 2019.

Whitaker, K. S. (2003). "Principal Role Changes and Influence on Principal Recruitment and Selection: An International Perspective", *Journal of Educational Administration, 41(1), 37-54,* https://doi.org/10.1108/09578230310457420

Yukl, G. (2010). *Leadership in organizations (7th, ed.)*. Englewood Cliffs, NJ: Prentice Hall.

5

ETHICS AND FAKE UNIVERSITY RESULTS

Linda Lilian

Introduction

A tale of a Teaching Medical Expert who doctored his student's marks spell bound by her beauty spans the dilemma.[33] Four years later this same beauty was assigned to conduct an operation on him when he was brought to the hospital in a coma. as he regained his conscious and caught a glimpse of who was about to cut into him on the theatre table he suffered a heart attack for he knew – this lady knew nothing about what she was going to do and more about experimenting. This story gives the pace for the discussion on what happens when immorality takes centre stage in training our human resource at tertiary level.

Myungjoon (1994) explains that Plato regards education as a means to achieve justice, both individual justice and social justice. The author opines that to Plato, individual justice can be obtained when each individual develops his or her ability to the fullest. In this sense, justice means excellence. For the Greeks and Plato, excellence is virtue. Myungjoon further argues that to Socrates, virtue is knowledge. Thus, knowledge is required to be just. From this Plato concludes that virtue can be obtained through three stages of development of

---

[33] Linda Lilian, Globethics.net National Contact Uganda, and member of the Globethics.net East Africa Advisory Board.

knowledge: knowledge of one's own job, self-knowledge, and knowledge of the Idea of the Good. Thus when education is compromised these three stages are severely affected.

Fouling marks in Universities is something tasted in the grapevine but as the cliché stands there is no smoke without a fire and the fire is within the hierarchy of the training staff as well as administrative staff who manage the grading and the records. The smoke is in seeing the most undeserving students getting high scores yet there attendance is lacking and initial performance deficient.

The stance of doctoring marks bargained for by sex or a bribe indicates an immoral act that had long grown to an amoral act. Philosophically immoral in that the candidates engaging in it and staff know it is wrong and may fear if caught it has penalties but go on to do it. Amoral in the sense that it has found commonplace in the academic arena and people engage in it as a normal activity to meet their ends without neglecting the moral feel of what is right or the ethical sense of what the action implies and penalties' therein.

Therefore this discussion hinges on the case of Makerere University where incidents of fouling marks has been recurrent, with no action taken until recently.

Case Scenario

Prior to the 2017 graduation ceremony, Makerere University management withdrew the names of 59 students from the final graduation booklet after it emerged that their names had been smuggled in the booklet. The university also withheld the transcripts of more than 14,000 students who graduated that year and ordered an investigation into forgery of marks. The university took the decision to withhold academic transcripts on March 9 2017, after suspending four staff from the academic registrar's department on suspicion that they participated in altering students' marks without permission from their bosses. The

Academic Registrar, Mr Alfred Masikye Namoah, on March 20 2017, wrote to the university staff, students and stakeholders indicating they had temporarily shut down the transcripts processing in order to clean up the mess (Damalie Mukhaye, 2018).

Problem Set

Christoph Stückelberger (2017:p.31-32) explains that integrity is the most important capital of a person and of an institution. He goes on to argue that scandals lead to a decrease in trust in individuals and institutions worldwide. According to the Webometric ranking Makerere University which was tenth on the continent at the beginning of 2014 had been relegated to the 13th position (Anguyo, 2014). In 2015 a BBC report pointed out officials at Makerere University had admitted that of 12,000 graduates from Makerere University, at least 600 did not meet minimum requirements. The Centre for World University Rankings 2018 – 2019 show Makerere University ranking at 771 in the world ranking and 448 in terms of quality education, however this could change, if its image is tainted.

Arguments

When Ethics is Given a Break

Using Lawlor's (2007) argument but placing it into the context of this paper, it should be examined as to whether students are either presented with a large amount of information regarding the various subtle distinctions and the nuances of the theory and, as a result, the students simply fail to take it in or, alternatively, the students are presented with a simplified caricature of the theory, in which case the students may understand the information they are given, but what they have understood is of little or no value because it is merely a caricature of a theory. In other words there may be a methodological problem in how knowledge is share that affects the moral sense to adhere to the ethical precepts and induces the students to connive with the lecturers or teacher or administrators to change results. When this happens the outcomes represent a society perverted by raw human resource not skilled human resource.

Ike (2017) explains that higher education institutions are bearers and catalysts for integral development which provides opportunities for many prepares women and men, privileged and underprivileged for the complex issues of society with broad values founded on ethics. This argument cites the pivot role of a tertiary institution. It's that part of the human resource value addition process that gives the fine tuning for students readying them to go impact the work space. When ethics is undermined at that level especially in the fine tuning that includes mentoring, training, skilling, examining and then grading, then the human resource churned out is contaminated and capable of causing destruction rather than constructing a positive product of their work.

"Kant believed that certain acts such as lying had to be wrong because if everyone lied there would be no way of knowing the truth. If everyone were false, how can anyone would have trust in anything? Thus truth telling is a universal duty. Humans live in communities. The need for assumed trust and truth is essential for social groups to survive," Iacovino Livia (2002:p.59) points out. To this assertion it is key to substantiate that just as the Golden Rule "do unto others as you would have them so to you," would suggest. No one would love to be lied to. Altering results is a lie to the potential clients a given University student will serve in his or her career.

A question posed here – if one knew the Doctor assigned to them had cheated on the examination to gain the qualification …how many people would want that Doctor to handle their health issue? This is a moral point to reflect on.

The New Zealand Education Council upholds a code of responsibility that emphasises promoting the wellbeing of learners and protecting them from harm. When a lecturer or a tertiary institution allows the student the temptation to alter their grades and cheat their way into graduating and practicing. They ethically do not promote the wellbeing of that student or protect them from harm. Harm which they will inflict on themselves in malpractice as well as the prospective clients they are to serve in the field.

Borrowing from the Community Tool Box a Resource from the University of Kansas, it is critical to note that always acting ethically brings some particular advantages with it. It makes your program more effective; it cements your standing in the community; it allows you to occupy the moral high ground when arguing the merits of your program and to exercise moral leadership in the community; and it assures that you remain in good standing legally and professionally. Where a University has its global image recognized with result altering the quality of students it produces become questionable. The efficiency of the education offered in that tertiary institution is doubtful as well.

Implications of Cheating the Grades

Biswal (2016: p.32) explains that schools are seen today suspiciously by parents, teachers, educators, administrators, union members & business persons, people inside and outside the school walls. Also schools face severe value crisis which has direct bearing on quality of the schooling as well as quality of outputs. A cheating student, a cheating training institute in this paper is presented as equivalent to a bank producing fake notes that circulate in the economy and cause doom.

Gilman (2005:p.7) explains that codes are not designed for "bad" people, but for the persons who want to act ethically. The bad person will seldom follow a code, while most people – especially public servants -- welcome ethical guidance in difficult or unclear situations. The average person is not grossly immoral but often tempted, and sometimes confused, by what appears to be a virtuous path. It is obvious we want the best and an 'A' score would tempt any student without ethical grounding to compromise. And when the system has no firm ethical management the mentor turns into the devil himself baiting the gullible or misguided student who thinks getting the qualification is the final cause not knowing it is a deficient cause.

Hutchings (2016p.7) confesses as an Educator "the uncomfortable truth is that we are in a high-risk position where seemingly insignificant missteps can, over time, cause irreparable damage to our students, our careers, our schools and communities, and the integrity of the profession — whether we break laws or school policies, or not." This citing has a background of the time, proximity and service a teacher offers a student. Amidst temptations of lower pay and low moral/policy enforcement, the teacher/trainer thus becomes a high risk factor in the education process of a learner. When ethical codes and laws are not sufficiently enforced the level of adherence may be low because human nature does have a close proximity with the ability to compromise.

Recommended Actions

Anh Tho Andres-Kammler (2017:p.14) suggests,

"To improve the image and regain trust among the public and social actor in the society administrators need to ensure the integration of values into their governance, management and daily practice." There the management of tertiary institutions or educational institutions even schools has to be ingrained in an ethical harmony that enforces professionalism in the teaching, mentoring and grooming of the students. This negates the act of altering grades or selling the examination out to the students ahead of the exam.

Biswal (2016: p.30) argues that a good schools pays equal emphasis to curricular aspects, teaching – learning and evaluation, research and extension, infrastructure and learning resources, student support and progression, organisation and management, healthy practices, value fostering practices among others. Even where the policies stand and structure exists ethics forms the conscious by which these will be operational, but only if it is enforced.

Quoting Gunzenhauser arguments Gluchmanova (2015: p.2) cites three tenets of professionalism for educators which this paper sees as prospects for remedying ethical dilemmas that is:

- As a professional, an educator is in a position to profess substantive beliefs about the meaning and value of education. In other words, a professional educator has a philosophy of education and engages others who may have different ideas about the meaning and value of education. A philosophy of education grounded on the care of the self is a philosophy of possibility.
- As a professional, an educator is in a position to exercise ethical and professional judgment. An educator is in a position to continually develop ethical and professional judgment throughout his career and in his various positions of responsibility. Further, professional judgment spans the positions of educators throughout the educational sector. Active/ethical professionalism applies to educators, school leaders, school boards, teacher educators, graduate educators, and policymakers.
- As a professional, an educator is in a position to acknowledge and resist opportunities to enact normalization on her, students, and colleagues. One very important part of articulating active/ethical professionalism is being clear on the role that resistance plays in order to achieve more defensible educational aims than those that are encouraged by high-stakes accountability

policy. To act ethically, an educator needs to understand how and why her work must at some level be resistant.

Puhan, Rasmi Ranjan, Lakshmipriya Malla, and Santosh Kumar Behera (2014) assert that in the belief that the quality of the services of the teaching profession directly influences the nation and its citizens, the educator shall exert every effort to raise professional standards, to promote a climate that encourages the exercise of professional judgement, to achieve conditions that attract persons worthy of the trust to careers in education, and to assist in preventing the practice of the profession by unqualified persons.

Conclusion

The paper covers the subject of results malpractice with the case of Makerere University which has recently been dogged by the immoral act. It shows the pros and cons of such practice based our scholarly arguments and the authors deductions. Ethics becomes the missing gem in ensuring policies are enforced, because it takes rationalized conscious to fix the dilemma of wanting to cheat or keep the standard and earn the qualification justly. Laws can be broken and ethics compromised but where an ethical foundation is embedded in the whole system. The argument put forward, is a difference can be realized. As well as a positive outlook of a tertiary institution in terms of the human resource it is grooming for the job market.

References

Anguyo (2014) Ugandan universities improve in ranking, New Vision Newspaper

Anh Tho, Andres-Kammler (2017) *Facing Changes: Making Use of the Full Potential of the Globethics.net*

Global Network, Globethics Consortium on Ethics in Higher Education Inaugural Meeting 2017 Report.

BBC (2015) *Makerere University: Uganda investigates 'degree fraud* https://www.bbc.com/news/world-africa-31426654

CWUR World University Rankings 2018-2019, https://cwur.org/2018-19.php

Education Council (2017) *The Code of Professional Responsibility: Examples in Practice*, New Zealand.

Ethical Issues in School Educational Management Bibhuti Narayan Biswal* Principal, Sri Sathya Sai Vidyaniketan, Ganeshvad Sisodra, N.H No. 8, Navsari396463, Gujarat, India

Gilman (2015) *Ethics Codes and the Codes of Conduct as Tools for Promoting an Ethical and Professional Public Service: Comparative Successes and Lessons*, Ph.D. Prepared for the PREM, the World Bank 2005 Washington DC.

Gluchmanova (2015) The importance of ethics in the teaching profession, Elsevier Ltd.

Hutchings Troy (2016) *Protecting the Profession — Professional Ethics in the Classroom,* https://www.ets.org/s/proethica/pdf/real-clear-articles.pdf

Iacovino, Livia (2002) Ethical Principles and Information Professionals: Theory, Practice and Education, Australian Academic & Research Libraries, 33:2, 57-74, DOI: 10.1080/00048623.2002.10755183

Ike, Obiora (2017) *Education in the 21st Century*: The Facing Changes: Making Use of the Full Potential of the Globethics.net Global Network, Globethics Consortium on Ethics in Higher Education Inaugural Meeting 2017 Report.

Lawlor, Rob (2007) *Moral theories in teaching applied* ethics, Journal of Medical Ethics, 2007 Jun; 33(6): 370–372.doi: 10.1136/jme.2006.018044.

Lee, Myungjoon (1994) *Plato's philosophy of education: Its implication for current education, Dissertations* https://epublications. marquette.edu/dissertations/AAI9517932

Mukhaye Damalie (2018) *Makerere University Expels Staff Over Forging marks,* Monitor Newspaper, Uganda.

Puhan, Rasmi Ranjan, Lakshmipriya Malla, and Santosh Kumar Behera (2014) *Current Ethical Issues in Teacher Education: A Critical Analysis on Pre-Service and In-service Emerging Teachers,* American Journal of Educational Research 2.12A (2014): 1-7.

Stückelberger, Christoph and D. Singh (2017) *Ethics in Higher Education: Values Driven Leaders for the Future,* Globethics.net.

The Community Tool Box (accessed online 2019), *Ethical Issues in Community Interventions, Centre of Community and Health Development,* University of Kansas, https://ctb.ku.edu/en/table-of-contents/analyze/choose-and-adapt-community-interventions/ethical-issues/main

6

INTEGRATION OF ETHICS IN TRAINING TEACHERS FOR SECONDARY SCHOOL EDUCATION IN KENYA

Rose Wambui Njihia

Introduction

Teaching is a profession which by its very nature requires a high level of integrity of life and aptitude in those who choose and train for it.[34] Formal education is essential at every stage of human development from pre-primary to primary levels, secondary to tertiary levels. This present paper places focus on secondary education and calls for intensified integration of ethics in the professional preparation of teachers due to the sensitivity of the age bracket of students they teach. Students at this stage are generally adolescents and are in search of discovering themselves and grasping clues on the vicissitudes of life. They need to find in teachers' authentic persons whom they can look up to as models. Instead, the recent events widely reported through mass media about some members of the teaching fraternity in secondary schools were absurd. Some teachers have been accused and even prosecuted for behavioural improprieties ranging from sexual involvement with students, examination malpractices to disorderliness while at work. The phenomena has prompted the desire to investigate into the quality of teacher training in the country, the state of integration

---

[34]Rose Wambui Njihia, Catholic University of Eastern Africa.

of ethics in teaching and the comparative study on the topic at hand from other countries for the purpose of obtaining insights on best practices that could be adopted where necessary in grooming a highly disciplined academic staff for secondary schools, with the objective of imparting holistic education to the young people to whom the thrust of a better future of a nation lies.

Teaching is a profession which by its very nature requires a high level of integrity of life and aptitude in those who choose and train for it. In Kenya, formal education plays a very significant role in all aspects of development; economically, socially and culturally. Formal education is equally essential at every stage of human development - pre-primary and primary levels, secondary and tertiary levels. Teachers in these different stages of education are seen as transmitters of skills, knowledge and values to their students. They are also seen as role models to the students they teach and they are always at the front line of developing students' understanding and core values (Patrinos & Kagia, 2008). Teachers are therefore very important in producing quality education hence they are expected to always be guided by ethical values.

Despite the fact that teachers play a very important role in education, and the values attached to them, there are professional misconduct and lack of integrity among teachers in Kenya which have been reported. Recent high profile cases such as teachers' sexual involvement with students, examination malpractices to disorderliness while at work have raised ethical issues in training of teachers from national to international arena. These cases stress the importance of ethical responsibility in the teaching profession, and further raise the need to educate students about their profession and ethical obligations. This paper attempts to call into action the importance of integrating ethics in training of teachers in secondary schools with specific focus in Kenya.

Literature across the world has shown that teachers and other educational administrators have been engaging in unethical behaviours in their profession. For instance Shakeshaft (2004) indicates that teachers in United States of America have been accused of involving in sexual misconduct with the students, such as, request for sexual favours, unwelcoming sexual advances and sexual touching. In Germany on the other hand, teachers have also been accused of indulging themselves with unethical practices such as selling examination materials to students (Chapman, 2002). Similarly, in Asian countries such as China, Transparency International (2007) found out that teachers' misconducts have been increasing tremendously; selling of examination materials and allowing someone else to sit for an exam for a certain candidate has been cited as common phenomena.

In Sub-Saharan Africa, there are numerous cases of professional misconduct involving teachers and other educational administrators. Teachers have involved in unethical behaviours while on duty; rape, sexual harassment, defilement, examination cheating, and drunkenness, just to mention but a few. In Tanzania, Oziambo (2013) discloses a number of teachers' professional malpractices which include examination fraud, unethical dressing, absenteeism, sexual misconduct, corruption, private tuition among others.

In Kenya, the recent events widely reported through mass media about some members of the teaching fraternity in secondary schools were absurd. Some teachers have been accused and even prosecuted for behavioural improprieties ranging from sexual involvement with students, examination malpractices to disorderliness while at work. The phenomena have prompted the desire to investigate into the quality of teacher training in the country and the state of integration of ethics in teacher training institutions in Kenya. In order to curb ethical and professional misconducts among teachers and school administrators, it is therefore important for the teacher training institutions to integrate ethical principles and values in teacher professional training exercise so as to produce teachers of integrity who will act as role models to the students.

Rationale

Education is widely recognized as key to national development in Kenya. Since independence, the government of Kenya has placed emphasis on the role of education in socio-economic development. As a result, the government has expanded teacher training institutions in the country with an attempt of ensuring that children receive quality education at all levels; the quality of teachers in schools is paramount in the attainment of educational goals.

However, the persistent increase in cases of misconduct among teachers and other educational administration staff in Kenyan secondary schools have been impeding the attainment and the implementation of educational goals. In an attempt to curb cases of misconducts among teachers and school administration, the government and other educational bodies like Teachers' Service Commissioner (TSC) have come up with measures to deal with integrity issues such as warnings, reprimands, dismissal, etc. In spite of all these measures, cases of teachers' misconduct in schools are still rampant in the country. This raises concern about the type and the quality of training offered to teachers in universities and other teacher training institutions.

Efforts have been made to decry and dissuade teachers from professional misconduct by various authors. Most of these writings are availed to the public through newspapers and other techno media. Nevertheless, an article of this nature is a piece of work that comes with its unique worth, not just to add a voice on a matter that has already been spoken about widely; a paper hosted by globethics.net is a sound way of delivering an idea of this kind. The audience is broad and the possibility of dissemination is guaranteed. The work is concise, thus allowing a quick perception of a difficult problem in a flash. The recommendations are timely and constructive for readers of all levels, both young and grown.

Perception of the Teaching Career in Secondary School in Kenya

In Kenya, many people do not perceive teaching as a future career which one can undertake to earn a living. Teaching in Kenya has been negatively perceived as a career for the poor and failures. The teaching profession is viewed as a low profession and a preserve for women (women in many African countries are poor, compared to men). In Kenya, the brightest form four leavers shun teaching. They do not even consider teaching as a career. This is mainly because many form four leavers who join the teaching profession are mostly with a lower grade which cannot make them secure more lucrative careers for example medicine, engineering, law, etc. This view has been supported by Thuranira (2010) who says that in Kenya, those students who take teaching as their career do it as last resort, having failed to enrol in other lucrative careers.

The teaching profession is associated with the poor in Kenya because people from high social economic status can afford to take their children to prestigious private schools and in turn score good grades which enable them to take prestigious courses in the best universities in the country. Following the media clips on the best performers in the national exams in Kenya, most of the students when asked about careers they would want to pursue, their options seem stuck on medicine, engineering, law, piloting or more recently actuarial science. This negative perception on the teaching career has got a huge impact on the education system in Kenya; the same parents who want their children to take only prestigious careers expect their children to be taught by qualified teachers and yet they do not want their qualified children to be teachers.

Quality of Secondary School Teacher Training in Kenya

Teachers are considered to be the nation builder. Teachers are very essential at every stage of students' development. It is therefore important to ensure that the quality of training programmes and the institutions are kept up to standard. This is because the quality of teacher training programmes and the institutions has direct consequences on the outcome of the teachers and the entire education system.

In Kenya, training of secondary school teachers is done in universities and colleges. In universities, training of teachers takes four year and a trainee acquires a bachelor of education degree (B.ED). In case an undergraduate has a bachelor degree in a different field, he /she take a one year post graduate course in education. In diploma colleges, training of teachers takes three years and a student acquires a diploma in education. Training of secondary school teachers takes place both in public and private universities.

Education is considered as one of the key elements to socio-economic development in the country. This therefore means that for Kenya to increase its rate of socio-economic development, teachers should receive high quality professional training. However, according to the Commission of University Education – CUE (2016), higher learning institutions in Kenya have been affected by countless problems ranging from irrelevant and low quality curriculum, ill equipped teacher training institutions, hesitancy in integrating new technologies among others.

Quality training of teachers is very critical. This means that the resources and facilities for preparing teachers need to be adequate and suitable in order to produce quality teachers. In Kenya, according to Wangari (2003), the current status of facilities and materials for training secondary school teachers is pathetic. Wangari further says that these materials and facilities for teacher training are inadequate, out-dated, dilapidated and unsuitable for producing competent teachers with the necessary skills and knowledge who can operate in this century.

This state of affairs raises concern about the quality of teachers serving in the school system and has negatively affected the image of these teachers. Their self-esteem is usually low, the society perceives them as people of low calibre and their integrity has always been compromised. While these teachers may appear incompetent and not reflecting the expected image of what a good teacher should be, the causes of this state lies elsewhere. They are victims of the teacher preparation programme in the country.

The mushrooming of private universities in Kenya for the last decades has led to the growth of secondary school teacher education leading to a very unhealthy trend that is commercialization. This trend has negatively impacted on the quality of secondary school teacher education in Kenya; teacher education has come into control of people who view training institutions as money making machines. These institutions lack or have dilapidated infrastructure necessary for facilitating teaching and learning activities. Resources and facilities are hardly in place, but exist only on papers. They are only provided during inspection but as soon as the inspection team leaves, the situation remains the same. This state of affair can be curbed by proper interventions from the Ministry of education and other educational bodies governing teacher education in the country.

Current Programme (Curriculum) of Teacher Training for Secondary Schools in Kenya

As the world continues to change with all its aspects of life, the education system must as well keep on changing so as to meet the needs of the teachers and the students. Unlike in the past, teacher-student relationships have become more complex. This therefore means that the curriculum for teacher trainees needs to be up-dated so as to provide them with the necessary knowledge on how to handle such relationships in a professional manner.

For the above goal to be realized, teacher trainees' education needs to be carefully made. In the views of Honey (2017), teacher education is the process by which a person attains training in an institution of learning in order to become a teacher. This therefore, means that teacher education prepares both in-service and pre-service teachers with the required skills as well as the necessary knowledge. In order to improve the quality of teacher trainees, teacher education should contain four main elements as quoted by Perraton (2010):

> "Improving the general educational background of the trainee teachers; increasing the trainees' knowledge and understanding of the subjects they are to teach; focus on pedagogy and understanding of children and learning; and the developing of the trainees' practical skills and competences" (Perraton, 2010).

The quality of the teachers teaching secondary school students in Kenya plays a very important role in education system of the country. This was heavily supported by the Ministry of Educational Implementation Framework III of 2011-2015 which states that:

> "The quality and effectiveness of the education system depend heavily on the quality of its teachers. They are the key persons in determining success in meeting the system's goals. In view of this, the calibre of teachers and the status of the teaching profession are of paramount importance. The educational and personal well-being of learners in schools, thus, hinge crucially on teachers' competence, commitment and resourcefulness."

The above view was supported by Karajaga (2012) who said that for a teacher trainee to become more effective in service delivery, he/she should as well be taught educational ethics, integrity and professionalism. The Sessional Paper No. 6 of 1988 has as well supported the need to improve the educational programmes of teachers in the country. The paper states that: "there is urgent need to develop and promote teacher education programme if the administration of education in Kenya is to succeed and therefore national development accelerated."

Ethics of teaching is a very important aspect in teacher education in Kenya. Ethics of teaching for secondary school teachers is neither formally designed in the curriculum nor taught to teacher trainees. Ethics of teaching are normally mentioned casually as aspects of principles and practices of teaching and only by those trainers who care to do so. This has led to the production of teachers who do not understand the teaching profession and its demands. Other than understanding the instructional responsibilities in teaching profession, secondary school teachers need also be well informed about ethics of teaching so as not to compromise the status, integrity and the image of the teachers in their profession as well as in the society.

According to Benninga (2003), universities and other learning institutions offering teacher education need to always to pay attention to values, ethics and service. Benninga further says that character education in teacher education should be part of philosophy of the institution as well as formal curriculum. The curriculum should examine moral development, ethics and the responsibilities of the teachers.

Studies have shown that the government of Kenya and other educational stakeholders are keen to support and improve teacher education programmes; but according to Kafwa, Gaudience and Kisaka (2015), the current teacher education curriculum in universities and colleges emphasises on the use of conventional teaching approaches rather than the modern approaches. A study by Allida, Ojunga,

Mvukiyehe, Okurut, Ndiwalana, & Muchemwa (2017), reveals that the curriculum for teacher trainees in Kenya does not always match well with the needs of the teacher trainees. The study further states that the training of teacher trainees is mainly theoretical in nature making it difficult for teachers to have an impact on classroom practice. The current curriculum does not emphasise the importance of ethics and professionalism in the teaching profession.

Gichure (1997) defines ethics as 'the systematic study of human actions from the point of view of their rightness or wrongness as a means for the achievement of man's ultimate happiness'. Similarly, Weiss (2006), states that: "good business means good ethics". In the same way, a good education means good ethics. This means that teachers as moral agents must always be guided by ethical values. Gichure (1997) states that: "teachers should always be guided by ethical values which include trustworthiness, honesty, integrity, reliability, loyalty, truthfulness, respect, caring, responsibility, accountability, transparency, diligence, perseverance, self-restraint, fairness and citizenship". The current teaching curriculum and the practices should therefore focus on the above ethical values so as to create a better society. This in return will enable the teacher training institutions to produce teachers who will always model strong character traits and demonstrate ethical behaviours, integrity and professionalism with their students and co-workers.

Current Issues on Professional Integrity Involving Secondary School Teachers

Safety in learning institutions is a concern of all stakeholders in education world over. Parents, educators, religious organizations, non-governmental organizations, policy makers, and governments all work to ensure that teachers, students and other members of the school community are safe from any imminent danger that could otherwise compromise the realization of schools' objectives. However, the current emerging evidence and incidents in Kenyan secondary schools indicate that issues on professional integrity involving teachers are predominant in schools. Cases such as rape, sexual harassment, examination malpractice, drunkenness and other forms of disorderliness in schools have become critical and threaten to tear apart the educational fabric in Kenyan learning institutions in general and secondary schools in particular.

Ethical decisions and actions are important in our personal and professional lives. This is certainly true in the teaching profession, where ethical misconduct continues to make attractive headlines in the media. A number of cases have hit the headline in Kenya involving some secondary school teachers engaging in rape and other forms of sexual behaviours with the students. The United Nations Educational, Scientific and Cultural Organization - UNESCO (2017) released a shocking report about the increasing cases of sexual harassment of students in secondary schools in Kenya aged thirteen to seventeen years, with perpetrators being their teachers. Thirty nine percent (39%) of the interviewed school principals stated that cases of teacher student sexual harassment had occurred in their schools. The current shocking cases were where one student was raped in June 2018 at Moi Girls' High School in Nairobi while the other students were reported to have been sexually harassed by male teachers in the same month at Maasai Girls' High School in Narok. To-date, the perpetrators are not known yet the incidences occurred inside the school's compound. In Kenyan secondary schools, much of the scope and the magnitude of sexual misconduct perpetrated by teachers and schools' administrators remain hidden.

Examination cheating is another common unethical behaviour among secondary school teachers and school administrators in Kenya. A report by Kenya Examination Council (KEC) revealed that during last years' (2017) Kenya Certificate of Secondary Exams (KCSE), teachers, students and the parents worked together mainly by use of mobile phones to transit exam materials (KEC, 2018). The report further says that ten teachers were implicated for sneaking examination materials into the schools' compound to help the students cheat. Some teachers have also been reported selling examination related materials to parents and students.

Drunkenness and disorderliness of teachers while at school is also an ethical issue which needs to be addressed by the relevant educational bodies in Kenya. Drunkenness and disorderly behaviours are more rampant in rural areas and in informal areas within the cities due to the presence of cheaper locally brewed alcohols. This scenario has made many teachers forget their professional responsibilities.

Teachers' absenteeism is a predominant issue of concern among secondary school teachers in Kenya. Many teachers have been reported to spending very few work hours at school while most of their time is spent in their private businesses. Absenteeism of teachers in Kenya is mainly attributed to low salaries making teachers to engage in private activities to supplement their income. This has resulted to poor academic performance of the students since teachers do not have enough time to complete the syllabi.

An Overview of Teachers' Training Practice in Foreign Nations

University of St. Francis in United State of America is one of the best examples of teacher education institution which embraces character education. The University has always paid much attention to ethics, values and service in the curricula. According to Bohlin, Dougherty & Farmer (2002), in the University of St. Francis, character education is part of the curriculum and the philosophy of the institution. Education students in this university are well equipped with the necessary knowledge and professional skills to integrate ethics, values, and service into their classroom teaching and learning experience. Most of the courses offered in education examine teachers' moral development, ethics and their responsibilities as character educators.

The university programs on the other hand, familiarize the students' teacher to community involvement and service (Bohlin, Dougherty & Farmer, 2002). In 1999, University of St. Francis formed the Values 99 committee which was mandated to identify key values to be included in the institution's mission statement. As a result, integrity, compassion, service and respect were emphasized and to-date all these values are integrated into all coursework offered by the institution. For instance, there is "Introduction to Theology" which is a course taken by all the students in the university. This course has the components of integrity and service.

Furthermore, the University of St. Francis offers character education for all teachers. This in an intensive one-week programme offered during summer. It is a professional development course where teachers are intended to respect and be responsible with the students. During this course, teachers are taught on how to integrate character education in what is taught to them. The course helps the educators to learn how to create a moral, influential and character building school and classroom environment.

In order to encourage students to practice habits of good character, the University of St. Francis has always provided a conducive environment. The university provides various activities which give students an opportunity to serve others. Student teachers are immersed in a conducive environment which nurtures their own development of good character. Furthermore, the coursework undertaken by these students enables them to shape and improve their teaching in a way that positively contributes to the development of character of the students they teach. This means that the graduates of the University of St. Francis are well prepared and always committed to promote and nurture character education throughout their teaching career.

Way Forward

In order to emphasise the importance of ethics in education and training, the following recommendation are put forward:

Universities and other teacher training institutions should integrate ethical discipline in all areas of education and teacher training. The learning institutions should therefore restructure the current education curricula to integrate ethics across all the teacher training programs. This can be achieved by inviting theologians, canonists and philosophical ethicists while developing the curricula so as to assist the curricula developers with the necessary content to include in the course. Once the curriculum has been developed, all the training institutions need to establish a centre of ethics where all the trainees will be required to undertake a course in ethics.

As the learning institutions try to reshape their structures to integrate ethics across all disciplines, it is important to note that an individual ethical behaviour is more likely to flourish within an impartial and fair society. The society forms individual values. This means that for one to live an ethical life, people must work harder in order to build a just and fair society even as they try to reshape its structures.

It is vital to appreciate the fact that a family where one grows is the basic institution for upbringing a human person who is not only law abiding but who is respectful and ready to adhere to ethical values in adult life. It's conceivably much difficult for adults to embrace prompt transformation of behavioural tendencies if attempts to holistic growth were not achieved early in life. It is compelling therefore, that parents should engage their offspring into a broad understanding of societal experience imbued with moral and ethical values. Exemplary teachers exist around the world, including in Kenya; their integrity of life is not merely a fruit of professional training in ethics, but is to be traced back to their childhood.

Conclusion

In order to solve the rampant unethical cases involving teachers and school administration in secondary schools in Kenya, it is very important that teacher training institutions restructure their curricula to include ethics across the entire teacher training programs. This in return will enable the teacher training institutions to produce teachers who will always model strong character traits and demonstrate ethical behaviours, integrity and professionalism with their students and co-workers.

This study touches into sensitive issues that would need quite a volume to stretch out ideas in all the aspects treated above; nevertheless in its brevity, it assumes a role of a launching pad towards an ambitious and elaborate research activity on the same theme in view of making education more meaningful. Despite the challenges secondary education faces in Kenya in regard to integrating ethics in teacher training curricula, there is hope of achieving transformation owing to the present efforts by government educational agencies and the good will of the public in embracing holistic education for a better future.

References

Allida, V. *et al.*, "Assessment of Teacher Education Curriculum in Kenya. Transforming for the future," in: *Baraton Interdisciplinary Research Journal*, 7, 1-9 (2017).

Benninga, J. S., “Moral and ethical issues in teacher education,” in: *Journal of Research in Character Education,* 1, (1), 17-30 (2003).

Bohlin, K. E. *et al.* (2002), “Practices of teacher educators committed to character: Examples from teacher education programs emphasizing character development. The Character Education Partnership”, http://www.University%20of%20Saint%20Francis.docx%202.pdf (accessed 12 September 2018).

Commission of University Education - CUE, In: *Daily Nation*, Sunday April 24 (2016).

Gichure, W. C., *Basic Concepts in Ethics*, Nairobi: Focus Publications Ltd, 1997.

Honey, N. (2017). “What is teacher education?”, https://www.reference.com/business-finance/teacher-education-8 (23 August 2018).

Kafwa, N. O. *et al.*, “Teacher preparation practices in Kenya and the 21st century learning: A moral obligation”, in: *Journal of Education and Practice, 6 (17)* (2015).

Kenya Examination Council (KEC), In: *Daily Nation*, Wednesday May (2018).

Karajagi, G. (2012). “Teachers as change agents: Academy for creative teaching”, http://www.academia.edu/4941833, (accessed 23 August 2018).

Oziambo, B., "The nature of teacher professional misconduct in Tanzanian Public

Primary Schools: The case of Sumbawanga Municipal and Rural Districts", In: *International Journal of Education,* 5 (1) (2013).

Perraton, H. (2010), "Teacher education: The role of open and distance learning", http://www.academia.edu/4941833/, (accessed 10 September 2018).

Thuranira, T. S. (2010), "Perspectives on the teaching profession in Kenya." University of Maryland, College Park, http://www.Perspective%20of%20teaching%20in%20Kenya.pdf, (accessed 4 September 2018).

United Nations Educational, Scientific and Cultural Organization (UNESCO) (2017), In: *Daily Nation*, (Wednesday, 13 December 2017).

Wangari, S., *Problems facing teacher education in Kenya: a case study of teaching practice in the University of Nairobi*, Nairobi, 2003.

7

BECOMING GLOBAL CITIZENS: LEARNING STRATEGIES IN ETHICAL DECISION-MAKING AND ITS IMPACT ON COMMUNITY MEMBERS A CASE STUDY ON CORRUPTION IN THE INDONESIAN CONTEXT

Alviani Permata

Introduction

Ethical decision- making is a skill that must be practice.[35] Misuse of this skill can lead to abuse of power. Learning from the PISA survey and several cases of violations of the power of young Indonesian leaders, the learning process in schools need to change. Indonesian teachers need to practice more learning strategies that develop higher- order thinking skills. These skills are to prepare younger generation to accommodate and face problems in their real life. Especially for Indonesian youth, the more skilled they are in ethical decision making, the more they can contribute to the international communities and become the best global citizens.

Abuse of power is an action that potentially happens in all organizations in the world. Indonesia is one of the countries that have

---

[35]Alviani Permata, Faculty Member of the Humanities Department of Duta Wacana Christian University, Yogyakarta, Indonesia.

many cases of this violation. According to a survey, the Indonesian Minister of Home Affairs has noted more than 70 out of 90[36] regional leaders are involved in corruptive cases. In 2016, 10 regional heads are involved[37] and in 2017, there are 12 cases involving regional leaders who are caught in the act. The leaders who did that abuse of authority were of various ages. The newest case involving young persons is the case of the president's millennial special staff who misused their authorities to bring in their companies for exclusive policy in community economic empowering.[38] Both of them then apologize and step back from their positions.

Abuse of power can take many forms, such as bullying or harassing behaviour, requesting staff to do personal errands or favours, pressuring staff to distort facts or break rules, and interfering with the ability of a colleague to work effectively.[39]

It is the act of using one's position of power in an abusive way.[40] What is intended by abuse which cross the boundary is carrying out activities or acting beyond limits of the authority stated in the law? This, in the course of performing work can occur both with external stakeholders and internally among staff.

It is no surprise that corruptive behaviours become more recurrent because it is "passed down" to younger generation. Even, husbands and wives in their positions can collusively do abuse of power.[41] The wives are in legislative board while the husbands are regional leaders. The misuse of ethical decision making is one of the causes of power abuse.

---

[36] Acch.kpk.co.id (18 Governors and 72 regional leaders as regents/mayors) in 2004-2017

[37] Based on Valid News Research. kompasiana.com online.

[38] Nasional.tempo.com online; https://www.bbc.com/indonesia/indonesia-52297462. Accesed July 4th, 2020.

[39] Unesco.org online. Accessed July 2020.

[40] Businessdictionary.com online. Accessed June 2020.

[41] These cases happened to some local leaders in some provinces in Indonesia.

Indonesian young people have this kind of issue. Thus, we have a challenging situation as a nation because Indonesia is facing 60% demographic bonus of productive age in the community. It is difficult to imagine should Indonesian young generation face this kind of issues on campus or at work while their ethical decision-making skills are weak.

This paper tries to describe the facts of how thinking skills can contribute to decision making competency of students that influence their ethical attitude and behaviour at work to be used they are adults, moreover when they become leaders.

Learning Strategies at Schools

Indonesia has participated in an international study on student performances since 2000. This study is called Programme for International Student Assessment (PISA) which is a worldwide study by the Organization for Economic Co-operation and Development (OECD). One of the aims for school projects is to measure students' knowledge, skills and competencies that will equip them for success in education and work. Every three years the PISA survey provides comparative data on 15-year-old performance in reading, mathematics, and science.[42] According to 2018 survey, junior high students in Indonesia scored lower than the OECD average in reading, mathematics, and science. This result has nothing to do with the low level of intelligence of Indonesian student but it is related to the learning strategies at schools.

Most teachers in Indonesia use traditional teaching methods. Such methods privilege conceptual integration over the practical testing of

---

[42] Pisa for schools - FAQS https://www.oecd.org/pisa/aboutpisa/pisa-based-test-for-schools-faq.htm

ideas, prioritizing abstract contents over empirical manipulation.[43] In this way, teachers perform expositive classes, and students must perceive, understand, and integrate information by themselves. Moreover, traditional methods aimed at the evaluation of learning ask for the recall and recovery of the contents presented in class, putting aside the accomplishment of practical activities in the empiric field, disregarding the use of problem-solving skills. (Freiberg- Hoffman, *et al.*, 2017). In Bloom's Taxonomy, the way teachers explain materials and students perceive and understand by themselves develops low order thinking skills (LOTS) which means that they only need to recall and understand. So, if a person is unable to achieve all lower thinking skills and move up to higher-order thinking, then this person will not be prepared for real-life situations.

The result of PISA surveys for Indonesian junior high students shows that teachers in Indonesia should revamp their methods in learning strategies to improve the students' thinking skills become high order (HOTS) to accommodate and face problems in their real-life situation.

According to Sternberg (2018), successful people use three kinds of intelligence: analytical, creative, and practical.[44] In Bloom's anatomy, these three kinds of intelligence need high order thinking skills (HOTS). Analytical intelligence uses critical thinking, which include judging, evaluating, comparing, contrasting, critiquing, explaining why, and examining. Analytical thinking is used to evaluate things and to decide. While creative thinking involves creating, discovering, imagining, supposing, designing, "what if-ing," inventing, and producing. It is substantial for students to exercise their creative "muscles." Lastly, practical thinking encompasses practicing, demonstrating, using,

---

[43]This situation is also supported by the national report card of Indonesian teachers which is only under 70 out of 100.

[44] http://www.intelltheory.org/sternberg.shtml

applying, and implementing information. Practical thinkers take knowledge and apply it to real life situations. They know how to use knowledge, how to adapt to different situations using their knowledge, and often how to get along with others.

Failure in practicing analytical, creative, and practical intelligence mentioned above implicates the skills to make ethical decision making. Ethical decision-making refers to the process of evaluating and choosing among alternatives in a manner consistent with ethical principles. In making ethical decisions, it is necessary to perceive and eliminate unethical options and select the best ethical alternative.

The ethical decision-making process requires three things. First, there is a commitment to the process. It ought to do with wanting to do the right thing. Second, there is awareness in the process. It is about the awareness to act undeviating and to apply moral beliefs to everyday behaviour. Third, it needs competence in the process. Competence here is the ability to gather and evaluate information, develop alternatives, and estimate potential risks and consequences.[45] So, Indonesian students, according to PISA surveys, face very fundamental problems since they are fifteen, which is the lack of training to have aforementioned competencies. This indicates that these young people have stunted awareness and low commitment in making and considering their choices.

Abuse of Power and Decision-making Skill

As stated above, ethical decision-making refers to the process of evaluating and choosing among alternatives in a manner consistent with ethical principles as high order thinking skills, which failed to be

---

[45] "Making Ethical Decisions Process". *blink.ucsd.edu* online. Accessed May 2020.

ingrained to Indonesian students since junior high according to PISA surveys. We can see some cases on Indonesian TV regarding the failure of practicing these skills of thinking, leading to some people being prosecuted in the court. Common cases that happens to some Indonesian leaders from various fields, like religion, politics, economics, even education. Some examples about is easily accessible in our newspapers. There is a case of bribery in sale and purchase of position in the ministry of religion[46], or the newest case of a young parliament member getting angry after being warned for texting and phoning in a plane while take off and landing[47] and the case of the president's millennial special staff due to conflict of interests.[48] A commissioner of The Indonesian Child Protection Commission is fired for her false and misleading statement about the cause of pregnancy that is not based on scientific evidence.[49] The news was about the ethical violation of individuals who are regarded as important persons in our community. They are religious leaders, a parliament member, a commissioner, and President's Staffs. All of them are categorized as young leaders.

The bribery case indicates that the religious leaders do not consider and evaluate other alternatives they have when deciding bribery as their solution. The only outcome they see is that they can earn a lot of money and do anything with the money. They fail to comply with the third process of the ethical decision- making skill. Meanwhile the case of the parliament member shows that he violates the first process of ethical decision-making, namely commitment. He does not have the commitment to do the right thing or the awareness to do so. He is talking on the phone while the plane is taking off which is something all passengers already know is wrong and is something that threaten the safety of many people on the plane.

---

[46] see Bernie, Mohmmad, 2019. *Tirto.id* online. Accessed August 2020.

[47] see Rizal, Jawahir Gustav. *Kompas*.com.Accessed August 2020.

[48] Kurniawati, Endri. Basarah. *Antara* online. 26 April 2020.

[49] *CNN Indonesia.* Online. 27 April 2020. Accessed August 2020.

Meanwhile, the president's millennial special staffs breach the third process of the ethical decision-making skill. They do not use the tendering processes which are the common way of being transparent, fair, and of avoiding conflict of interest in business. Finally, the commissioner's case also disregards the third process because she did not research the information she can simply find in books, researches, or newspapers before issuing her statement. This sensitive statement has impacted her capacity and competency as a commissioner of the National Commission for Child Protection.

Learning from these cases suggests that the first and second processes of ethical decision-making have been neglected. As noted above, the first process is a commitment to doing the right thing; the second is awareness to act consistently and apply moral beliefs to daily behaviour. Neither is easy to be put into practice, especially in today's world where norms have changed. Although values are the kind of principles people are not ready to compromise on[50], it is undeniable that values nowadays have changed. Parents and teachers ought to have more perseverance to practice both processes for themselves and also for their children and students. The perseverance will work best if there are supports from the government to be the example. In good governance, there are individuals who do their best not to break the laws or rules which they have established themselves.

Becoming a Global Citizen: Managing Power with Ethical Decision-making Skill

Global citizenship nowadays is a new phenomenon. This is a symbol of a person who has the initiatives to be more aware of the world. He or she respects and values diversity. A global citizen participates in

[50] Girardin, Benoit, 2012: 66.

communities at all levels, from local to global, and takes responsibilities for their actions and beliefs. To become a global citizen means to be creative, flexible, dedicated, and proactive. Global citizens take active parts in the emerging international communities and are concerned in helping to build the values and practices of these communities.

With the low competencies mentioned above, it is difficult to have hope that Indonesian young people can contribute in building the values and involving in world communities unless there are changes in the way teachers educate their students. This can be done through training their students to have more opportunities in making choices, considering and evaluating their choices, and judging their own choices in peer-meetings or seminars.

The more creative learning strategies employed in the class are, the more motivated students are in learning and awakening their curiosity, which leads to improvement on their competencies in ethical decision-making skills. Should this is applied, it is possible that Indonesian young people become the leaders for global communities in more ethical ways, without the chances of abuse of power will happen, and they will be more prepared to face and handle the VUCA (volatile, uncertain, complex, and ambiguous) situation in the future, and hopefully, they can contribute more in international communities and become the best global citizens. The long-way-to-go journey really needs a complex and an outstanding strategic plan which involves many stakeholders while the Indonesian minister of education is preparing for it to happen.

References

Bernie, Mohammad. 2020. "Suap Jual Beli Jabatan Kemenag: Reformasi Birokrasi Tak Berjalan? - Tirto.ID". *Tirto.Id.* https://tirto.id/suap-jual-beli-jabatan-kemenag-reformasi-birokrasi-tak-berjalan-djQ3.

Freiberg Hoffmann, Agustín, Juliana Beatriz Stover, and Natalia Donis. 2017. "Influence of Learning Strategies on Learning Styles: Their Impact on Academic Achievement of College Students from Buenos Aires". *Problems of Education in The* 21^{St} *Century* 75 (1): 6 - 18.

Girardin, Beno□ 2012. *Ethics in Politics: Why It Matters More Than Ever and How It Can Make A Difference*. 1st Ed. Geneva: Globethics.net Focus No. 5.

"Jokowi Teken Keppres Pemecatan Sitti Hikmawatty dari KPAI". 2020. *CNN Indonesia.com*. https://www.cnnindonesia.com/nasional/20200427095823-20-497540/jokowi-teken-keppres-pemecatan-sitti-hikmawatty-dari-kpai.

Kurniawati, Endri. 2020. "Basarah: 2 Staf Khusus Milenial Mundur, Hindari Abuse of Power". *Tempo*. https://nasional.tempo.co/read/1335805/basarah-2-staf-khusus-milenial-mundur-hindari-abuse-of-power.

Paramita, Rahadian. P. 2018. Rapor Guru dalam Hasil Uji Kompetensi https://lokadata.id/artikel/rapor-guru-dalam-hasil-uji-kompetensi

Rizal, Jawahir G. 2020. "Ramai Soal Kasus Mumtaz Rais, Ini Penjelasan Soal Pentingnya Keselamatan Udara Halaman All - Kompas.com". *KOMPAS.com*. https://www.kompas.com/tren/read/2020/08/15/212531165/ramai-soal-kasus-mumtaz-rais-ini-penjelasan-soal-pentingnya-keselamatan?page=all.

Stella, Felisitas. 2020. "Maraknya Penyalahgunaan Wewenang Kepala Daerah". *KOMPASIANA*. https://www.kompasiana.com/stellanathania/5c015155677ffb642912d805/maraknya-penyalahgunaan-wewenang-kepala-daerah.

"What Is Abuse of Power? Definition and Meaning". 2020. *Businessdictionary.Com*. http://www.businessdictionary.com/definition/abuse-of-power.html.

Yosephine, Liza. 2020. "Andi Taufan Garuda Putra, Staf Khusus Milenial Presiden Jokowi Mundur di Tengah Tuduhan Konflik Kepentingan - BBC News Indonesia". *BBC News Indonesia*. https://www.bbc.com/indonesia/indonesia-52297462.

8

RETRIBUTION OF PLAGIARISM FOUNDED ON REASON-BASED ACTIONS

Reason-based Actions and the Virtue of a Gift

Ignace Haaz

Introduction

Plagiarism and Applied Ethics as a Reason-based Practice

Reasons for action in the field of research and higher education and the retribution of wrongs

Practical reason is the capacity for resolving, the question of what one is to do by applying reflection. The focus for practical reason can spans across applied ethics of research in higher education, to the understanding and management of wrongs.[51] Reflections on reasons for action and clear definition of what research-wrongs are concern the difference between expressionist and reason based actions[52]. There is a difference between taking action with good reason, and taking action simply because the action is fun or troublesome. If additional

---

[51] Ignace Haaz, Managing Editor, Globethics.net.

[52] Similar views on reason-based practice are found in the work of Joseph Raz and I ought him the comparison between expressive actions and practical reasons, and the concepts of first and second-order reasons.

responsibilities exist in taking a specific action, they are not merely expressive acts, but reason based actions. Once the concept of a reason based responsible action is defined, we shall see that the idea that *we ought to answer to research wrongs* becomes clearer, but does not entail one unique and clear option on the type of *retributive* answer. Although we might distinguish between situations where *a sanction must be engaged*, from situations where *a sanction ought to be engaged* against a wrongful conduct and action, retribution might not only be seen as a closed and simple answer to the author of the negation of research rights. Further education ethics objectives and virtue based actions might also be valuable parts of the answer to the wrong.

The framework for a reason based actions

As a general framework for a reason based action, we first need to distinguish between reasons taken in the wide sense, or *first-order reasons,* from a more technical definition of reasons as second-order reasons. First-order reasons are any type of ground for action, which exist on balance, or *immediate reason for performing* therefor should be considered as comparable reasons. By contrast, if we say that we have a good reason P to act or refrain from acting under some circumstances, and have a reason Q to act or refrain from acting, in similar circumstances, if P entails non-Q, we have an exclusionary reason non-Q of a new type of reasons. It is a reason to act or refrain from acting *for a reason*, which we would call a second-order reason. P is not a first-order reason but a *rule-type* or *promise* type of reason, which entails that we as subject stop to consider competing options, as equally valid possible reasons for the action, once we decide initiating the action based on that reason. Stopping to put on a same balance of values a reason for action can be based on the fact that *a reason entails itself another reason*, typically a reason related to the exclusion of any possible overriding options, as in promise-keeping. When we say we book an appointment we arrange it at a particular time t1 which excludes t2. Such reasons are in most usual cases not expressionist reasons, since they entails some further reasons as the management of some activities, but need not to exclude direct motives as the pleasure to meet and see again a colleague, we have not seen for a while. Not all actions are done for some reason, an exemplary case are actions performed under hypnosis[53]. If a subject acts under the influence of post-hypnotic suggestion, or for kleptomaniac actions, such as picking up a book in a bookshop and leaving the shop without paying, neither first-order nor second-order reasons seem to work. In these cases, the subjects may well admit, after interrogation, that there was no reason to do what they did (Raz, 1999[54])[55].

---

[53] We may also ask with Swift, and later the Romantic thinkers, how far reason without faith in reason is practically possible, could we not imaging that instead of being an "animal rationale", the human being could be considered only "rationis capax" [with the capacity to use reason]. In our chapter we resist this view, without falling into the intellectualist view of believing that knowing a multitude of truth propositions, without knowing why they are truth and what for they are relevant, as the autodidact of the *Nausée* of Sartre who simply reads everything.

[54] Raz, Joseph (2011). *From Normativity to Responsibility*. Oxford: Oxford University Press, p. 71. See also: Raz, Joseph (1999). *Engaging Reason: On the Theory of Value and Action*. Oxford: Oxford University Press.

[55] We might think that the *something wrong* which occurs in hypnosis, is on both levels: on a first-order cognitive level, when hypnotic suggestion is present, it does not concern yet a second-order judgement, but directly what the belief is, and how we judge about things. If some abrupt change occurs in the brain, for the sake of the argument, a non-reasonable mental confusion occurs, hallucination, delirium, etc. Obviously a person could act without reason, as we observe with Alzheimer, or dementia induced mental states. Then second-order ways of dealing with the issue may also not work, as a person might not be in position to correct the lack of relevance of some impressions. Instead of rejecting the validity of a doubt, on some odd impression, and say that some first-order belief may be wrong, a way of regulating our beliefs may be missing

On the contrary, the classical example of a reason based action could be seen as a second-order reason related action, when I not only act for the reason that my action relates to some value based central feature, but when I decide not to choose between competing options anymore, due to an exclusionary reason. A good way of representing what an exclusionary reason may be is the mental state of fatigue which prevents me from considering the different options at hand clearly (cf. Raz, 1978[56]). It is not a state of mental confusion, which would lead to do as if I would be able to consider many options, but simply recognizing that I am not able anymore to choose in a balanced way, therefor I exclude any choice and suspend in a wise way of considering any range of options until I feel I recovered my mental capacity.

Excluding options as including options in a balanced way are essential modalities of our mental activity of choosing, not only in research and knowledge related domains but overall, in any non-cynical but "educated" manner and behaviour, when we act with moderation. Applied into the field of research practices, we find a wide range of reason based actions under the heading of "integrity based research". Typically questions of property or copyright function on the model of promise, by setting up a set of exclusionary options on the model. If this reason P to act on R's work and to borrow it is a good reason, then it might entail a set of exclusionary conditions such as "but I should not sell R's work, transform it in such a way that R's work would not be recognizable integrally as R's work, and I may even not be in position to copy or distribute copies of R's work, under specific exclusionary reasons". Of course reasons to copy and distribute could be also defined

---

in the first place. Since, from Raz's point of view we cannot choose to believe or not to believe, the situation becomes different, we need to reject fairly simply that reason exist in the first place.

[56] Raz, Joseph (ed.) (1978). *Practical Reasoning*, Oxford: University Press.

as granted, the set of reasons is open for transformation and should always remain adapted to the needs of the given practices[57].

We can generally agree across domains, disciplines and cultures that a necessary condition for carrying on good practice in research is a clear discernment of the reasons to act in such a way that the value of the work of another person is respected. These reasons will in turn entail the integrity based formation of new ideas or research results[58]. In particular the set of exclusionary reasons against various ways of the negation of others rights, and consequently jeopardizing trust and respect for the

---

[57] Globethics.net Foundation (*www.globethics.net*) aims at sharing teaching and networking services in an inclusive and empowering way. Open access publication and internet technologies play a key role in setting inclusive standards of education in place. The value of *integrity* is not less important, as the Switzerland based international organisation have both in its value statement. In our chapter we focus on integrity and argue that exclusionary reasons do play an important role in the ethics of higher education, research and information technologies ethics. Since education institutions emphasise usually inclusion and solidarity, it is worth showing the limits of inclusion, when balancing the distinctive values of responsibility and integrity. The puzzling aspect of these different norms is that precisely exclusion based reasons are founded on the very idea that we stop balancing options at some point. We shall argue that we are not abandoning our respect for all these values by respecting the value of integrity.

[58] Mistaken belief of what is valuable is not a sufficient for identifying a higher education research wrong, as long as respect for the other and for other's work is given. It might still be a illegitimately partial belief, since it seems a misperception of values. It may also be the case that a mistaken belief related partial belief or a form of legitimate partiality as choosing in favour of our family and friends, to be partial in favour of our country or city, ends up in choices based on anything different from maximising reason and reasoning. Then does it not follow that partiality is inconsistent with reason based actions to some degree? As valuable options are often incommensurate, and leave room for partiality, we tend to believe that reason based actions is an essential component for integrity based research in education, and thus being reluctant to reason, in the education field, is being weak-willed, lazy, foolish but not wrong.

work, should be considered with strong emphasis. The conditions around engaging with specific values, which are entailed by the production of research results, and the communication of these results, are essential features of an integrity based framework of responsible research. When identified, the communication of what constitutes a wrong is crucial and our aim and reflection on retributive sanction will be to show that a wide range of options is available. The individual teacher or the education institution, empowered with the capacity to assess the value of a research work, ought (and in limited cases must) respond by engaging seriously the author of the wrong with his wrong doing.

Let's first consider a central assumption made when we talk about respecting the value of a work. Building on available sources and then referring to them correctly denotes a respect for the work and the person. Typically respect and engagement with research values mean that the author, who presents his personal contribution to a field of knowledge, discriminates reasons to act on some other person's work. It is very difficult to see how one could be seen responsible for their research results without any given exclusionary reasons, a reason superior to reasons to perform this or that act. A reason to do one's duty for duty's sake may not entail negative or exclusionary reasons but in most cases, these duty founded reasons are special reasons called second-order reasons. In fact research individuals and institutions should be proud to show the amount of efforts made to understand research fraud through the disciplined use of observation and reason. Let us present four examples: i) fabricating results without relying on real results, ii) unduly changing, omitting or suppressing data, iii) using other's work and ideas without giving credit, or iv) manipulating integrity of the research process, without direct violations of rights. All of these examples are to some extent ways of not taking into consideration exclusionary reasons not to engage into the negation of the other's rights to be considered with respect.

Borrowing ideas and lacking respect for other's work

A borrowed idea is not necessarily wrong, but each part of a text should be documented so that the reader knows exactly where the ideas of one person end and where those of someone else's begin. The difficulty with a *prima facie* definition is that there is a set of sources classified as "common knowledge," in each discipline of university studies. Common knowledge is assimilated to information "that the average, educated reader would accept as reliable without having to look it up" that is without needing the validation of a source reference[59].

In the broader sense, some statements would need citation in a paper for a non-expert audience, while it would not need citation in an audience of students or teachers of a given discipline. In a nutshell, given the interdisciplinary and transversal character of knowledge formation today, common knowledge depends on what we assume others already know. It is therefore based on an evaluation of comparatively similar degrees of knowledge which may also, in fact rather seem incommensurate. As we said earlier, we nevertheless need a clear definition of what type of reason to act on other's work is a wrong reason, if we strive to have a reason-based practical rules.

The rules according to which we borrow from—and build on—the work of others cannot be a 'rule of the thumb' type of criteria if it is to remain fair. As we find clearly expressed, the manner remains unambiguous:

---

59 Academic Integrity At MIT, What is Common Knowledge? https://integrity.mit.edu/handbook/citing-your-sources/what-common-knowledge, accessed 2020.01.20

> "Since generating new knowledge requires an investment of time, money, and hard work, by meticulously documenting every borrowed idea we acknowledge our debt to others who have made the investment". [...] a code of conduct [on fair borrowing] does not merely protect intellectual property" [60]

In order to consolidate the protection of intellectual property of others, the very specificity of intellectual work should qualify for being an invention, and not only a transposition, translation, contextualization, or repetition of older models. Political ideological reasons, or partiality based values always coexist with other more universal type of reasons and values. Both universal and partial norms can have a historical dimension. They are subject of transformation at different times, in a wide range of diverse situations[61]. Honesty and originality of research describe central universal values specific to the field of higher education, they participate to the global and universal value of the university. They are the very core of knowledge virtues and apply across different disciplines: mathematical, natural and human sciences. Borrowing and building on existing knowledge are not self-sufficient values:

> "[the ethics of fair borrowing] also keeps us pushing academic knowledge forward in small increments. Compiling existing

---

[60] "Antiplagiarism policy and guidelines on integrating sources in academic writing", Wrocław University, 2012

[61] Access to Internet has brought a range of positive new experiences and values in the course of the 20th century, as the pleasant reading of texts - without needing to carry any physical print copies of our favourite books, journals and correspondence. Historical and political falsification occurred in Eastern European countries after 2nd WW and the Treatise of Trianon, in Middle East after the domination of the Ottoman Empire, in Africa after colonization by Western European countries, which are on the negative side of the transformations of values, etc.

> knowledge is the work of encyclopaedia and textbook writers. By contrast, [research practices] are expected to go beyond recycling and to contribute something new. This need not be a ground-breaking theory or discovery. [It may simply consist in] testing a hypothesis, proposing a new way of classifying a text, or exploring an old idea/text from a new angle." (Ibid.)

In conclusion, borrowing is very acceptable but needs a set of reasons, as second-order reasons, entailing reasons to exclude a range of further options and simply "recycling old ideas". Reason-based actions are clear means of a process of discovering not only communicating knowledge, in order to determine comparatively similar degrees of knowledge between an ideal emitter and a receptor of knowledge. Omitting reason-based actions often leads not only to a more problematic definition of knowledge formation and knowledge communication, but it may lead to research fraud.

Complementing a Rights-based Approach Built on a Reason-based Practice of Research

Many publishers, research centres and universities have developed clear policy documents over the past twenty years, to establish good research practice rules. In particular when it comes to possible consequences of plagiarism, precise reasons for action are considered as essential, because learning without responsibility seems incomplete and integrity placed at the core of research values. Description of the psychology of the author of plagiarism may be used for providing a virtue ethics approach on plagiarism as an intellectual vice. Both approaches differ in how on one side we define the morality of practical reasons, and on the other a virtue-based comparative balance of possible degrees of virtuous/vicious attitudes.

Retribution: as closed system of payback

Many would prefer concrete and short rule to swiftly deal with plagiarism. The reason for this attitude is related to the symbolic meaning of most wrong doings. An author who commits a fraud or a falsification shows contempt for the rules and law and for his victim. This expression of contempt damages the relationship of trust and mutual recognition and respect previously presumed to exist between all members of the research community. While many wrong doing seek some illegitimate but clear competitive advantage, contrary to many other offences, intellectual fraud or falsification as *an act* causes another person limited material injury, and the author often limited benefit[62]. Plagiarism as contempt for other's scientific work is less act oriented, as a community oriented symbolic signal. Therefore, when we use terms such as "a moral retribution" and proportionate answer to x misbehaviour, retribution as negation of "x negation of rights", mixed retribution as partly "a signal in the communication about a wrong" and as "prevention" for further harms such are reputational risks, it is important to note that not all of these expressions are equivalent, and that non goes beyond the action of the author towards reconciliation and trust. All form of retributive repayment of a debt, be it an offence or of the negation of a right, have in common the fact that they relate to retributive punishment, and retribution does not posit an end outside of itself. Retribution by essence gives *the only reason* and shows *the extent* for punishment (Garvey, 2004, p.1335)[63]. The author of a research fraud should be sanctioned because he or she deserves it. Fraud does cost people money, when individuals or institutions have to go to court.

---

[62] This is not truth for the practice of fraud which extends far beyond a single action, and creates a situation of loss of credibility of the research programme, as many corrupt the research on the long term, across different places.

[63] Garvey, Stephen P. "Is it Wrong to Commute Death Row? Retribution, Atonement, and Mercy", (2004). Cornell Law Faculty Publications. Paper 278. http://scholarship.law.cornell.edu/facpub/278

Fraud would normally not injure victims physically, but they entail a distinctive form of moral injury. We compared various justifications for punishment in our work *Solidarity*, where we have argued that there should be *a beyond* the retributive answers to an action:

> "[A] classic form of legitimation by mutual recognition[64] [...] which conserves full significance today[65]. This approach is immediately easy to grasp and carries an important normative hope, it allows at the same time to move away from a formalism of the moral law, by the presentation of the ethical life proper to a community. [It] presents the pain [related to a harmful conduct] on different levels of foundation, such as the restoring the balance of human rights, after a suffering caused by an unbalanced will."

The centre of philosophical interest for a philosophy of rights is to answer the question, valid for a narrower focus on plagiarism, on "How

---

[64] I can see a problem related to the understanding of mutual recognition, as product of a partial attachment to local values. In some dark chapter of human history, and if respect is not granted and values are mistaken, values can create discord. Instead of some sort of harmless competition for excellence, which entails a strong universalistic dimension, value may be seen as remotely related to the common bond of humanity which unites us. See: "Racism and Rationality in Hegels Philosophy of Subjective Spirit", Darrel Moellendorf, *History of Political Thought*. Vol. XIII. No. 2. Summer 1992, 243-55, https://www.fb03.uni-frankfurt.de/58976054/Racism-and-Rationality-in-Hegel_s-Philosophy-of-Subjective-Spirit.pdf

[65] We suggest to take the claim *cum grano sali* and to read Hegel's "abstract rights" literally as abstract achievement of personhood, not depending on very concrete and narrow historical data but on some rational common bond on values. After all "Given that everyone is partial to something which is genuinely of values, the universality of values is respected" (Raz, J. Introduction, *Value, Respect, and Attachment*, p. 3).

to introduce a sanction in a system of reciprocal recognitions, without unbalancing the very rule that we fix to measure a harmonious balance of human relationships?[66]" Contrary to contractual or convention based views on justice, a human rights-based view can be based on a dialectical process without contradiction, similar to the formation of rights. As restorative process, the response to the negation of rights constituted by stealing the other person's work, is also beyond retribution a matter of restoring equality on the grounds of inequalities.

Trust in the research community and unequal distribution of science

Unequal distribution of science and the constitution of unevenly distributed large knowledge centres explain a knowledge divide, where some basic encyclopaedic knowledge understandable and accessible by all is a problematic precondition to the formation of a core "common knowledge". Unequal access to a common knowledge complicates the conditions of legitimate borrowing of knowledge. We could without ambiguity say that since common knowledge is needed in order to have clear discipline oriented knowledge (scientific, cultural), which is not simply controlled language, but a place where knowledge could and should be expanded. A divided common knowledge makes discipline oriented knowledge difficult to define. It is not to forget that ethical progress could and should exist in parallel to a simple expansion of knowledge. Trust within the research community and the existence of a knowledge divide outside of the community is based on the assumption that knowledge and education needs to be to some extent competency oriented systems. In transdisciplinary, and technically enhanced transversal learning environments the comprehension of the situation of an unequal starting point has evolved out of simplistic relativistic

---

[66] We transpose here to the field of publications' ethics some our key arguments from our previous work on the philosophy of law and punishment: Ignace, Haaz, *Solidarité* (Paris: L'Harmattan, 310pp., here p. 8-9, on punishment see in particular pp. 39-72, 2012.).

understanding of the human being and learning institutions. If the belief in the universality of values is not mistaken, as the spirit of optimism bred by the enlightenment argues, then altruism which stress the universality or *common bond of value* can emerge but is not sufficient. An ideal of justice is necessary in order to answer a possible *aporia* of the principle of mutual recognition, which should be placed in:

> "[a] set of rational principles of ethical life, nested in the notion of justice. Applied to sanction and blame, the originality of this view [on the ethics of sanctions] is to situate reciprocal recognition in relation to an axiological structure of experience, towards an […] understanding of existence, which results in two ethical postures.

In our book (ibid.) we showed that we could postulate:

> […] an ethical and religious optimism, […] which rests on an absolute principle which should, first of all, be understood as an ethics of flight from the world, the abandonment of external things, so that the mind turns to the inner life, and pursues the unity of experience which organizes things. Secondly, it is to take into consideration that […] ethical principles [should] converge on the hypothesis of a gift, of solidarity. This is addressed to all living beings, beyond punishment and moralism, by a kind of overflow, a communication of good, that is to say by sympathy and by a movement of assimilation towards transcendence and the example of virtue[67]."

Applied to plagiarism classical errors one might be tempted to commit dealing with sanctions are of two types. If the principle of a gift, solidarity or altruism applies, it could first change the whole scope of a

---

[67] *Solidarité*, pp. 8-9, ibid.

narrow reading of the retribution of rights, or of the communication of the retributive signal, related to a setback of interest of the author of the fraud. Some virtue of mercy and atonement could lead beyond the preventive aim of simply signalling the importance of integrity-based system of values ad minima. Second, if reconciliation is the end toward which punishment is a means, then a giving virtue should be part of the process of applying sanctions, and counterbalancing the expression of contempt which damages the relationship of trust and mutual respect. This relationship and trust is previously presumed to exist, in a system impacted by an unequal access to knowledge. Unlike *consequentalism* and *utilitarianism*, which can live with a purely contingent relation between the sanction and the aim of punishment, a principle of gift, solidarity, mercy or atonement can add a necessary relation between the sanction of plagiarism and the possible end in view, when an institution puts not only sanctions but *wise sanctions* in practice.

For sure, in contrast to utilitarian means, to define the rightness and the severity of a sanction is very different from, for example agreeing to ban a person from a community of teachers or researchers to safeguard a high education standard. Education and research wrongs should not be considered as purely utility-based measures, as in most of pandemic public health measures. Institutions have limited means to answer wrong doings, but it is not a reason for neither agreeing with academic anarchism and opt of a *coulant* laisser-faire[68]. Nor should we prefer, if solidarity is key, purely preventive considerations on sanctions, as they are unfitting the ethical scope of sanctions, even if they bring consequential results in deterrence. Integrity in research should be

[68] Following e.g. Jeff Shantz and Dana M. Williams, Postscript: Anarchists in the Academy, in: *Anarchy and Society, Reflections on Anarchist Sociology*, Studies in Critical Social Sciences, Vol. 55, Brill, 2013, pp. 175-89, "the last ten years have seen anarchists carve out spaces in the halls of academia - and (...) likely at a quicker rate than any other politically-radical ideology" (p.176).

promoted, but engaging in the value of justice should not be realized by the instrumental criminalization of individuals, without a wider view on the context. The justification remains that it is simply unsure that real progress in behavioural change could be achieved by harsh measures of constraint. *Atonement*, or education through sanction, should not be directly the final objective of a sanction, as it gives space to all sorts of abuses in the name of an integrity-based ideal situation. In particular regarding academic fraud, if the aim of the sanction is only the education of the wrongdoer, through atonement, beyond a principle of retribution, atonement fails to remain partly related to the process of retribution. *Retribution as principle* focuses on the *action which deserves a precise response* and relates to the *proportionality* of a sanction. If a virtuous gift of mercy takes a dominant place, without some degree of equality, two individuals who deserve the same sanction for academic fraud could receive a different treatment. Furthermore not applying a sanction on the ground of *a gift tempering the demand for justice* enters in conflict with the idea of justice itself. As principle, this central idea of justice says that an instance has the obligation to punish provided an offender deserves it. The status of a virtuous gift of mercy, as an act of grace, and genuine virtue could be questioned[69].

Outside of the perspective in which retribution is defined, an institution should not impose sanctions as long as necessary to change the behaviour of the wrongdoer, even if there are reasons stated not to agree on the wrongdoing. We can remind ourselves that the severity of a sanction is a category, which should be seen as very different from the nature and scope of a sanction. If we focus on the social bound in the research community, we need to take very seriously the integration of

---

[69] Cf. the comparison of Garvey on mercy and retribution; Garvey, Stephen P. "Is it Wrong to Commute Death Row? Retribution, Atonement, and Mercy", (2004), op cite, p. 1324.

trust and all means of reconciliation after corruption based practices are discovered and wrongdoing isolated in a justice-based procedure.

In order to show that solidarity can complement other models of backward looking or forward looking justifications punishment, we first need have the complete range of possible misconducts as academic frauds in mind, on a line proposed by the All European Academies (ALLEA)[70]. ALLEA interestingly has adapted a principle of gift and restoration to their set of rules. ALLEA does not include conceptually the context of justice related to unequal access to knowledge which, as we argued, gives further reasons to consider solidarity-based ends. We rely also on *a mixed model of retribution*, which, we think, is adapted as entailing an expressive function, to academic frauds and plagiarism, precisely because they are not, in most cases, criminal or civil offenses. Research wrongs are usually seen as infringing an author's intellectual property rights, including copyright or trademark. Equally important, an academic fraud is a matter a reputation risk management, which entails restorative procedures when there is over sanctioning. ALLEA's focus on integrity as constructed on reasons for actions doesn't necessarily account for a further process for responsible altruism, as objective of rebuilding trust in the research community. However, the typography should be taken as sufficient set of reasons, and should be used in a reason-based explanation of practical morals in the domain of higher education.

A typography of possible wrongs in relation to the positive value of integrity in research can be drafted, based on the extensive semantic of ALLEA, which clearly differentiates between serious misconducts entailing the *modality* of not only *should* punish but also *must*. A first observation is that *plagiarism* is a *serious intellectual misconduct*, but

---

[70] ALLEA stands for "All European Academies". See their impressive ethical code for research: (2nd Ed., 2017), https://allea.org/wp-content/uploads/2017/05/ALLEA-European-Code-of-Conduct-for-Research-Integrity-2017.pdf

most of the misconducts are far more subtle manipulations, which contradicts the general definition of the primary principle of reputation risk prevention. Since misconduct in the grey area are abuses, it may not be possible have secondary enforcement procedures clearly foreseen in each case.

In most cases, it is possible to copy from sources that are not protected by copyright, e. g. works that are already in the public domain, without committing copyright infringement. By contrast, ideas and facts, not protected by copyright should not be plagiarized as they may have precise sources. Finally, copying and reusing short passages without attribution is a form of plagiarism, but it is unlikely that it is a violation of copyrights. For all these reasons, training and monitoring the issues related to plagiarism might become far more efficient than civil law or penal legal law and procedures. In private contract law, the breach of a contract can result in a lawsuit and heavy fines, and accepting undeserved research grants could even be sued as a criminal fraud. Although some countries assimilate plagiarism with theft (Poland), knowledge divide, interdisciplinary and transversal learning models soften the boundaries for common knowledge, and thus for knowledge wrongful appropriation. Controlled knowledge transmission with regards to plagiarism is an ideal context. By contrast, institutional communication and political communication follow other standards of honesty. Even for textbooks and scientific literature, things are not so easy to assess where the consequence of plagiarism is less important, because the originality of the work transmitted (i.e. the creative component of a body of knowledge) is not presupposed.

Research misconducts as exclusionary statements of reasons

1. Misconduct categories or reasons to consider P as a wrong reason of doing research:[71]

   1.1. *Serious* research misconducts (which *must be sanctioned*)

   1.1.1. *Fabrication* - making up results and recording them as if they were real

   1.1.2. *Falsification* - manipulating research by unduly changing, omitting or suppressing data or results

   1.1.3. *Plagiarism* - using other's work and ideas without giving credit, violating the rights to intellectual outputs

   1.2. Violations of good research practice and damaging integrity of the research process, without direct violations of rights (*which should be sanctioned*) as:

   1.2.1. Manipulating authorship and denigrating the role of other researchers in publications

   1.2.2. Self-plagiarism - re-publishing substantive parts of own earlier publications or translations, without duly citing the original

   1.2.3. Selective citing - as citing selectively to enhance/support own findings or to please colleagues

   1.2.4 Withholding research results

   1.2.5 Allowing sponsors to jeopardize independence in the research process so as to promulgate bias

---

[71] We have based our typology of statements of reasons on the ALLEA's code of ethics in research. *The European Code of Conduct for Research Integrity Revised Edition*, published in Berlin by ALLEA - All European Academies, 2nd Ed. 2017, https://allea.org/wp-content/uploads/2017/05/ALLEA-European-Code-of-Conduct-for-Research-Integrity-2017.pdf

1.2.6 Unnecessarily expanding the bibliography of a study

1.2.7 Accusing a researcher of misconduct in a malicious way

1.2.8. Misrepresenting research achievements

1.2.9 Exaggerating the importance and practical applicability of findings

1.2.10. Delaying or hampering the work of other researchers

1.2.11. Misusing seniority to encourage violations of research integrity

1.2.12. Ignoring putative violations of research integrity by others (or covering up inappropriate responses to misconduct or other violations by institutions)

1.2.13. Establishing or supporting journals that undermine the quality control of research as predatory journals

2. Prevention of misconducts (as training, supervision and mentoring incl. development of a positive and supportive research environment)

2.1. Integrity-based action with violations and allegations of misconduct

2.1.1. Investigation processes as fair processes

2.1.2 Declaration of conflict of interest during investigation by all parties involved in procedure

2.1.3 Confidentially and rights of whistle-blowers during investigations

2.1.4. Transparency and uniformity (assuring public procedures)

2.1.5. Principle of applying proportionate sanction to severity

of the violation
2.1.6. Restorative action (after exoneration of allegations of misconduct, or after punishment privileged upon simple retribution)

If it is clear that based on our ALLEA rules, an institution confronted with academic fraud needs to communicate very clearly with the wrongdoer so that "he/she knows the institution knows" about the wrong, opening ways of directly dealing with restoration as gift of solidarity and need for reconciliation, in all cases where we only ought to sanction.

Based on the assumption of unequal access to knowledge, any subject could be considered as a socially constraint entity, where the value of a life as a social construct, takes the aspect of various possible historical burdens, unequally shared in society. A social and cultural bias exists, it is part of our attachment to partiality, which has legitimate grounds when based on values and the possibility of counterbalancing universality-based reasons. Partiality may invite to a special effort beyond the retributive framework of a sanction in the education sector. Sociologist J. Galtung introduced the idea of *structural violence* to show a real situation where justice norms are derivate from power relations:

> "There may not be any person who directly harms another person in the structure. The violence is built into the structure and shows up as unequal power and consequently as unequal life chances. Resources are unevenly distributed, as when income distributions are heavily skewed, literacy/education unevenly distributed, medical services existent in some districts and for some groups

only, and so on. Above all the power to decide over the distribution of resources is unevenly distributed[72]".

"By doing away with giving explicitly to everyone what it implicitly demands of everyone, the education system demands of everyone alike that they have what it does not give. This consists mainly of linguistic and cultural competence and that relationship of familiarity with culture which can only be produced by family upbringing when it transmits the dominant culture". (Bourdieu, 1977, p. 494).[73]

Common Knowledge as Unequal Capital

The hypothesis of deep structural inequalities in the access to information and knowledge is not at all an isolated phenomenon with regard to other types of more commercial goods and services. For centuries, "pirate publishers" and "Robin Hoods of Science" emerged, reprinting materials that were in the course of political and social economical struggles left for a small minority. Nowadays, with the power of internet technology "infodemics" are spread by social medias[74], illegal borrowing of knowledge results culminates in huge grey libraries (Sci-Hub), clearly refusing to play with the established

---

[72] Galtung, Johan, "Violence, Peace, and Peace Research", *Journal of Peace Research*, Vol. 6, No. 3 (1969), pp. 167-191, 170.

[73] Bourdieu, P. (1977). "Cultural reproduction and social reproduction". In: J. Karabel & A. H. Halsey (Eds.), *Power and ideology in education*, pp. 487-511, New York, NY: Oxford University Press.

[74] See the well-balanced analysis of the ethical problem of infodemics (p. 104) by Christoph Stückelberger: "You Shall not Lie: From Covid-19 Fake News to Truthfulness", in: *Who Cares About Ethics*, Obiora Ike, Amélé Adamavi-Aho Ekué, Anja Andriamasy and Lucy Howe López (Eds.), Geneva: Globethics.net 2021, pp. 99-109.

rules of dominant publishers such as the Dutch-British Elsevier[75]. If piracy and fake news are as widespread, academic fraud and plagiarism should not be understood as a simple failure of reaching common standards in mainstream education systems but as a strong potential to overcome these unequal contexts.

Bourdieu has underlined the fact that common knowledge depends on "a cultural capital" and the idea of a reproduction of social and cultural inequalities across social classes. By contrast to economic capital, social capital is essentially cultural capital in the wide sense, including not only essentially scholarly restricted definition of culture, but as common cognitive and behavioural competencies (Draelants, Ballatore 2017; Diewald, Schupp 2006; Weiss, 2006)[76]. Cultural capital as marker of social class is therefore essential in order to see hidden

---

[75] We find a good résumé by Bodó: "Pirate publishers played two key roles in this context: they printed censored texts, and they introduced cheap reprints that reached new reading publics. Both actions fuelled the development of a deliberative public sphere in Europe and the transfer of knowledge between more and less privileged social groups and regions." Bodó, Balázs (2011): "Coda: A Short History of Book Piracy", in: *Media Piracy in Emerging Economies*, Karaganis, Joe (Ed.), Social Science Research Council, p. 399.

[76] Diewald, M., & Schupp, J. (2006). «Kulturelles und soziales Kapital von Jugendlichen - die Bedeutung von sozialer Herkunft und der Qualität der Eltern-Kind-Beziehung». In: Rehberg, K.-S. (Hrsg.), *Soziale Ungleichheit, kulturelle Unterschiede: Verhandlungen des 32. Kongresses der Deutschen Gesellschaft für Soziologie in München.* Teilbd. 1 und 2, pp. 910-927. Frankfurt am Main: Campus Verl. https://nbn-resolving.org/urn:nbn:de:0168-ssoar-144887 Weiß, A. (2006). «Hochqualifizierte MigrantInnen: der Kern einer transnationalen Mittelklasse?» In: K.-S. Rehberg (Hrsg.), *Soziale Ungleichheit, kulturelle Unterschiede*, ibid., pp. 3643-3652. Frankfurt am Main: Campus Verl. https://nbn-resolving.org/urn:nbn:de:0168-ssoar-142661; Draelants H., Ballatore, M. « Capital culturel et reproduction scolaire. Un bilan critique », *Revue française de pédagogie* [En ligne], 186 | 2014, mis en ligne le 01 janvier 2017, consulté le 22 janvier 2020. URL: http://journals.openedition.org/rfp/4430 ; DOI : 10.4000/rfp.4430

expectations of the education system, some of which are explicitly left on the background of Bourdieu's method such as gender and ethnicity (Adkins and Skeggs 2004[77]). If Bourdieu makes a justified claim for unequal access to knowledge, the analogy between common knowledge and cultural capital is partly right, and fraud based on the misunderstanding of some reason-based structure of education becomes clear:

> "students [...] plagiarize primarily because they are concerned that not only are their vocabulary and writing skills subpar, but that they do not fit into the college student role. Their [...] decisions to plagiarize are rooted in the outcomes stemming from educational practices that reinforce class hierarchies."

For Strangfeld "students' plagiarism experiences are contextualized within their broader educational histories rather than limited to the immediate circumstances surrounding their academic dishonesty[78]". Unintentional plagiarism may occur because students lack sufficient knowledge of citation technique. Many are unsure if the information they are presenting is common knowledge[79].

On the other side, it is easy to use the technology of machine learning to rewrite a text, in such a way that the initial text is totally masked. The method consists of passing "through [...] translators applying a series of translations to different languages before returning

---

[77] "Elite Higher Education admissions in the Arts and Sciences: Is cultural capital the key?" Zimdars, A., Sullivan, A. and Heath, A., preprint, http://hdl.handle.net/ 20.500.12424/2332137

[78] Strangfeld, J. A. (2019): "I Just Don't Want to Be Judged: Cultural Capital's Impact on Student Plagiarism", *SAGE Open*. https://doi.org/ 10.1177/2158244018822382

[79] Strangfeld, J. A. (2019): "I Just Don't Want to Be Judged", p. 2, ibid.

to English. The purpose of this is to attempt to preserve the semantic meaning while rewriting the text[80]".

As general rule, once detected the research and teaching supervision authority considers three aspects of: *severity*, the *scale* and the *resilience of the target* of the harm:

> "to decide where governance responses are most needed—it is necessary to consider the following three dimensions: severity (the level of harm caused by the [plagiarism] deep fake), scale (how widespread the harm is) and resilience (the ability of the "target" to withstand the impact). We suggest that there is a prima facie case for prioritizing responses to the [plagiarism] deep fakes that cause intense harm to individuals or that contribute to systemic societal risks such as the erosion of trust and truth[81]."

Conclusion

Retributive sanction to academic fraud and plagiarism is as proportionate response justified by the will, in terms of general governance of risks, of avoiding that deterrence goes too far, and certainly not wanting that unproportioned measures be the rule. Nor do we want to punish in order to focus on only educating others, without preventing harms/risks and without the wider framework of justice and reattributing wrongs which are deserved.

The aim of an ethical gift of solidarity or atonement is oriented toward not so much the transformation of persons and institutions, by producing atonement or mercy, but it is based on the aim of

---

[80] Kalleberg, Rune Borge (2015): Towards Detecting Textual Plagiarism Using Machine Learning Methods, The University of Agder, Faculty of Engineering and Science, Department of Information and Communication Technology, 12.

[81] *Forged Authenticity Governing Deepfake Risks*, Executive Summary, ibid.

reconciliation beyond the objective of the sanction. Reasons for active sanctions are not limited only to intentional and voluntary reasons, as we can be held responsible for unintentionally harming others. Reasons for actions that go beyond the thin limits of our clear intentions should not close the reasons on the retributive component without a chance to operate transformations toward a more genuine academic community, one in which offenders and victims share that degree of trust and respect, upon which communal existence depends. If reasoning and reasons are maximised, instead of dismissed and devaluated, reason-based actions show that it is excluded for serious wrongs to hide away from sanction, which may likely have direct impact and consequences on trust in the research and learning process. In this case, we would tend to believe that wrongdoers should be allowed to move forward by wrong habits and character, and without prevention measures, we might be facing the same problem soon in a slightly different way[82].

References

Academic Integrity At MIT, What is Common Knowledge? https://integrity.mit.edu/handbook/citing-your-sources/what-common-knowledge, accessed 2020.01.20

ALLEA's code of ethics in research. *The European Code of Conduct for Research Integrity Revised Edition*, published in Berlin by ALLEA - All European Academies, 2nd Ed. 2017,

[82] We found interesting the observation Bergadaà which corroborates other research experts' warning, pointing out that fraudulent activities by research directors is likely to spread among the collaborators of the research institute or laboratory, after an author of sever research misconduct managed to find another workplace, and could not help reproducing his mechanical way of abusing others trust.

https://allea.org/wp-content/uploads/2017/05/ALLEA-European-Code-of-Conduct-for-Research-Integrity-2017.pdf

"Antiplagiarism policy and guidelines on integrating sources in academic writing", Wrocław University, 2012

Bergadaà, Michelle, « Quand parler du plagiat, c'est déjà agir », Le plagiat, entre banalisation et diabolisation. Conférence de la Bibliothèque de l'UNIGE sur le plagiat, https://mediaserver.unige.ch/ play/123658

Bodó, Balázs (2011): "Coda: A Short History of Book Piracy", in: *Media Piracy in Emerging Economies*, Karaganis, Joe (Ed.), Social Science Research Council.

Bourdieu, P. (1977). "Cultural reproduction and social reproduction". In: J. Karabel & A. H. Halsey (Eds.), *Power and ideology in education*, pp. 487-511, New York, NY: Oxford University Press.

Collins, Aengus. (2019), *Forged Authenticity: Governing Deepfake Risks*. Lausanne: EPFL International Risk Governance Center.

Diewald, M., & Schupp, J. (2006). «Kulturelles und soziales Kapital von Jugendlichen - die Bedeutung von sozialer Herkunft und der Qualität der Eltern-Kind-Beziehung». In: Rehberg, K.-S. (Hrsg.), *Soziale Ungleichheit, kulturelle Unterschiede: Verhandlungen des 32. Kongresses der Deutschen Gesellschaft für Soziologie in München.* Teilbd. 1 und 2, pp. 910-927. Frankfurt am Main: Campus Verl. https://nbn-resolving.org/urn:nbn:de:0168-ssoar-144887

Draelants H., Ballatore, M. « Capital culturel et reproduction scolaire. Un bilan critique », *Revue française de pédagogie* [En ligne], 186 | 2014, mis en ligne le 01 janvier 2017, consulté le 22 janvier 2020. URL: http://journals. openedition.org/rfp/4430 ; DOI : 10.4000/rfp.4430

Galtung, Johan, "Violence, Peace, and Peace Research", *Journal of Peace Research*,Vol. 6, No. 3 (1969), pp. 167-191.

Garvey, Stephen P. "Is it Wrong to Commute Death Row? Retribution, Atonement, and Mercy", (2004). Cornell Law Faculty Publications. Paper 278. http://scholarship.law.cornell.edu/facpub/278

Haaz, Ignace (2012): *Solidarité: Chez Hegel, Von Hartmann, Tocqueville et Mill*, Commentaires philosophiques, Paris: L'Harmattan, 310pp..

Himmelstein, Daniel S. et alii, (2018):"Research: Sci-Hub provides access to nearly all scholarly literature", *eLife Sciences Publications, Ltd*, DOI: 10.7554/eLife.32822

Kalleberg, Rune Borge (2015): Towards Detecting Textual Plagiarism Using Machine Learning Methods, The University of Agder, Faculty of Engineering and Science, Department of Information and Communication Technology.

Moellendorf, Darrel. "Racism and Rationality in Hegels Philosophy of Subjective Spirit", *History of Political Thought*. Vol. XIII. No. 2. Summer 1992, 243-55, https://www.fb03.uni-frankfurt.de/58976054/Racism-and-Rationality-in-Hegel_s-Philosophy-of-Subjective-Spirit.pdf

Raz, Joseph (2011). *From Normativity to Responsibility*. Oxford: Oxford University Press.

Raz, Joseph (1999). *Engaging Reason: On the Theory of Value and Action*. Oxford: Oxford University Press.

Raz, Joseph (Ed.) (1978). *Practical Reasoning*. Oxford University Press.

Raz, J. (2001): *Value, Respect, and Attachment*, Cambridge: CUP.

Shantz, Jeff and Dana M. Williams, "Postscript: Anarchists in the Academy", in: *Anarchy and Society, Reflections on Anarchist*

Sociology, Studies in Critical Social Sciences, Vol. 55, Brill, 2013, pp. 175-89.

Strangfeld, J. A. (2019): "I Just Don't Want to Be Judged: Cultural Capital's Impact on Student Plagiarism", *SAGE Open*. https://doi.org/ 10.1177/2158244018822382

Weiß, A. (2006). «Hochqualifizierte MigrantInnen: der Kern einer transnationalen Mittelklasse?» In: K.-S. Rehberg (Hrsg.), *Soziale Ungleichheit, kulturelle Unterschiede*, ibid., pp. 3643-3652. Frankfurt am Main: Campus Verl. https://nbn-resolving.org/urn:nbn:de:0168-ssoar-142661

Zimdars, A., Sullivan, A. and Heath, A. "Elite Higher Education admissions in the Arts and Sciences: Is cultural capital the key?", preprint, http://hdl.handle.net/ 20.500.12424/2332137

9

ETHICAL DECISION-MAKING AND BEHAVIOURAL ETHICS: EXPLORING THE LINK BETWEEN ORGANISATIONAL CULTURE AND ETHICAL BEHAVIOUR

Maria Rosario G. Catacutan

Introduction

Investigations into recent business scandals have shown that ethical breakdowns in organisations are not necessarily caused by a few bad people who lack a moral compass but also by the presence of organisational cultures that can drive good people to engage in unethical behaviour.[83] Research on behavioural ethics has shown that ethical decision-making is a complex process; it is influenced not only by individual traits but also by contextual variables that impact employees' decisions to engage in unethical behaviour. The purpose of this paper is two-fold: to expound on the role of organisational culture in ethical decision-making and to highlight some of the limits of behavioural ethics as a model for human behaviour in ethical decision-making processes. Despite its important contribution to understanding the

---

[83] Maria Rosario Catacutan, Senior Lecturer in Business Ethics, Strathmore University, Kenya.

influence of situational factors in ethical behaviour, this paper argues that some of the assumptions about behavioural ethics can lead to an eclipse of moral agency and moral responsibility.

Interest in business ethics has once again come to the fore with corporate scandals on the rise. Prominent companies with reputable brands such as Volkswagen, Wells Fargo, and JP Morgan, have been involved in these scandals, and suffered enormous losses. Wells Fargo, for instance, accepted to pay a $3 billion fine to the U.S. government this year for engaging in fraudulent sales practices with numerous employees opening millions of fake customer accounts. Similarly, Volkswagen was ordered by a U.S. federal judge in 2017 to pay a fine of $2.8 billion for rigging its diesel-powered vehicles to cheat on emissions tests. In 2013, JP Morgan had to pay $13 billion in settlement over allegations that it had misled its investors about the soundness and risks of mortgage-backed securities that triggered the 2008 subprime-mortgage crisis. In the wake of these scandals, companies used the 'bad apples' argument attributing ethical failures in the organisation to a few individuals lacking some personal quality such as moral character (Treviño & Youngblood, 1990). Volkswagen's former U.S. top executive, Michael Horn, blamed the emissions scandals on a couple of rogue software engineers who designed the programme to cheat on the emissions tests (Morgan & Gardner, 2015). Similarly, Wells Fargo executives laid the blame on dishonest individuals who opened bank accounts to reach their sales quotas leading to the firing of more than 5,300 employees over a period of five years (Glazer & Rexrode, 2016). However, as details from the investigations of these scandals emerged, business academics are increasingly convinced that ethical failures in organisations are not exclusively caused by a few bad employees who are dishonest and lacking in moral character but also by the existence of 'bad barrels' or organisational cultures that can potentially drive good people to make unethical decisions (Treviño & Youngblood, 1990; Soltes, 2017; Schipani, 2017). Unrealistic sales targets, improper incentives, repeated ethical violations, and poor leadership are among the organisational factors cited as contributing to these scandals (Tayan, 2019; Merenda & Irwin, 2018). The aim of this paper is to discuss the relationship between organisational culture and ethical behaviour from the perspective of behavioural ethics. Prior to this discussion, an overview of the behavioural ethics as a field of study and as an alternative approach to understanding ethical decision-making in business will be provided. This paper also aims to highlight some of the limits of behavioural ethics as a theoretical model for human behaviour in ethical decision-making processes.

Behavioural Ethics as a Field of Study

The application of behavioural ethics as a theoretical framework in the study of ethical decision-making emerged as a critical response of scholars to a perceived inadequacy of the philosophical approaches traditionally used in business ethics teaching (Treviño, 1986; Bazerman & Gino, 2012). It contrasts itself from traditional approaches as it promotes a descriptive rather than a normative approach to understanding ethics, drawing its principles from psychology and behavioural decision research. As a field of study, behavioural ethics research can be traced to the earlier works of Treviño (1986) that examined individual and situational variables that explain and predict ethical decision-making behaviour of individuals in organisations. Over time, studies of individual ethical and unethical behaviour within organisations have been collectively classified as part of behavioural ethics research. Most of these studies were informed by the works of Lawrence Kohlberg (1969/1984) and James Rest (1984) on cognitive moral development, as well as the works of Stanley Milgram (1963) and Albert Bandura (1991) from the field of social psychology (Treviño, Weaver, & Reynolds, 2006). As a sub-domain within the field of ethical decision making, behavioural ethics is concerned with individual behaviour that is subject or judged according to generally accepted moral norms of behaviour. Its focus is on explaining individual behaviour that occurs in the context of larger social prescriptions (Treviño, Weaver, & Reynolds, 2006). Bazerman and Gino (2012) offer a lengthier definition of behavioural ethics as "the study of systematic and predictable ways in which individuals make ethical decisions and judge the ethical decisions of others that are at odds with intuition and the benefits of the broader society" (p. 90).

Behavioural Ethics: a Critical Response to Normative Approaches in Teaching Ethics

Initial studies on ethical decision-making in business focused on the application of normative ethical theories in resolving ethical dilemmas. Normative ethics pertains to the realm of philosophy and focuses on providing guidelines on how individuals ought to behave (Beauchamp & Bowie, 2004). From this perspective, students are taught that ethical decision-making involves the process of evaluating the morality of actions by applying normative ethical theories or frameworks such as virtue ethics, consequentialism, and deontological ethics in solving ethical problems. Common among these theories is a key assumption that there is only one ultimate criterion for correct moral conduct, each proposing a different and competing perspective as to what such a standard may be (Velasquez, 2001).

The virtue ethics theory is described as an attempt to recover the insights of Aristotelian-Thomistic moral philosophy; it maintains that rational activity is the specific human function and that to act according to reason is the specific human good (McInerny, 2007). The rightness of actions therefore depends on their moral quality, whether the actions embody the virtues or not. Further, virtue ethics theory claims that moral reasoning is not a purely cognitive activity and that character exerts great influence over the moral reasoning process. Proponents of virtue ethics argue that good ethical reasoning skills by themselves do not guarantee sound reasoning in moral matters. Equally important are the lived experiences of the moral agent because an upright moral life predisposes a person towards sounds ethical reasoning. Classical philosophy identifies the habit of sound reasoning in moral matters within practical wisdom or prudence (in Greek, phrônesis). Aquinas (1273: p. 47) defines prudence as "right reason in action".

Consequentialist ethics stipulate that the rightness of an action depends on its outcomes or consequences. Under this perspective, an act is morally right if it could be established that it would result in more good than bad consequences. Foremost among consequentialist theories is utilitarianism, which prescribes the maximisation of any form of utility as the sole criterion for the goodness of actions. Represented by John Stuart Mill (cited in Velasquez, 2001), consequentialists propose that actions and rules of conduct be analysed in terms of their favourable and unfavourable consequences, considering as moral those actions and rules that would most likely produce the greatest happiness, pleasure or utility for the greatest number of people.

Deontological ethics, in turn, prescribes the fulfilment of duties as the basis for the rightness of actions. Its most prominent representative, Immanuel Kant (cited in Velasquez, 2001), argues that actions are morally right when one follows the inner dictate or imperative of one's conscience that commands us to act out of a sense of duty. To act out of duty then is to act in response to a categorical imperative. Further, Kant maintained the categorical imperative ought to have a universal character in that it could be willed that the dictate of one's subjective conscience could become a universally accepted law binding all persons. To avoid deception, to keep promises, and to treat people fairly are ethical maxims that one could will to be universally binding, granted that all reasonable people would agree that it is in the interest of society that such duties be observed. Hence, such actions are considered morally correct. For deontological ethics, therefore, morality of actions would depend on the duty imposed on the moral agent by his own conscience — the categorical imperative — the duty being expressed as a rule or maxim that could be willed to become a universal law.

The normative approach in teaching business ethics entails explaining these various ethical systems or theories as a theoretical framework for ethical decision-making. Primarily, its aim is to develop moral reasoning skills by asking students to critically analyse and apply these theories in solving moral dilemmas embedded in case studies. For instance, to explain the distinction between utilitarianism and deontological ethics, teachers in business ethics typically ask their students to make a decision using a scenario described in the so-called "trolley problem", a thought experiment in ethics. Students are expected to discuss, argue and explain which one of two options would be appropriate to solve the ethical dilemma embedded in the trolley problem (Bazerman & Gino, 2012). Despite its popularity, a few scholars argue that the normative approach in teaching business ethics is inadequate because discussion of these normative theories in class often leads to endless debates as to whether a utilitarian or deontological approach is more appropriate in solving moral dilemmas (Bazerman & Gino, 2012). Others also maintain that developing students' moral reasoning is useful, but such an approach does not motivate students to practise ethical behaviour (Melé, 2005). Lastly, some theorists highlight evidence provided by descriptive research on actual decision-making processes of white-collar criminals (Soltes, 2017). Overall, this body of research suggests that people who commit white-collar crimes were not necessarily bad or evil people; rather a good number were well-intentioned individuals who ended up doing bad things as a result of pressures they faced in their work environments (Bazerman & Gino, 2012). Ethical decision-making is therefore a complex process that is influenced by more than individual traits such as moral reasoning and character. A whole set of contextual variables also come into play such as surrounding norms, situational pressures and institutional incentives that impact employees' decisions to engage in unethical behaviour (Soltes, 2017). Consequently, scholars propose the need to shift away from a philosophical-normative approach in teaching ethics, which conceptualises how people *ought* to decide or act, to an empirical-descriptive approach that describes how people *actually* decide/behave in moral contexts (Bazerman & Gino, 2012). As Soltes (2017, p. 460) explains:

> "Despite compelling academic evidence showing how people respond to perverse incentives and difficult circumstances, management education often continues to espouse individual character as the motivating factor that influences [ethical] success or failure when placed in these circumstances. As a result, management education may not be providing students all the tools needed to most effectively confront the murky decisions they will inevitably face."

For Bazerman and Gino (2012), this emphasis on how human beings actually behave in moral contexts describes the focus of behavioural ethics research. It adopts a descriptive or empirical rather than a normative or theoretical approach to the study of ethics and draws primarily from theories on psychology and behavioural decision research.

Behavioural Ethics and Cognitive Moral Development Psychology

To date, numerous studies in ethical decision-making utilise a descriptive or empirical approach (O'Fallon & Butterfield, 2005; Treviño, Weaver, & Reynolds, 2006; Bazerman & Gino, 2012). Earlier studies were inspired by the works of cognitive developmental psychologists Lawrence Kohlberg (1969) and James Rest (1984), which focus on the influence of individual cognitive processes – such as moral reasoning, moral awareness, and moral motivation – and on ethical decision-making.

Lawrence Kohlberg (1969) worked towards a greater understanding of moral development by undertaking an empirical investigation of people's moral beliefs. In his theory of moral development, Kohlberg identified six stages of moral reasoning, representing six problem-solving strategies, used to arrive at moral judgements: (1) the morality of obedience; (2) the morality of instrumental egoism and simple exchange; (3) the morality of interpersonal concordance; (4) the morality of law and duty to the social order; (5) the morality of consensus building; and (6) the morality of personal autonomy. At the lowest or pre-conventional level, individuals' judgements about what is right are based on authority (stage 1). Motivated by fear of punishment, individuals at this stage adhere to norms set by authority as the main criteria for making decisions. On the next level (stage 2), individuals' judgements are primarily influenced by instrumental motives. Motivated by self-interest, individuals at this level judge what is right on the basis of advantages that they can derive from it. At the middle level or the conventional level, individuals' judgements are made in reference to the expectations of significant others (stage 3), behaving in ways to achieve some semblance of goodness in one's social circle. In the next category (stage 4), judgements on what is right are based on conformity with social norms or conventions seen as necessary foundations of law and order. At the post conventional level, judgements are made out of a sense of duty, choosing to act in ways that respect individual rights and democratically accepted laws (stage 5). Finally, at the highest stage, judgements are based on one's conscience in reference to universally held moral principles (stage 6). In these most advanced stages, individuals are characterised as fully autonomous, principled, and highly consistent with their moral thought.

Utilising Kohlberg's work, James Rest (1984) developed the Four Component Model of Moral Behaviour. According to this theory, there are four processes that are involved in moral behaviour, namely: moral awareness, moral judgement, moral motivation, and moral character. All four components are necessary to enact moral behaviour and moral failure could be attributed to failure in any of these processes. The first component, moral sensitivity, entails interpreting the situation surrounding the action and being aware of the consequences of one's actions. Moral judgement, the second component, is the act of judging which action is morally right or wrong. This process was the focus of Kohlberg's theory of moral development (1969). The third component, moral motivation, is the process that involves prioritising moral values over other personal values. Finally, moral character, the last component, refers to an individual's strength of convictions as well as his/her courage and persistence in overcoming obstacles in order to carry out a good action. Rest (1984) is known for having constructed the Defining Issues Test (DIT), an instrument that has been validated and used in hundreds of studies (Treviño, Weaver, & Reynolds, 2006). Using hypothetical stories patterned after Kohlberg's dilemmas (1969), subjects taking the DIT are engaged in moral problem solving. A variety of scores could be derived from the DIT but the most frequently used is the P score (Principled moral thinking). This indicates the extent to which a subject uses a reasoning process characteristic of stages 5 and 6.

Research has found that most adults are at the conventional level; that is, their moral reasoning is largely influenced by significant others (stage 3) and by rules and laws (stage 4). According to Rest (cited in Treviño, Weaver, & Reynolds, 2006), fewer than 20% of American adults actually reach the principled level. Empirical evidence of adults reaching stage 6 is rare, such that it is considered to be only a theoretically postulated stage.

Organisational Culture and Ethical Decision-making

A significant body of research on the behavioural aspects of ethical decision-making are based on the frameworks of Kohlberg (1969/1984) and Rest (cited in Reynolds & Ceranic, 2007). Initially, studies focused on the influence of an individual's level of cognitive moral development on ethical decision-making processes (O'Fallon & Butterfield, 2005). However, over time, scholars also explored the role of situational variables in the ethical decision-making process (Treviño, Weaver, & Reynolds, 2006).

The influence of organisational culture on ethical decision-making is a widely researched topic as evidenced by the extent literature available on the topic (O'Fallon & Butterfield, 2005; Treviño, Weaver & Reynolds, 2006; Tenbrunsel & Smith-Crowe, 2008; Bazerman & Gino, 2012). Given the size of this body of research, this paper will focus on providing an overview of organisational culture's influence on ethical decision-making. This will be done by expounding on the theoretical propositions advanced in the person-situation interactionist model of ethical decision-making by Treviño (1986). This study was chosen because it is one of the pioneering models on ethical decision-making that incorporated the influence of organisational culture as one of the situational variables in the ethical decision-making process. The model combines the influence of individual variables (moral development and psychological traits such as ego strength, field dependence, and locus of control) as well as situational variables (organisational culture, immediate job context, and job characteristics) in ethical decision-making. The work of Bazerman and Gino (2012) will also be considered as this study incorporates a specific set of assumptions drawn from the field of behavioural ethics and focuses on the link between organisational culture and unethical behaviour.

Culture is defined as the common set of tacit assumptions, values, and beliefs that influence the way a group of people think or behave (Schein, 1985).

Melé (2009) makes a distinction between organisational culture and corporate culture. The organisational culture is the actual culture, described as "the way we do things here". By contrast, the corporate culture is the desired or ideal culture, expressed through the company's mission, vision, values, guiding principles, and codes of conduct. It depicts "how a company ought to do things". The ethical culture represents a slice of the organisational culture that influences employees' ethical behaviour through formal and informal organisational structures and systems (Treviño, Weaver, & Reynolds, 2006).

One of the assumptions maintained by Treviño (1986) in the person-situation interactionist model of decision-making, is that most adults operate at the conventional level (stages 3 and 4) of cognitive moral development as found by Kohlberg (1969). This suggests that people's ethical decision-making processes are generally susceptible to the influence of organisational culture and other job context variables. Treviño (1986) theorised that the following components of organisational culture influence the way people make moral judgements: collective norms, referent others, obedience to authority, responsibility for consequences, codes of ethical conduct, reinforcement contingencies, and external pressures of time, scarcity of resources, competition, and personal costs.

Both collective norms and referent others are situational factors that guide ethical behaviour in organisations. Collective norms refer to an organisation's shared values, goals, purposes, and a belief regarding what is ethical or unethical behaviour. In organisations that have a strong ethical culture, members have a clear understanding of these norms and rely on them when making decisions. In contrast, individuals from organisations that have a weak ethical culture are likely to rely on referent others regarding ethical or unethical behaviour (Schein, 1985). This is consistent with the social learning theory which maintains that much of human behaviour is learned by observing referent others (Bandura, 1991). It suggests that organisations can influence the ethical behaviour of their members if they propose appropriate referent others through the organisation's choice of heroes and heroines. Further, it highlights the importance of leaders acting as moral exemplars or role model virtues to their subordinates (Dobson & Armstrong in Melé, 2005).

Apart from collective norms and referent others, the way organisations define authority, can also influence ethical/unethical behaviour. Typically used to support this proposition are studies based on social psychology experiments conducted by Yale psychologist, Stanley Milgram (1963). These studies are known as the obedience-to-authority experiments. In a nutshell, they provide evidence which shows that individuals are capable of acting against their own moral judgement of what is right or wrong and inflict harm on others if asked to do so by an authority figure. Treviño (1986) posits that individuals who work in organisations with authoritarian leaders are likely to carry out the orders of those in authority, even if those orders are contrary to the person's determination of what is right.

Take for instance the case of Angelo Mozilo, former CEO of Countrywide Financial Corporation, who was charged by the U.S. Securities and Exchange Commission (SEC) with securities fraud for hiding the high-risk nature of Countrywide's loan products from its investors. Mozilo and other senior executives of Countrywide were described as bullies who ruled their employees with fear and manipulation. Cynder Niemela, former senior Vice President for culture and communication, and Michael Winston, former Chief leadership officer, described Countrywide's organisational culture as a toxic culture ruled by fear and top-down intimidation. Dave Sullivan, another senior management official, described Countrywide as "definitely the most top-down company I've ever seen. Mozilo was God. Whatever he said went" (Hudson, 2014). One employee maintained that so much fraud was being committed between loan brokering, document alteration, and overstating a borrower's length of employment and actual income. Although a few individuals reported the fraudulent lending activities, Countrywide's executives refused to open a full-scale investigation within the company for fear of reprisal from top management. As America's biggest sub-prime mortgage lender, Countrywide Financial collapsed during the 2008 financial crisis and was bought by the Bank of America to save it from bankruptcy. In 2011, the Bank of America was found liable for fraud over defective mortgages sold by its Countrywide-unit (Raymond, 2013). Mozilo and other executives from Countrywide were convicted of fraud and insider trading by the U.S. SEC in 2009.

The manner in which organisations promote individual responsibility and awareness of consequences for one's actions at all levels of the organisation is another element of how organisational culture shapes ethical behaviour. This finds support in early research, which suggests that being aware of the consequences of one's actions on others and ascribing responsibility to oneself are likely to influence individuals to make ethical decisions (Schwartz cited in Treviño, 1986). In contrast, unethical behaviour is more likely to occur in organisational contexts where responsibility for the consequences of an action is diffused by promoting external definitions of responsibility based on formal role definitions and hierarchy (Maclagan cited in Treviño, 1986).

Consider the case of Oliver Schmidt, former general manager of Volkswagen's U.S. Environment and Engineering Office, sentenced to 7 years in prison over the emission scandal. Schmidt told a judge that he was coached by company executives to lie about diesel emissions in a meeting with U.S. regulators. According to Schmidt, he was given "a script or talking points" approved by VW management and high-ranking lawyers to use for that said meeting. He confessed that he "should have gone to that meeting, ignored the instructions given to [him]" and admitted that "there was a defeat device in VW diesel engine vehicles and that VW had been cheating for almost a decade" (Smythe, 2017). Apart from Schmidt, another VW employee, James Liang, a senior engineer who worked for VW for 34 years, was also sentenced to 40 months in prison for his involvement in the emission scandal. Liang's lawyer, Daniel Nixon, however argued that Liang was not a "mastermind" of the emissions fraud and "blindly executed a misguided loyalty to his employer" (Shepardson & White, 2017). In this case, Schmidt and Liang were emboldened to take part in the fraudulent activities of VW because the involvement of high-ranking officials led to a diffusion of responsibility for the unethical acts.

Another way organisations attempt to guide members' ethical behaviour is by developing formal codes of ethics and legal compliance programmes including ethics training, ethics advice lines and offices, and systems for anonymous reporting of ethical misconduct (Treviño, 1986; Treviño & Brown, 2004). However, the existence of codes and programmes, by themselves, cannot guarantee ethical behaviour in organisations. Code effectiveness depends to a great extent on whether or not they are consistent with the organisational culture and are enforced. Employees need to perceive that management is intent on managing ethics, incorporate ethics into decision-making, and keen to enforce the code. This is shown by management's commitment to follow up on ethical concerns raised by employees, identify rule violators, and demonstrate consistency between ethics compliance programmes and actual organisational practices (Treviño & Brown, 2004). It is also important that employees perceive that ethical conduct is rewarded and unethical conduct sanctioned by their leaders in the organisation. This is in accordance with reinforcement theory which maintains that individual behaviour is a result of its consequences. This also suggests that organisations can influence the behaviour of its members through the types of rewards and punishments they set for ethical/unethical behaviour. Some reward or incentive systems, however, may lead to unethical behaviour.

Take the case at Wells Fargo where executives created an incentive system for cross-selling that pushed lower level employees to create fake accounts for customers. An investigation into the fake accounts scandal blamed a "sales-oriented culture" at Wells Fargo. The report highlighted the role of Carrie Tolstedt, former head of Wells Fargo's community bank unit, stating that "even when challenged by their regional leaders, the senior leadership of the Community Bank failed to appreciate or accept that their sales goals were too high and becoming increasingly untenable" (Wells Fargo Sales Practices Investigation Report cited in Frost, 2017). For Schipani (2017), organisations that reward employees for unrealistic sales targets and apply excessive pressure to meet these goals become a breeding ground for ethical lapses leading to illegal and criminal behaviour. The Wells Fargo case shows that employees may be encouraged either subtly or explicitly to find ways to cut corners to meet expectations and earn promotions or even just to retain their jobs.

Behavioural Ethics and Ethical Decision-making: Scope and Limitations

Despite its significant contribution to expanding understanding of the role context plays in individual decision-making, this paper argues that some of the assumptions of behavioural ethics can lead to an eclipse of moral agency and moral responsibility. Treviño and Brown (2004), for instance, use the bad barrel argument to explain why people make unethical choices. They maintain that:

> "Most people are the product of the context they find themselves in. They tend to 'look up and look around', and they do what others around them do or expect them to do. They look outside themselves for guidance when thinking about what is right. What that means is that most unethical behaviour in business is supported by the context in which it occurs- either through direct reinforcement of unethical behaviour or through benign neglect". (p. 72)

Similarly, Bazerman and Gino (2012) argue that morality is something malleable and dynamic. Hence, situational and social forces overwhelm individual differences to the extent that "although [people] value morality and want to be seen as ethical people, [they] regularly fail to resist the temptation to act dishonestly or even fail to recognize that there is a moral issue at stake in the decision they are making" (p. 91). Of late, however, there is marked prevalence of whistleblowing on organisational misconduct. Whistleblowing is defined as the disclosure by an organisation's members of illegal and immoral practices under the control of their employers, to persons or organisations that may be able to effect action (Near & Miceli cited in Mesmer-Magnus &

Viswesvaran, 2005). Significantly, extant research characterised whistle-blowers as individuals who tend to score higher on moral reasoning and to value whistleblowing when faced with unethical behaviour (Mesmer-Magnus & Viswesvaran, 2005). Hence, contrary to the assumptions of behavioural ethics, these findings indicate that individuals do have the capacity to resist commands of authority figures when such commands conflict with one's moral values.

Another assumption made by behavioural ethics theorists, is that individuals who commit unethical actions are actually well-intentioned people who engage in unethical behaviour because they are unaware of the moral dimensions of their actions. Bazerman and Gino (2012) termed these actions "unintentional dishonesty" arising from "bounded ethicality". Bounded ethicality leads people to engage in behaviours of which they would otherwise disapprove and judge as unethical after considerable reflection. Using Rest's theory on moral development, Bazerman and Gino (2012) argue that dishonest actions carried out under conditions of bounded ethicality should be considered *unintentional* because individuals made unethical decisions without awareness of the ethical dimension of their actions, and likely without deliberate intent to engage in unethical behaviour arising from this lack of moral awareness. For instance, citing the case of investors who sold investments of Bernie Madoff, jailed for operating a multi-billion dollar Ponzi scheme, Bazerman and Gino (2012) say: "While some investment firms that sold Madoff's investments may have been crooks who knew that the fund had problems, we believe that many others never considered the morality or legality of the fund. *They had defined the problem as an investment decision, and ethics were not even on their radar screen* [emphasis added]. Thus, the need to assess the ethics of the situation never arose" (pp. 21-22). From the perspective of behavioural ethics, therefore, individuals who engage in unethical behaviour under conditions of bounded ethicality would be considered blameless, free from any form of moral responsibility, and their actions described as forms of "unintentional dishonesty" (Bazerman & Gino, 2012).

This paper, however, argues that actions carried out under conditions of bounded ethicality (unawareness of the moral dimension of an action) are not necessarily unintentional acts as advanced by Bazerman and Gino (2012). Support for this argument can be found in research studies which provide evidence that moral awareness is a key component of ethical decision making and that individuals can be intentional in acquiring and developing moral awareness or sensitivity to improve their ethical decision-making processes (Myyry & Helkama, 2002; Catacutan & De Guzman, 2016). Additional support is also provided by studies that conceptualise moral awareness as a conscious and deliberate mental process; how it is exercised can be linked to individual character (Blum, 1991; Melé, 2010).

Moral sensitivity or awareness was conceptualised by Rest (1984) as one of the components of moral behaviour. According to Rest (1984), the first component involved in making a moral judgement and in taking moral action is moral awareness or the ability to recognise the existence of a moral issue. It also entails the ability to interpret the context or situation surrounding an action, and the consideration of the possible actions that one could take, of the people that will be affected by these actions, and the manner in which these people will be affected by the likely consequences of these actions. It is also linked to the notion of empathy and perspective taking (Johnson, 2007), and moral imagination (Werhane, 2002). The Four Component Model theorises that moral judgement is not the only process in the psychology of morality nor does moral judgement account for moral behaviour (Thoma, Rest & Davidson cited in Jordan, 2007). Significantly, Rest (1984) maintains that all four components – sensitivity, judgement, motivation and character – are necessary to enact moral behaviour, and moral failure could be attributed to failure in any of these processes.

Recent theoretical and empirical research has given significant attention to moral sensitivity because scholars argue that individuals' inability to recognise ethical issues in complex situations absolutely precludes the process of moral judgement (Clarkeburn, 2002). Studies have shown that moral awareness varies significantly among individuals and that individuals with higher levels of moral awareness are more likely to make ethical decisions (Wittmer, 1992). Research has also shown that it is an ability that can be acquired and developed through ethics instruction (Jordan, 2007; Clarkeburn, 2002). The effect of educational interventions on moral problem recognition has been explored, especially in the domain of professional ethics, and found that moral problem recognition can be promoted by professional ethics training (Myyry & Helkama, 2002).

Other studies also underscore the role of the decision-maker's character in moral problem recognition. In this sense, a person's failure to be aware of the moral components of a situation could constitute an ethical fault since the consequent failure to act and respond to such situations could have serious negative consequences for other persons. Blum (1991), for instance, claims that failure in moral awareness is likely caused by an individual's tendency towards self-absorption and attentional laziness. Tenbrunsel and Messick (2004) attribute the inability to recognise moral problems to ethical fading or the process by which a decision-maker consciously or subconsciously ignores the moral aspects and implications of an ethical decision. Bird (cited in Drumwright & Murphy, 2004), for his part, considers failure in moral problem recognition as arising from moral muteness or individual failure to voice ethical concerns in settings where it is appropriate to do so. Drumwright and Murphy (2004) maintain that problems in moral issue recognition are largely due to people's rationalisation or their unwillingness to focus on the problem; such rationalisations, in turn, contribute to and reinforce the perceptual problem. Finally, proponents of virtue ethics theory identify the capacity for moral issue recognition as an essential component of practical wisdom or the virtue of prudence (Melé, 2010).

Conclusion

Investigations of recent business scandals have shown that ethical breakdowns in organisations are not necessarily caused by a few bad people who lack a moral compass but also by the presence of organisational cultures that can drive good people to engage in unethical behaviour. Research on behavioural ethics has shown that ethical decision-making is a complex process; it is influenced not only by individual traits but also by contextual variables that impact employees' decisions to engage in unethical behaviour. The purpose of this paper was two-fold: to expound on the role of organisational culture in ethical decision-making and to highlight some of the limits of behavioural ethics as a model for human behaviour in ethical decision-making processes. Despite its important contribution in understanding the influence of situational factors in ethical behaviour, this paper argues that some of the assumptions of behavioural ethics can lead to an eclipse of moral agency and moral responsibility.

References

Aquinas, St. Thomas (1273). *Summa Theologiae,* trans. (1947) by Fathers of the English Dominican Province. New York, NY: Benziger Brothers.

Bandura, A. (1991). Social cognitive theory of moral thought and action. In W. M. Kurtines & J. L. Gerwitz (Eds.). *Handbook of moral behavior and development (Vol. 1).* Hillside, NJ: Erlbaum. 45-103.

Bazerman, M. & Gino, F. (2012). Behavioural ethics: Toward a deeper understanding of moral judgment and dishonesty. *Annual Review of Law and Social Science, 8*, 85-104.

Beauchamp, T. L., & Bowie, N. E. (2004). *Ethical theory and business practice*. Upper Saddle, NJ: Pearson.

Blum, L. (1991). Moral perception and particularity. *Ethics, 101*(4), 701-725.

Catacutan M. R. & De Guzman, A. (2016). Moral sensitivity practice in academic deanship: Does it really matter? In I. Amzat & B. Yusuf (Eds.). *Fast forwarding higher education institutions for global challenges*. Singapore: Springer. 173-184.

Clarkeburn, H. (2002). A test for ethical sensitivity in science. *Journal of Moral Education, 31*(4): 439-453.

Drumwright, M. & Murphy, P. (2004). How advertising practitioners view ethics: Moral muteness, moral myopia, and moral imagination. *Journal of Advertising, 33*(2), 7-24.

Freeman, E. (1994). The politics of stakeholder theory: Some future directions. *Business Ethics Quarterly, (4)*4, 409-421.

Frost, W. (2017, 10 April). Wells Fargo report gives inside look at the culture that crushed the bank's reputation. *CNBC*. Retrieved from https://www.cnbc.com

Glazer, E. & Rexrode, C. (2016, 13 September). Wells Fargo CEO Defends Bank Culture, Lays Blame with Bad Employees. *Wall Street Journal*. Retrieved from https://www.wsj.com/

Hudson, M. (2014, 19 May). Management gurus claim they were blindsided by toxic environment at Countrywide. *The Center for Public Integrity*. Retrieved from https://publicintegrity.org

Jordan, J. (2007). Taking the first step toward a moral action: A review of moral sensitivity measurement across domains. *The Journal of Genetic Psychology, 168*(3), 323-359.

Kohlberg, L. (1969, 1984). Stage and sequence: The cognitive-developmental approach to socialization. *Essays on Moral Development: The Psychology of Moral Development (Vol. 2).* San Francisco: Harper & Row Publishers. 1-169.

McInerny, R. (2007). Ethics and virtue ethics. In Pontificia Academia Sancti Thomae Aquinatis, *Doctor Communis, Proceedings of the Pontifical Academy of St.Thomas Aquinas: The human person, natural law, human rights in a complex and globalised world.* Vatican City: Pontificia Academia Sancti Thomae Aquinatis. 177-186.

Melé, D. (2005). Ethical education in accounting: Integrating rules, values and virtues, *Journal of Business Ethics, 57*(1), 97-109.

Melé, D. (2009). *Business ethics in action: Seeking human excellence in organizations.* Palgrave Macmillan.

Melé, D. (2010). Practical wisdom in managerial decision making. *Journal of Management Development, 29*(7), 637-645.

Merenda, M. & Irwin, M. (2018). Case study: Volkswagen's diesel emissions control scandal. *Journal of Strategic Innovation and Sustainability, 13*(1), 53-62.

Milgram, S. (1963). Behavioural study of obedience. *Journal of Abnormal and Social Psychology, 67*(4), 371-378.

Morgan D. & Gardner, T. (2015, 8 October). Volkswagen's U.S. chief blames emissions scandal on 'individuals'. *Reuters.* Retrieved from https://www.reuters.com/

Myyry, L. & Helkama, K. (2002). The role of value priorities and professional ethics training in moral sensitivity. *Journal of Moral Education, 31*(1), 35-50.

O'Fallon, M. J. & Butterfield, K. D. (2005). A review of the empirical ethical decision-making literature. *Journal of Business Ethics, 59*(4), 375-413.

Raymond, N. (2013, 23 October). Bank of America liable for Countrywide mortgage fraud. *Reuters*. Retrieved from https://www.reuters.com

Rest, J. R. (1984). The major components of morality. In W. M. Kurtines & J. L. Gewirtz (Eds.), *Morality, moral behavior & moral development*. New York: John Wiley & Sons. 24-38.

Reynolds, S. & Ceranic, T. (2007). The effects of moral judgment and moral identity on moral behavior: An empirical examination of the moral individual. *Journal of Applied Psychology, 92*(6), 1610-1624.

Schein, E. H. (1985). Organizational culture and leadership. San Francisco: Jossey-Bass.

Schipani, C. (2017, 24 March). Is your company as ethical as it seems? *Harvard Business Review*. Retrieved from https://hbr.org/

Shepardson, D. & White, J. (2017, 25 August). VW engineer sentenced to 40-month prison term in diesel case. *Reuters*. Retrieved from http://reuters.com

Smythe, C. (2017, 3 December). VW bosses coached me to lie, jailed manager tells U.S. judge ahead of sentencing. *Automotive News Europe*. Retrieved from http://europe.autonews.com

Soltes, E. (2017). Teaching vs. living: Managerial decision-making in the gray. *Journal of Management Education, 41*(4), 453-468.

Tayan, B. (2019, January 8). The Wells Fargo cross selling scandal, *Stanford University Graduate School of Business Research Paper*, No. 17–1. Retrieved from https://ssrn.com/

Tenbrunsel, A. & Messick, D. (2004). Ethical fading: The role of selfdeception in unethical behavior. *Social Justice Research, 17*(2): 223-235.

Tenbrunsel, A. & Smith-Crowe, K. (2008). Ethical decision making: Where we've been and where we're going. *The Academy of Management Annals, 2*(1), 545-607.

Treviño, L. (1986). Ethical decision-making in organizations: A person-situation interactionist model. *The Academy of Management Review, 11*(3), 601-617.

Treviño, L. & Brown, M. (2004). Managing to be ethical: Debunking five business ethics myths. *Academy of Management Executive, 18*(2), 69-83.

Treviño, L., Weaver, G. R., & Reynolds, S. J. (2006). Behavioral ethics in organizations: A review. *Journal of Management, 32*(6), 951-990.

Treviño, L. & Youngblood, S. (1990). Bad apples in bad barrels: A causal analysis of ethical decision-making behaviour. *Journal of Applied Psychology, 75*(4), 378-385.

Velasquez, M. (2001). Moral reasoning. In N. Bowie (Ed.). *The Blackwell guide to business ethics,* Malden, MA: Blackwell. 102-106.

Wittmer, D. (1992). Ethical sensitivity and managerial decision-making: An experiment. *Journal of Public Administration Research and Theory, 2*(4), 443-462.

10

ETHICAL IMPLICATIONS OF THE FEMALE IN IGBO CULTURE: A LITERARY EXCURSION IN CHINUA ACHEBE'S THINGS FALL APART AND BUCHI EMECHETA'S THE JOYS OF MOTHERHOOD

Mary Rose-Claret Ogbuehi

Introduction

Nigeria and most African countries are oppressively masculinist.[84] According to Rose Ure Mezu (1995:1) in her work "Women in Achebe's World", "Nigeria's traditional culture, Muslim as well as non-Muslim, had been masculine-based even before the advent of the white man".

Many female writers have been of the opinion that female subordination and oppression have become problems in African literary debates. "Writers such as Ama Ata Aidoo of Ghana and (Flora) Nwapa of Nigeria have insisted that the image of the helpless, dependent, unproductive African woman was one ushered in by European imperialists whose women lived that way while Buchi Emecheta

---

[84]Mary Rose-Claret Ogbuehi, Lecturer, Department of Foreign Languages and Literary Studies, University of Nigeria.

maintains that African women were traditionally subordinated to sexist cultural mores". (Ibid:1)

Fictions have been used to portray the society and its cultural lives and activities. Literary excursion in these pre- and post-colonial literatures has shown the position which women occupied not only in Igbo culture but also in other African cultures. This paper takes a look at various ways in which women have been projected in these novels. Secondly it seeks to know if there has been improvement in women's position in the African society after many decades of their publication and concludes with recommendations.

Position of Women in the Novels, *Things Fall Apart* and *the Joys of Motherhood*

In the novels, *Things Fall Apart* and *The Joys of Motherhood,* women are designated as weak, foolish or not very reasonable, indecisive, reproductive object, inherited object and second-class citizens belonging to their men. They are also victims of domestic violence and polygyny. Igbo culture, as well as many African cultures, is patriarchal. Patriarchy denotes a structural system of male domination. In it, family names and inheritance are transferred through the male lineage. In her work, *Of Woman Born (1976)*, Adrienne Rich captures most of the variations and nuances of African traditional social milieu which she describes as patriarchy:

The power of the fathers: a familial, social, ideological, and political system in which, by direct pressure or tradition, law and language, customs, etiquette, education, and division of labour men determine what parts women shall or shall not play, and the female is everywhere subsumed by the male.

In the novel, *Things Fall Apart*, patriarchy rules in Okonkwo's world and that of his people. It is a world in which the man is everything and the woman is nearly nothing. Okonkwo, the main character represents the patriarchal figure. The number of women a man is able to acquire and keep, as well as the size of his yam barns and the number of his titles, determine the man's worth and show his success in the society. This success is ascribed to Nwakibie "who has three huge barns, nine wives and thirty children, and the highest but one title which a man can take in the clan (21)". Unoka, Okonkwo's father is an untitled man, a weak person which connotes femininity (21). Okonkwo bemoans his father's weakness. He (Okonkwo) did not inherit anything, "He neither inherited a barn nor a title, nor even a young wife (18)". Women become part of objects to be inherited. Besides, Okonkwo calls Osugo his fellow man "a woman", just because the man has not taken any title and contradicted him in a meeting, saying "this meeting is for men" (26), indicating that the man is a non-achiever and therefore a woman. Non-achievement and dependency become the hallmark of being a woman.

Women are beings who are supposed to be controlled. The ability of a man to control his women shows his strength as seen in *Things Fall Apart*. "Okonkwo believes that no matter how prosperous a man is, if he is unable to rule his women and children, especially his women, he is not really a man" (53). Women are projected as beings that ought to be controlled by men. Because they need to be controlled, "Okonkwo's wives live in perpetual fear of his fiery temper" (13). To be under the control of a man denotes submissiveness and allowing the man to dictate what the other does. Therefore, Achebe's women are voiceless and inconsequential. When Ikemefuna is brought to stay at Okonkwo's household, he hands him over to his first wife, who asks; "Is he staying long with us?" In response, "Okonkwo thundered and stammered, when you became one of the *ndichie* of Umuofia (14)". This means that the woman has no voice and cannot even ask a simple question.

In Igbo cultural milieu, folktales and storytelling are normally told by women to their children after evening meals as a means of transmitting the cultures of the people. Okonkwo enjoins Nwoye and Ikemefuna to join him in his obi, where he tells them stories about tribal wars. Nwoye, Okonkwo's son enjoys the story being told by his mother, "but he now knew that they were for foolish women and children (54)". Stories about wars signify strength and valour while the ones about vultures and tortoise usually told by women testify to weakness and foolishness. Women are custodians of oral tradition. Oral tradition is a traditional teaching method with unlimited potential in transferring knowledge. It is an important aspect of traditional African education theory and practice, concerned with teaching the oral tradition as well as helping them to learn to use the language both creatively and effectively. It is through oral tradition in form of stories and folktales that values, morals and beliefs are passed on to future generations.

Apart from classifying women as foolish, they are also victims of domestic violence. With little or no provocation, women bear the brunt of men's anger, sometimes transferred anger. They serve as an outlet through which men's anger is relieved. "Okonkwo, who had been walking about aimlessly in his compound in suppressed anger, suddenly found an outlet. Who killed this banana tree?" On founding out that his second wife cut a leaf from there, Okonkwo gives her a sound beating. In the same manner, Uzowulu forms a habit of beating his wife Mgbafo even when pregnant till her brothers decided to beat him up and take back their sister. The elders of Umuofia in settling the matter affirm that "It is not bravery when a man fights with a woman (93)". Violence perpetrated against women by their partners or ex-partners is often accompanied by emotionally abusive and controlling behavior. People have argued that physical force and threats are resources which are used to control the action of others. Many acts of domestic violence have led to the death of women while others have been maimed by such means as through acid baths. Many women keep quiet about abuse from their partners. Reasons for keeping quiet are sometimes based on cultural beliefs which encourage men to punish their wives and keep them under control through beating. It is still the case that the stigma that goes with divorce and broken marriages no matter who is the cause of the break also encourages women to bear the almost unbearable. Some other times, the financial dependence of the woman and perhaps her family on the man also exposes the woman to domestic abuse without recourse.

In many African cultures, polygyny is practiced. Polygyny is the custom of marrying many wives. Polygyny dehumanizes women in numerous ways and is destructive to women's autonomy and psychology. Marriage, which is supposed to bring about happiness and companionship, has turned out to be an institution in which women are stifled, dominated, and exploited. Polygyny brings about envy, distrust and tension in the family. Newell (1997: 128-129) expresses this view stating "Polygyny is the epitome of female denigration, exploitation and domination in West Africa. If home represents the place where one is most at peace and at ease, the polygynous home is not home but hell for the co-wives and their children as tensions reign supreme, fuelled by envy, distrust, intrigues and all sorts of destructive passions".

Though women are relegated to the background, Ani, the earth goddess is respected in Igbo cosmology. According to Achebe in his *Things Fall Apart*, "*Ani or 'Ala'* (depending on the Igbo dialect in use), played a greater part in the life of the people than any other deity. She was the ultimate judge of morality and conduct. And what was more, she was in close communion with the departed fathers of the clan whose bodies had been committed to earth (36)". The Earth Spirit, 'Ala' as the mother of Igbo people is characterized by sacredness and peacefulness. She can punish as well. She sees all things and all human beings. No secret is actually hidden from her. She is like the hidden eye that sees even our nakedness. Ike and Edozie 2001: 54 explain:

The Earth goddess can thus give life or destroy it, she loves immensely, but it is true also that nobody can hurt more than she (can). Her justice is believed to be next to that of Chukwu, because she, like Chukwu, weighs all the circumstances surrounding the action.

It is therefore not a surprise that Okonkwo is punished for killing his clansman mistakenly. "It was a crime against the earth goddess to kill a clansman, and a man who committed it must flee from the land" (124). Okonkwo has committed *Nso-ala* or desecration of the earth/land. Thus, Okonkwo flees to his maternal land Mbanta and spends seven years before returning to Umuofia. As Okonkwo buries himself in despair, his maternal uncle Uchendu addresses Okonkwo in these words;

Can you tell me, Okonkwo, why it is that one of the commonest names we give our children is Nneka, or Mother is supreme---- A man belongs to his fatherland and not to his motherland. And yet we say Nneka. Why is that? ....Yes it's true that a child belongs to its father. But when a father beats his child, it seeks sympathy in its mother's hut. A man belongs to his fatherland when things are good and life is sweet. But when there is sorrow and bitterness, he finds refuge in his motherland. Your mother is there to protect you. (134).

The only women respected in *Things Fall Apart* are likes of Chielo, the priestess of the Oracle of the Hills and Caves, who by the virtue of their work, is removed from the pale of normalcy. Engaged in her work of prophecy, she transforms from the ordinary to the extra-ordinary and thus can reprimand anybody even as she does Okonkwo. "Beware, Okonkwo, she warned. Beware of exchanging words with Agbala. Does a man speak when a god speaks? Beware" (101). In this case, on account of her work and of the god for whom she speaks, Chielo acquired a status not normally reserved for women.

African male writers create a false impression of women who are contented with their subordinate roles. The literature produced by men tends to glorify and uphold patriarchal powers where the woman has only subjugated existence without an essential voice. Men have legitimised patriarchal ideologies in their writing, which promote inequality between the two sexes through enabling tropes of post-colonial male domination as well as colonialism. Eko (1986: 211) states;

Between the 50s and 60s, the image of women changed considerably. Works by Achebe, Amadi, Aluko, Munonye, Ngugi and many others, which fall within the traditional mode, share basically a conventional attitude towards women with only slight variations. The writers appear to be both noncommittal and uncritical of the status quo. They invariably cast all women in the strict sexist role of mothers and wives, submissive to the norms and regulations that restrict them.

African women writers are trying to rewrite the image of women already created by men. In *the Joys of Motherhood*, Emecheta exposes the subjugated existence of a woman's life in a traditional society. She demonstrates that in a traditional Igbo society, a woman gains more status when she increases the lineage of her husband by giving birth to baby boys. Women are recognized in their reproductive ability of giving birth and not in their productive abilities as individuals and what they can offer their societies. This task becomes one of the sources of women's slavery.

Emecheta begins her novel, *The Joys of Motherhood*, with the notion of barrenness in Igbo culture and its concomitant effect on the woman. Marriage is contrived to raise a family. A woman becomes enslaved in her biological ability to bear and to rear children. If a woman cannot be impregnated to perform this primary function, she lives in misery and is taunted by her in-laws and neighbors (and sometimes even by her husband in real life). The taunt that a childless woman gets from the society can be so excruciating and can even lead to suicide for many women. Thus, the barren African woman is seen as an incomplete woman. She becomes as John Mbiti puts it; "the dead end of human life, not only for the genealogical level, but also for herself" (Christian 1985: 216). Nnu Ego remains childless after some years in marriage and so her husband Amatokwu divorces her. "What do you want me to do? Amatokwu asks. I am a busy man. I have no time to waste my precious seed on a woman who is infertile. I have to raise children for my line" (Emecheta 1979: 37). So, he marries a second wife and when she can no longer bear the taunts, she returns home to her father.

In Igbo culture as well as many other African cultures, the man is encouraged to marry another woman, who can bear him children. Her father Agbadi, returns the bride price and decides to give her to another man. She is given to a man whom she does not know and whose physical appearance she does not like, but who makes her a woman by making her conceive and have children (Ibid:79). The primary role of a woman is thus reduced to the production of babies otherwise the woman is classified as a failure. Nnu Ego in her second marriage lives up to the expectation of the society. She gives birth to her first son. Unfortunately, the child died after some weeks. Nnu Ego sees herself as a failed woman, who has failed both her father and the society and decides to commit suicide. The intervention of passers-by and the woman who slaps her for abandoning her child and husband makes her exclaim; "But I am not a woman any more! I am not a mother any more. The child is there, dead on the mat. My chi has taken him away from me. I only want to go in there and meet her" (65). The crowd who have gathered agreed that a woman without a child for her husband is a failed woman (Ibid: 65).

To prove that she is not a failure but a woman who lives according to the dictates of her society, Nnu Ego has to give birth successively. She believes in the reward and status she would get as a mother and most especially giving birth to male children. This ideology becomes the bedrock of her slavery. She becomes a prisoner, imprisoned by the love for her children and imprisoned in her role as the senior wife.

Moreover, female figures in the novel are victimized by the oppressive forces of race, gender and class. Emecheta in her novel portrays women who are subjugated by the patriarchal society. The effect which colonial patriarchal discourse has on the native patriarchy is further criticized. "In this regard, colonialism intensified patriarchal oppression, often because native man increasingly disenfranchised and excluded from the public sphere, became more tyrannical at home" (Barfi et al 2015: 28). The novel depicts the Igbo colonial society of 1934. Nnu Ego is married to her second husband Nnaife in Lagos, who is a washer-man to his British master. Nnaife tells Nnu Ego that he has to marry her in the church lest he will lose his job and Madam here will not take it. Nnu Ego bemoans that her husband has become a slave to the white woman, whose underwear he washes and snaps at Nnaife;

> "You behave like a slave! Do you go to her and say, 'Please madam crawcraw-skin, can I sleep with my wife today'? (50). Following her discussion with Cordelia whose husband is a cook to the white man, Cordelia confirms that the manhood of their husbands has been taken away from them and says; "They are all slaves, including us. If their masters treat them badly, they take it out on us" (54).

Apart from the slavery brought about by colonialism, traditional gender roles enslave women in African culture. Nnu Ego realises that after giving birth to her children, she has to feed and cater for them, lest they die of hunger. She says: "Yes I have many children, but what do I have to feed them on? On my life, I have to work myself to the bone to look after them. I have to give them my all. And if I am lucky enough to die in peace, I even have to give them my soul" (187). To avert such calamity, Ibuza Women Lagos branch, who converge at their monthly meetings lend her five shillings from the women's fund and advised her to buy tins of cigarettes and packets of matches, which she can sell in front of their house. This solidarity shows how women help themselves in their economic struggles.

> "The other women taught her how to start her own business so that she would not have only one outfit to wear…she was so thrilled with this that, as the other more experienced women had foretold, she had no time to be lonely or worry about her husband's humiliating job, or bite her fingers about her coming child" (54).

In this regard, the patriarchal division of labor defines a woman's role in the family. Besides her domestic work; she is expected to do everything to feed her children. As Barfi (2015:31) puts it:

> "Nnu Ego in this colonial society has to do a petty business in order to feed her children and even her husband. She knows, according to the tradition of Ibuza, she is responsible for her children. When she demands her husband more money to feed her children, Nnaife asserts cruelly: It is your responsibility to feed your children as best (as) you can. Sell your lappas. You are the chief wife, use your head." (152)

Nnu Ego is expected to feed her family even when the means of feeding them is not there but Nnaife the husband, who has meagre resources, is busy impregnating the wives to give them more mouths to feed. Nnu Ego has no life of her own. She cannot complain lest the society reminds her that she is a senior wife and has to behave accordingly. She realizes that:

She was a prisoner, imprisoned by her love for her children, imprisoned in her role as the senior wife. She was not even expected to demand more money for her family; that was considered below the standard expected of a woman in her position. It was not fair, she felt, the way men cleverly used a woman's sense of responsibility to actually enslave her. They knew that a traditional wife like herself would never dream of leaving her children (153).

Another female character depicted in the novel is Cordelia, Nnu Ego's neighbor. Though squabbles and quarrels exists among them, they do not take it to heart. They devise means of assisting each other and practiced mutual aid to each other. It is Cordelia that delivered Nnu Ego of her son, Ngozi. When Nnu Ego expresses her gratitude, Cordelia responds; "We are like sisters on a pilgrimage. Why should we not help one another?" (55). Mama Aby is also another neighbour of Nnu Ego, who assists her in getting out money from Post-Office sent by Nnaife during the period he was recruited into the army to fight in Burma. These women prove that they can be of help to themselves especially in difficult times.

Emecheta highlights the problem of gender inequality in the character of Adaku. Adaku is Nnu Ego's co-wife. She is inherited by Nnaife at the death of her husband, Nnaife's brother. She has two girls. She gives birth to a boy who died after few weeks of convulsion. Adaku cannot be consoled. As Nnu Ego tries to console her with soothing words of being young and has the possibility of conceiving again, she says:

You can say that now. Do you remember how sad you were, senior wife, when you had the two girls? You would have been happier if they had turned out to be boys instead. Now I had a boy, my only son, and he did not live. O God, why did you not take one of the girls and leave me with my male child? My only man child (142).

Having waited for male children who were not forth-coming, Adaku decides to be independent and to make her own decision. Adaku's sense of independence is seen when she initiates a strike by refusing Nnaife supper until he increases his wives' food allowance. Adaku is called an "ambitious woman" by Adankwo, who not only has accepted the patriarchal hierarchies but is using it in silencing her fellow woman. Adankwo admonishes Nnu Ego:

> "Can't you see that you are running from the position your chi has given you leaving it for a woman your husband inherited from his brother, woman whom we here all know to be very ambitious, a woman who has not even born a son for this family" (158).

Adaku is despised for not giving birth to a boy. Giving birth to a boy becomes one of the characteristics through which a woman gains respect in her husband's house.

Adaku's quest for equality is reiterated when she walks out on her husband, to live a dignified life and be a single woman, educating her daughters alone. She tells Nnu Ego;

> "I am not prepared to stay here and be turned into a mad woman just because I have no sons.... I am going to make some of our men who return from the fighting happy... I will spend the money I have in giving my girls a good start in life" (189).

Adaku who is no longer interested in what patriarchal society demands of her and what women have been made to think of themselves, says to Nnu Ego;

"The more I think of it, the more I realise that we women set impossible standards for ourselves. That we make life intolerable for one another. I cannot live up to your standards, senior wife. So, I have to set my own standard" (189). With that Adaku concentrates on her business and becomes a successful businesswoman. She moves out of the traditional norm and lives an independent life.

Moreover, when Nnu Ego had her first set of twin girls, their birth did not bring any delight to Nnaife. He simply said; "Nnu Ego, what are these? Could you not have done better? Where will we all sleep, eh?

What will they eat?" All these lamentations show that boys worth more than girls among the Igbos. Besides the naming ceremony was not performed for them. "Nnaife did not even suggest their names", Nnu Ego moaned. "Twins don't deserve special names. This one came first so she is Taiwo and the (other) one is Kehinde" (141). As if relegating the girls to the background is not enough, Adaku tells Nnu Ego; "These girls when they grow up will be great helpers to you in looking after the boys. Their bride price will be used in paying school fees as well" (141).

Education of the boys is of paramount importance. The bride price of the girls will be used for the education of the boys. The self-actualization of the girls and the education of the girls are not important and hence not to be considered. Nnu Ego sacrifices her life for the education of her sons with the hope that her sons will look after her. Unfortunately her sons travel to America and Canada and forget their mother, and she dies on the road side of the village.

Emecheta's *Joys of Motherhood* portrays also the extent to which women and their sexual pleasure are disregarded. Agbadi neglects his women. "He would be reminded to do his duty by them, then when they became pregnant, he would not be seen in their huts until the time came for him to mate them again. But whenever he returned from his many wanderings he would go and stay with his Ona" (8). She further criticizes the manner women are treated like commodity, such that whilst Agbadi's wives wish to speak with him, he brings his mistress to sleep and to give her pleasure. In the same vein, when Adaku, the inherited wife of Nnaife comes to live with them in Lagos, Nnu Ego shows her discomfort and resentment. At night Nnu Ego is disregarded:

Nnu Ego fought back tears as she prepared her own bed for Nnaife and Adaku. It was a good thing she was determined to play the role of the mature senior wife; she was not going to give herself any heartache when the time came for Adaku to sleep on that bed. She must stuff her ears with cloth and make sure she also stuffed her nipple into the mouth of her young son Adim, when they all lay down to sleep (138).

The polygynous system does not favor the woman. It rather treats the woman as the 'other'. The man rather hops from one woman to the other disregarding the hurt and the bad feelings it brings to the first wife. Nnaife seeing that Nnu Ego finds it difficult to sleep mocks her and says to Adaku; "My senior wife cannot go to sleep. You must learn to accept your pleasures quietly, my new wife Adaku" (139). The first wife is not only treated as the other but she is forced to accept it and be mature lest she brings dishonor and disgrace to her family. In all these, Emecheta shows various ways in which women are subjugated and treated as second-class citizens in Igbo culture.

Improvement in the Position of Women after Decades of Publication of the Novels

Many decades after the publication of *Things Fall Apart* and *The Joys of Motherhood,* one can say that there is a gradual improvement in the situation women found themselves then and now. It is gradual because patriarchy is endemic in Igbo and many African cultures. Patriarchy fosters the system of male domination. Culture is not static but dynamic. The coming of the missionaries eroded some of the cultural practices through which women are exploited such as polygyny and as inherited objects. Many men out of Christian practice engage in monogamy, whereby a man is married to one wife but that does not inhibit many from engaging in extra-marital affairs. Polygyny is not totally wiped out in Igbo culture. Monogamy is accepted only to the extent that it remains compatible with certain traditional requirements. For instance, the need for a male heir to carry on the family lineage is seen as a justifiable reason to take another wife. There is still quest for preference for sons, even though, many couples are advised to go for adoption but it all depends on the education and understanding of the couples involved.

Seen as a powerful instrument through which national development is attained, education is available also to girls. During the colonial era, education was designed for boys. It prepared boys to qualify for employment as clerks, teachers, interpreters, catechists for government offices. Girls were not considered for such employments. Even when they went to school, they were taught domestic science and cookery which would prepare them to be good wives and mothers and nothing more. This explains the reason Nnu Ego's twin girls did not attain the same level of education with her boys. The development of any nation cannot be fully effected without women's contribution. Realising that education is one of the powerful instruments of empowering women with the knowledge and skills that would help them to participate actively in the development process, Nigeria became a member country to the United Nations 1979 convention known as Convention on the Elimination of all Forms of Discrimination Against Women (CEDAW). Though Nigeria signed against all forms of discrimination against women, women are still subjected to various forms of discrimination. A lot of cultural and traditional factors inhibit women from having access to educational and economic opportunities like the men folk.

Violence against women which is one of the means through which women are dehumanized is still on the increase. There has been an increase in the cases of wife battery/beating, rape, and psychological abuse. The rate at which young girls and women are raped in Nigeria is on the increase. The perpetrators are people in key positions of trust such as fathers, step-fathers, uncles, friends, family friends, cousins, grandfathers and religious personnel. Violence against women increases day by day. There are cultural and social norms that support different types of violence. There exist traditional beliefs that men have a right to control or discipline women through physical violence like beating. This makes women vulnerable to their intimate partners and places girls at risk of sexual abuse in the hands of men.

Many women who are victims of abuse by their spouses have been abused many times. Violence against women remains one of the social malaises that needs to be improved. Many acts of domestic violence have led to the death of women while others have been maimed by such means including acid baths. Yet, many women keep quiet about abuse from their partners. There is still great need for improvement in matters concerning violence against women.

Moreover, there still exists gender inequality between men and women. In Igbo culture, a woman is allowed to buy a land only when accompanied by a man or a boy irrespective of his age. Gender plays an active role in such a situation which points to the superiority of a boy-child over a girl-child, of a boy over a girl, and of a man over a woman. In some situations as shown above, even a day old boy-child could be valued in Igbo culture more that an adult woman. This value system makes a woman dependent.

For decades, Igbo women are not allowed to have a share or an inheritance of their father's property or wealth. It is normally divided among the men and the boys of the family. This long-held tradition of dispossessing women of their rights in their families is termed discriminatory by the Nigerian Supreme Court, which declared such practice as a clear violation of the constitution around ten years ago.

Besides, there still exists preference of boys over girls. Many women who did not give birth to boys are still taunted in many villages and their husbands take on second wives in a bid to have boys for their lineages. Many women are still deprived of active voice in their marriage and in the communities where they live. They cannot take decision in what concerns them. In issues concerning marriage, many girls are allowed to choose their husbands but there are still many cases in which marriage is contracted based solely on the arrangement and agreement of the parents.

Recommendations and Conclusion

Patriarchy, Socialisation and Discrimination

In this twenty-first century, there is need for improvement in the position of women. Knowing that Igbo women have been facing multiple forms of discrimination since the colonial era of 1900, whereby women have suffered and continue to suffer from various forms of discrimination, simply because they are women, hence an urgent need for equity and social justice. The literary works of Chinua Achebe (*Things Fall Apart*) and Buchi Emecheta (*The Joys of Motherhood*) have shown how women are perceived in Igbo culture during and after colonial era. In order to enhance gender equality in public and private domain, certain cultural practices such as patriarchy is perpetuated through the socialization process which begins in the family and penetrates into other sectors of the society like religion, education, the economy and politics need to be re-examined, reviewed and bettered with more humane considerations for women inserted into it.

The family serves as a place where patriarchal practices are nurtured and taught to the young to accept gendered roles. In this domain, boys and girls are given roles that limit the girl child from the outset. The boy is taught to be strong in preparation to being later the head the family while the girl is taught to become later a wife and a mother, and as required by the custom to be submissive and dependent on her husband. This act of dependency is not part of the Igbo culture of pre-colonial era. The economic power and control of women in the pre-colonial era as well as the complimentary role of women before the advent of the colonial masters should be re-introduced.

Patriarchal attitudes are found in Christianity, which strengthens the traditional beliefs that women are weaker sex and need to be controlled. The biblical narrative of the creation of Eve from Adam's rib makes it possible to view women as dependents and as such second-class citizens. Christian churches should be able to teach their members that women are also created in the image and likeness of God, not that of man. The Bible is adopted from Jewish tradition which relegates women to the background. No wonder, not minding the progress and betterment introduced by Jesus on the situation of women, one could still read in the passages of the New Testament that; "Jesus fed five thousand people not counting the women and children" (cf. Matthew 14: 21 depending on the translation). This gives the impression that that which is important has been counted. Women bundled together with children do not count much.

Education

Education of boys and girls should be encouraged. Many families would prefer to educate their boys as seen in *The Joys of Motherhood.* Nnu Ego's sons travelled to Canada and America to pursue their education. They learnt the culture of individualism and forgot their mother, who died eventually out of heartbreak. The twin girls are not given any formal education because they are girls. Boys are seen as those who would bear the family names while girls will be married off. At home, the boy-child is given cars, puzzle games that require mental ability while the girl-child is given dolls or kitchen utensils that direct her to motherhood and the kitchen. Girls should be given toys that will prepare them to read science and engineering. These negative patriarchal socializations which begin from home should be abolished. Education of girls leads to self-fulfilment, self-confidence, self-identity and economic independence.

The Economy

Patriarchal attitudes do not allow many women to take part and play their role in the control of the economy. It is obvious that men control the economy. Few women are allowed to occupy ministerial positions in Nigeria even though many Igbo women of reputable character like late Prof. Dora Akunyili and Dr. Okonjo-Iweala have shown their abilities when they were called to serve. Women should be given the opportunity to serve in their respective areas of specialization. They should be accorded the opportunity to serve when they do better than men.

In the corporate sector, many women are victims of sexual harassment by their bosses. Some have to accept to be abused in order to be promoted. It is the submission of this paper that such sexual harassment and abuses should be stopped. Sexual abuse has led many women to depression, suicide, unwanted pregnancy and transmission of HIV or other sexually transmitted diseases.

Politics

Women constitute half of Nigeria's population, yet they are discriminated against in the political process. Women in Nigeria hold less than 7% of decision-making positions. Entering politics and aspiring to a political position have a lot of financial implications. Politics has a lot to do with resource availability and control. Many women do not have enough resources to sponsor themselves to political posts. Political parties should be organised in such as a way that women can have access to resources and participate actively in politics.

Were these recommendations taken and implemented, the country would certainly gain a lot from these improved positions that would eventually allow women fulfill their potentialities in the society for the good of all, both for men and for women, for the present generation and for future generations.

References

Achebe, Chinua. *Things Fall Apart*. Heinemann, 1958.

Barfi, Zahra et al. "A Study of Buchi Emecheta's The Joys of Motherhood in the Light of Chandra Talpade Mohanty: A Postcolonial Feminist Theory. *European Online Journal of Natural and Social Sciences*, vol.4, no.1, 2015, pp. 26-38. www.european-science.com

Christian, Barbara. *Black Feminist Criticism: Perspectives on Black Women Writers*. Pergamon, 1985.

Eko, Ebele. "Changes in the Image of the African Woman: A celebration". *Phylon*, vol. 47, no. 3, 1986, pp.210-218.

Emecheta, Buchi. *The Joys of Motherhood*. Braziller, 1979.

Ezegbe, Bernedeth and Felicia Akubue. "An Appraisal of the Status of Nigerian Women: Educational Implications and National Development". *American Journal of Sociological Research,* vol. 2, no. 2, 2012, pp. 27-31.

Ike, Obiora and Ndidi Nnoli-Edozien. *Understanding Africa: Traditional Legal Reasoning Jurisprudence & Justice in Igboland.* CIDJAP Publications, 2001.

Kambarami, Maureen. "Femininity, Sexuality and Culture: Patriarchy and Female Subordination in Zimbabwe. Africa Regional Sexuality Resource Centre, 2006.

Mezu, Rose Ure. "Women in Achebe's World". Womanist Theory and Research 1.2 (1995) www.uga.edu/-womanist/ 1995/ mezu.html

Newell, Stephanie, editor. *Writing African Women: Gender, Popular Culture and Literature in West Africa.* 1st ed., Zed Books, 1977.

Powell, Andrea. "Problematizing Polygyny in the Historical Novels of Chinua Achebe: The Role of the Western Feminist Scholar". *Research in African Literatures*, vol. 39, no. 1, 2008, pp.166- 184.

Rich, Adrienne. *Of Woman Born: Motherhood as Experience and Institution*. W.W. Norton and Company, 1976.

11

ETHICS IN HIGHER EDUCATION: A RETHINK FOR A TRANSFORMATIVE MODEL IN AFRICA

Aidan G. Msafiri

Introduction

Ethics in higher education serves as both the soul and heart of true and holistic human transformation and empowerment. Ethics constitutes the fundamental principle of value based, inspirational, and practical education.[85] It is informative, formative and has the potential to be transformative, particularly against the present-day profit-oriented education models, trends and brands. Values that are the "DNA" of transformative education do not simply fall from the sky. Such values are nurtured and safeguarded, and passed onto future generations. Amidst the ever-growing "void" or "vacuum" of values, especially in higher education, there is an urgent need to rethink a new model and paradigm of education.[86] New models should be based on the

[85] Aidan G. Msafiri, Climate Change Ambassador for the United Republic Of Tanzania, Kilimanjaro.

[86] This section was previously released on Globethics.net website, and is republished with authorisation of Globethics.net Foundation.

fundamental ethical values of: care, concern, trust, responsible leadership, accountability, foresight, true love, dignity, honesty and patriotism.

Ethics

The term "*ethics*" has its origins from the Greek language "*ethos*". It implies an 'outlook shaped by the awareness of moral values'. It involves reflection and action of what is objectively good, to be pursued, and what is objectively bad, to be avoided. This reflection on action is founded on three key pillars: the objective good, the self, and the others.

Non-Humans

Ethics transcends faith, race, political affiliations, cultural status and gender and is therefore cross-boundary by nature. Ethical living implies practicing what is objectively good, on personal, social, economic, political and other levels.

From both Christian and Interfaith perspectives, there is agreement that ethics orients, motivates and empowers, harmonizes and inspires personal faiths, families, communities and nations. Ethics aims to know what is objectively 'good' and what is objectively 'bad', and facilitates decision-making to avoid the 'bad'.

It must be well understood that ethics are not laws stipulated by governmental forces. Ethics is made up of inner values, virtues, habits, norms, attitudes, beliefs, criteria and principles. Unlike laws, ethics is motivated by the inner, non-tangible values such as: peace, faith, Agape (love), solidarity, fairness, care, compassion, trust, justice, empathy, wellbeing, joy, equity, accountability, transparency, sustainability, forgiveness, mercy, and moderation.

NB: We cannot measure such values empirically; neither can we touch them, as we simply live them.

Ethics is also motivated by transcendent/metaphysical beliefs or revelations. The may include reward after death, punishment after death and eternal happiness. A human being is capable of knowing these super natural realities. In these instances, ethics and ethical living do not fall from the skies. These realities are reflected, lived, and passed onto future generations through religious and societal norms and values

Higher Education

The term "education" originates from the Latin "*educare*", which implies 'to inform, to inspire, to share, to mentor or to enlighten with values, life views and world views'.

It must be well noted that learning, be it primary, secondary or tertiary, is not simply an event ,but rather a value-based, life-long process of transforming the cognitive, affective and psychological dimensions of the human being's mind, soul, body and will.

More generally, higher education refers to post-secondary education. It is usually delivered at educational establishments such as universities, colleges, academies, seminars or institutes. However, there can be a difference between higher education and further education.

Rationale/Justification

A value-based ethical education model is key to a holistic, transformative and developmental process. It is the best cure against Nyerere's "cancers" of development, namely ignorance, disease and poverty. It also poses arguments against Mahatma Gandhi's Seven Blunders Theory. The theory stipulates

> "wealth without work, pleasure without conscience, knowledge without character, business without morality, science without service, worship without sacrifice and politics without principle."

At present, at the centre of the Tanzanian ethical educational system lays the infamous dictum from President John Magufuli, 'Kutumbua Majipi', which translates 'Operating on Boils'. The dictum exists as a result of corrupt practices within Tanzanian society. This highlights the need for a shift into a new paradigm truly reflective of values.

Thought-provoking Ethical-based Questions

What are the short, medium and long-term consequences of dissociating ethics in families and in the educational curricula? Where is the absence of ethics in academia and intellectual professionalism leading us (*quo vadis*)? What are the impacts of the commercialization and commodification of education in Africa and worldwide? Do we believe that ethical behaviours are rewarded more than unethical behaviours? Do we agree that, when good people do nothing, evil increases? What are the weaknesses of the information revolution to society? Are they not emptying their minds and filling their databanks? (Ref. "*Homo Idioticus*") Is the present day knowledge-based society transforming the human person ethically, socially and as a human? What are the implications of observations such as "operation well done, but patient died", "graduation done, but graduates remain illiterate"? What are the implications of value-free education trends or models, "patchworks", and "bluff society"? Are university students' mere consumers, or innovative producers of knowledge and skills? Do we agree that ethics is the key incubator and protector of transformative higher education? What are the impacts of political interests in the process of curricula development and policy? What are the effects of "academic inbreeding"? Is the academia managing or damaging its own image and mission? Do the mission, vision and core value statements of a university mean anything today, especially without ethical engagement and transformation? What are the roots of the ever-growing "copy and paste" plagiarism and laziness cultures among college students?

These questions will be addressed in three key parts.

Ethical and Value-based Education as a Transformative Tool against Destructive World and Life Views Today

Economic Illusions in Higher Education today

"I am because I consume" vs. "I am because we are" or "I am because I think". This line of thinking manifests itself within the complacency syndrome, catalysed by the 'Speed maniac' culture we experience in present day. The following quotes adequately capture this line of thought: "All what matters is the bottom line structure", "The survival of the fastest syndrome" and "When in Rome, do like the Romans do."

Cultural-Religious and Anthropological Illusions in Higher Education Today

Common illusions which roam in higher education point towards a sense of superiority. This may include, but is not limited to: "Educated men are superior to others", "My tribe is more than your tribe" and "Our religion is superior to theirs."[87]These anthropological illusion contribute to the growth of religious fanaticism, intolerance, fundamentalism and Bokoharamism

Academic Professional Illusions in Higher Education Today

The illusions which circulate amongst academics, may include, that "PhD holders and Professors are awarded with more rights and dignity than certificate, diploma and Bachelor Degree holders" and "the longer the CV, the greater the respect." This exemplifies how values, such as respect are awarded due to academic achievement and accolades, opposed to a values-driven environment, in which all can flourish.

---

[87] Luciano Mattei, P. Wambura, A Guide To Christian Ethics And Formation In Moral Maturity, Philosophical Studeis 12, Nairobi, CUEA Publications 2000, pp. 17-19.

Ethics-driven Higher Education and Wisdom as a Post-colonial and Post Modern Liberation Toolbox

Liberation from Nyerere's three major enemies namely, ignorance, poverty and diseases, requires dismantling corruptive practices, abolishing the "Big Result Now" mindset and ridding the educational system of egocentrism, abuse or misuse of power, leadership vacuums and resource depletion. It is of equal importance to fight against gender discrimination, oppression and indifferentism. Liberation in itself is as an authentic African/ "*Tanzanian Renaissance*" for true peace, sustainable growth and common welfare. As Samuel Kobia observes,

> "Authentic renaissance must lay down the foundation of democracy as a way of life; so that the whole body of social systems and constraints are subject to ethical evaluation...The late Mwalimu Julius Nyerere once said that peace was another word for development". "Development is about peace, it is about an abundant life, it is about justice, and it is about happiness"[88]

Ethics-driven Higher Education and Wisdom as a Therapy against Educational "Boils" and Disasters of Today

The more knowledge one attains the more power one has. There is a constant struggle between the knowledge-based societies and the illiterate, marginalized and less privileged. Recent trends have noted a rise in"*Shule za Sekondari za Kata*" ("Ward Secondary Schools"), meaning, more emphasis on quantity than quality or 'quantity over quality'.

The current trend of 'quantity over quality 'in higher education is led by the need to collect professional and academic accolades, simply to compete for employment . It lacks the formative and transformative values, virtues and core competencies for affirmative action.

---

[88] Samwel Kobia, The Courage To Hope, (Geneva: WCC Publications) p. 131

There is an absence of core communication skills, but greater pressure for current graduates to become "multi-linguists", "multiplayers", "job creators and not job seekers". Graduates lack the courage to stand for truth and advocate for their beliefs. The emergence of 'I culture' opposed to a 'We culture' presents a major challenge within the educational system.

There has also been an increase in destructive solidarity, with phrases such as "birds of the same feather flock together' becoming increasingly politicized within educational systems.

Ethics-driven Higher Education and Wisdom as "Best Practice" For Self-sufficiency and Sustainable Livelihoods

The famous Afro-Caribbean writer C.L. James makes the following observation on the relevance of the Arusha Declaration

> "Julius Nyerere in theory and practice laid the basis of an African State which Nkrumah had failed to do…In the Arusha Declaration Nyerere laid down his principles. This is one of the greatest documents of the past World War II."[89]

In the same vein of thought, Saju Chachalachal noted that

> "One of the best means of empowering others, especially the youth generation is through different modes of education…we have a great responsibility to offer a method of education that would enhance life…If our educational institutions and programs become centres of empowering others, including the downtrodden and the marginalized, it opens up the horizons of growth and success to everyone…"[90]

---

[89] C.L. James, Nkrumah and Revolution: (London: Allison & Busby) p. 7.

[90] Saju Chachalachal Cmi, Ignitig Minds to Transform the Society, (Bangalore: 2013) p.x.

Ethics-driven Higher Education as a Key Trigger for a Humanizing, Civilizing and Liberating Process

First, education must be a credible means of acquiring formative wisdom for practical life; it must provide a truly dynamic liberating culture. True education should by its very nature empower humans to effectively and efficiently utilize their spiritual, intellectual, physical, cultural, economic and technological potential for a quality and fulfilled life. As a civilizing process, education must enable humans to think for them,[91] to decide for themselves, and to be creative, innovative and proactive.

Ethics-based Higher Education and Wisdom as the "DNA" and Trigger for True Self-reliance

Nyerere's noble paradigm of "Education for Self-reliance" (ESR) cannot be exaggerated. *For Nyerere,*

> "Agricultural and food sovereignty was priority number one. It underpinned its practical and particularly its service-oriented objectives. For Nyerere "...education in Tanzania should not be designed just to produce passive agricultural workers of different levels of skills, who simply carry out plans or direction received from above. It must produce good farmers; it has also to prepare people.

For they are free workers and citizens, in a free and democratic society, albeit a largely rural society. They have to be able to think for themselves, to make judgements on all the issues affecting them, they have to be able to interpret decisions made through the democratic institutions for our society and to implement them in the light of peculiar local circumstances where they happen to live..."[92]

---

[91] Saju, p. 62.

[92] Unpublished paper by Rwekaza S. Mukandara UDSM- Redet Workshop Jan. 2015.

Ethics-promoting Higher Education as a Trigger for Sustainable Peace, Coherence and Common Wellbeing

Firstly, a true and credible education model in Tanzania must be established, in order for education to play a key role in building sustainable peace. Such education models should belief-promoting, whilst protecting traditions of care, and promoting empowerment, inclusivity, fairness and equality. By doing so, this creates more opportunities for meaningful dialogue, and ultimately strengthens national unity. Secondly, a holistic educational model must proactively fight gender inequalities, and reflect on its role in tackling social conflict, gender based violence, and female genital mutilation. It has to avoid the gender bias, which very often promotes extreme masculinity at the expense of balanced/moderate femininity. A YouTube TV Advertisement in 2013 noted that:

> "In March, 2013 Safari Lager won the title of the No. 1 beer in Africa at the Inaugural Africa Beer Awards, which reinforced its positioning of Tanzania's Champion for Champion Men. Admittedly, this grand and gorgeous TV advertisement was made to showcase moments in the lives of various men, not women worldwide in welcoming others to the World of Champions and Heroes not Heroines."

Ethic-based and Pro-active Higher Education as a Platform to Prevent Risky "Operations" against Human Rights

"*Operesheni Tokomeza*" was launched on the 4th October, 2014, which aimed to curb poaching and illegal ivory trade. This effort organized by Tanzanian scholars, graduates and leaders proved to be unsuccessful. It contributed to abuse of human rights, in particular by the deployment of 885 Army Force officers of the Tanzanian Defence Forces (TPDF), who forcefully and violently responded to poaching acts. Karlon N. and Crosta A concluded that:

> "The deadly path of conflict, ivory starts with the slaughter of innocent animals and ends with the slaughter of innocent people. It is a source of funding for terrorist organizations that transcends cruelty. It is the "white gold" for Africa Jihad, white for its color and gold for its value. If we fail to act now, militant groups like Al-Shabaab will lay down their roots deep in the African landscape destroying its heritage for generation to come. Dangerous and unpredictable Al-Shabaab's involvement in ivory trade brings with it an alarming dimension".[93]

Are scholars and graduates aware of these dangerous dimensions? If yes, is it wise to simply ignore them?

Ethics-driven Higher Education Curricula as a Promoter of Sustainable Centres for Excellences and Growth, and R&D in Society Today

Excellent scholars, students, educators and graduates need to regard themselves top performers in demonstrating noble service in their respective disciplines and professions. They are key stakeholders, and they must translate their passion into their profession. They must be the engine for future research and development. They must dully demonstrate a new culture of service for humanity, and not the mere "service for money" culture or simply serve their own interests.

As Peter Eichhorn aptly comments:

> "Researchers, librarians, technicians and administrative staff involved, but also PhD Students, graduates… are part of the

---

[93] Karlon N., Costa A. ("An Undercover Investigation on Ivory And Terrorism." This is available at: http://elephantleague.org/project/africas-white-gold-of-jihad-al-shababandconflict-ivory/

process of scientific work... and primarily active as producers and not consumers or even customers..."[94]

Ethics-driven Higher Education as Means Against Destructive Anti-life Ideologies and Slogans

Upon Marguerite A. Peeters observations, he stated that "Slogans of social engineers are manipulative and play on self-evident truths. They seem to propose a program to which nobody can be opposed... they betray common sense. They do so in a seductive manner".[95]

From a Tanzanian perspective, the unethical slogans, nouns and adjectives, have become increasingly engrained in the youths' life. These sayings are conflicted with traditional values, especially from a religious perspective. One of the phrases which have been normalised includes: "Kula Bata" which translates to 'Be immoral'.

Ethics-driven Higher Education and Wisdom as an Effective Means for Sustainable Use and Management of Natural Resources in Tanzania

Service-oriented education and wisdom must be value-driven, and build on the values of 'responsibility, trust, freedom, peace, justice, inclusiveness, transparency, solidarity, common welfare, happiness and hope'.[96] A 'wise scholar' should embody democracy and lead by example for their communities, and the 'Anawim' (poor).

---

[94] Peter Eichhorn "Determinants For University Excellence" in Paolo Rondo-Brovetto, Iris Saliterer (Eds) The University As A Business (Wiesbaden: VS Research, 2011) p. 37.

[95] Marguerite A. Peeters, The Globalization Of The Western Cultural Revolution, (Institute for Intercultural Dialogue Dynamics, asbl) p. 167.

[96] Aidan G. Msafiri "Democratic And Sustainable Governance In Natural Resources in Tanzania" in CETA and Konrad Adenauer Stiftung Journal, Vol. II, March, 2013 p.19.

Towards a Rethink and Paradigm Shift: Rediscovering Educational Principles and Values Today

The Principle of Human Dignity and Rights in Higher Education

Human dignity and rights underpin both the intrinsic and inalienable values of all humans created in the image and likeness of God (Gen. 1:26).

The principle of Education for Self-reliance (ESR) in Higher Education

Education for Self-Reliance underscores the values of self-actualization and self-realization of each and every human, as noted by Julius K. Nyerere. It attempts to inculcate the "*Know what*", "*Know how*" as well as the "*Know why*" aspect of the learning process. In the same vein of thought, Bill Gates states: "If you are born poor, it is not your mistake, but if you die poor, it is your mistake."

The Principle of a Mind Set of Destruction in Higher Education (Rom. 12:1-8)

A mind set of destruction re-thinks and re-assesses, introducing a new world and life view. Such mind set challenges the "*status quo*", as well as the 'business as usual' syndrome. Deconstruction needs to "think outside the box", and embrace a constructive new way of responding to diverse socio-economic, academic, technological and cultural challenges.

The Kerygmatic Service-oriented Enculturation Principle in Higher Education

This principle emphasizes on the on-going proclamation of Jesus' formative attitudes, teachings, norms, values for integral liberation, and development and enlightenment of humanity. From an osteological point of view, Pope Francis asserts that proclaiming Christ necessarily means

> "Showing that to believe in and to follow him is not only something right and true, but also something beautiful, capable of filling life with new splendour and profound joy... We must be bold enough to discover new signs and new symbols, new flesh to embody and communicate the word..."[97]

The Principle of Responsible Scholarship in Higher Education

Responsible scholarship emphasizes the unique role of academia, "Scholarly gurus" and "intellectual Think Tanks", particularly in rendering dignified and sustainable service to humanity and society. Responsible scholarship and leadership must be both value-based and service-oriented. It differentiates itself from irresponsible models of leadership, which quite often lack, vigour, focus, and creative engagement of selfless giving and holistic liberation.

Last, this principle guarantees not only "*future fitness*," but also provides what Paul Tilich (1886-1965) affirms, "The power of creating beyond oneself without losing oneself" through a transformative faith or religious belief. Hence, reinventing a formative "*Christian Avant-garde*".

The Principle of Globalisation as a Concern in Higher Education

Globalisation as a concern to higher education is a relatively new model, and introduces transformative view by Aidan G. Msafiri (2013). This principle calls for new value-based commitments, and collective responsibility in globalizing life-promoting values, such as: virtues, ethos, attitudes and principles.[98] As the quote states, "when good people do nothing, evil increases." Globalization is inevitable, it is inescapable,

---

[97] Pope Francis, Evangelii Gaudium (EG) No. 167.

[98] Aidan G. Msafiri, Globalization of Concern II pp.1-45 passim Ibid

but as academics, we need to globalize good, when the world and society is globalizing evil.

The Principle of Success Factors Consciousness in Higher Education

This principle demands both personal and collective awareness, and readiness for strategic thinking, planning and decision making for affirmative action. The edifice of the principle is built on the following key trajectories and pillars: the what, the how and the why. This principle must also be built on 'SMART' goals (*S*trategic, *M*easurable, *A*chievable, *R*elevant and *T*imely), discipline, competence, teamwork, efficiency and communication.

The Golden Rule Principle in Provision of Education Services (Mt. 25:34-36) In Higher Education

This principle encapsulates a profound, broad-spectrum, and love-based approach in life. It highlights both the verticality and horizontality of human obligation for selfless giving and agape.[99] This must be demonstrated through service to others.

The Principle of Deep Change (Transformation) and the Middle Path Education in Higher Education

Deep change goes beyond mere quantitative, arithmetic and geometric meanings and metrics of change. From a Judeo-Christian perspective, deep change (Greek: Metanoia) is pivoted on the value and virtue of moderation, in contradiction to the vices of extravagance and aviary. Accordingly, to Jeffrey D. Sachs' reflections on Buddhism and Aristotelianism is worthy paraphrasing:

---

[99] Aidan G. Msafiri, "Ethics For Climate Justice And Sustainability Through Value-Based Approaches: A New Tanzanian Model And Paradigm Shift" in Oliver Rupel, Christian Roschmann, et Climate Change Vol. III (Baden, Nomos: 2013) p.679.

"The essential teaching of both Buddha and Aristotle is the path of moderation pursued through life-long diligence, training and reflection. It is easy to be addicted to hyper consumerism, the search for sensory pleasures and the indulgence of self-interest, leading to brief but long-term unhappiness."[100]

The Principle of Dignified Value of Values in Higher Education

This value-oriented view attempts to uncover the value of prioritization as a viable and credible vehicle for integral development and transformation. Admittedly, values do not simply fall from the sky. They are formed, nurtured, cared for, preserved, transmitted etc. The "value of values" principle, especially in responding to pedagogical challenges, goes beyond the North Atlantic, quantitative-driven solutions, methods and approaches. It prioritizes the fundamental values of peace, service, empathy, stewardship, care, honesty and justice.

Practical Ways Forward and Conclusions

Our need to reassess the multidisciplinary and liberating role and relevance of ethics in higher education cannot be overemphasized. It must not only be both purpose oriented and value promoting, but also of relevance and sustainable, especially in the concrete "*Sitz im Leben*" (Life context). This calls for effective and sustainable deconstruction of the project paradigm. It provides both the "*Kairos*" (opportune time) and the "*Praxis*" (Practice). At this juncture, few but very pertinent conclusions need special focus. Firstly, ethics in higher education and knowledge are not dead artefacts for mere intellectual gymnastics and satisfaction. They must be for the sustainable service of all humans.

---

[100] Jeffrey D. Sachs, The Price of Civilization: Economics And Ethics After The Fall (London: The Bodley Head 2011) p. 156.

Truly, the future empires of the future will be knowledge-based empires and societies. Liberating ethical and service loaded education is the heart and cornerstone of vibrant and sustainable opportunities for Africa and the entire globe.

Secondly, service-oriented wisdom and education must first and foremost be an option for poor. That is, for and with the "*anawin*" the (poor), the marginalized, the oppressed and the downtrodden. It must include the values of inclusivity and osteology. In this regard, university graduates, scholars, educationists, philosophers, theologians and "Think Tanks" must hear the voice cry of the poor, in the same way Yahweh heeded to the misery of the Israelites in Egypt.

As Pope Francis aptly observes in his Evangelii Gaudium, "If we, who are God's means of hearing the poor, turn deaf ears to this plea, we oppose the Father's will and his plan…" (EG. No. 187). As academics, we need to shift from "talk shops" to "workshops", from indifferentism to true empathy, from "academic arrogance" to self-giving professionalism. As one of West Africa Theologians once said, "*Theologians and scholars need to have long ears like those of a Rabbit.*" This powerful symbolism needs to be enculturated, adopted and contextualized for an affirmative action. I conclude by calling all of you to this short reflection of mine:

Be still… we are still the Platonic cave;

Be still… we are becoming victims of the cancer of 'graduation done', graduates illiterate;

Be still… we need to avoid making education "a commodity". It has to be a service for values and dignity;

Be still… our education models are increasingly becoming less ethical and patriotic;

Be still… we are becoming the best products of a plagiarist copy and paste culture, without acquiring clear, critical, creative or transformative minds;

Be still… we can see the ever growing "Lucuric" (gap) between knowing and doing, information and action, professionalism and ethical behaviour;

Be still… we need to integrate not only the aspects of ethical "Know what" and "Know now" but also "Know why" in our academic syllabus today;

Be still… we need to ethically ignite minds, hearts, hands, heads for self-reliance, self-actualization, self-realization, so that we may render a dignified and sustainable service to all of humanity.

References

Chachalachal, Saju CMI, *IGNITING MINDS TO TRANSFORM THE SOCIETY*, (Bangalore: 2013)

Davis R. Anna, Frances Fahy, Henrike Rau (2014) *Challenging Consumption: Pathways To A More Sustainable Future*, New York, Routledge

Eichhorn, Peter "*Determinants For University Excellence*" in Paolo Rondo-Brovetto, Iris Saliterer (Eds) The University As A Business (Wiesbaden: VS Research, 2011)

Hubert Wolfgang (2013) "*Die Grundfragen Unseres Lebens*" Muenchen, Verlag C.H. Beck HG

James, C.L. *Nkrumah And Revolution*: (London: Allison & Busby)

Karlon N., Costa A. ("*An Undercover Investigation on Ivory And Terrorism*." This is available at: http://elephantleague.org/project/africas-white-gold-of-jihad-al-shababandconflict-ivory/

KISDI *Megatrends KOREA*, Seoul 2007

Kobia Samwel, *The Courage To Hope*, (Geneva: WCC Publications)

Mattei Luciano, P. Wambura, *A GUIDE TO CHRISTIAN ETHICS AND FORMATION IN MORAL MATURITY*, Philosophical Studeis 12, Nairobi, CUEA Publications 2000.

Msafiri Aidan G., "*Redefining Ethics of Land Justice and Use in Tanzania Today: Quest for A Paradigm Shift in Land Justice For Sustainable Peace in Tanzania*". Kimaro D., A. Munga, (EDs) ELCT & Sebastian Kolowa University College.

Msafiri, Aidan G. "*Democratic And Sustainable Governance In Natural Resources in Tanzania*" in CETA and Konrad Adenauer Stiftung Journal, Vol. II, March, 2013

Msafiri, Aidan G. "*Ethics For Climate Justice And Sustainability Through Value-Based Approaches: A New Tanzanian Model And Paradigm Shift*" in Oliver Rupel, Christian Roschmann, et Climate Change Vol. III (Baden, Nomos: 2013)

Msafiri Aidan G., *Globalization of Concern Vol. I* Dar es Salaam University Press 2008.

Msafiri Aidan G., *Globalization of Concern Vol. II*, Essays on Education, Health, Climate Change and Cyberspace. Geneva: Globethics.net Focus No. 8, August, 2012.

Msafiri Aidan G., *Globalization of Concern Vol. III*, Essays on Justice, Education, Sustainability and Technology. Geneva: Globethics.net Focus No. 32, 2016.

Msafiri Aidan G., "*Rediscovering Christian and Traditional Values for Moral Foundation*", (Nairobi: CUEA Publications, 2010).

Msafiri Aidan G., "*Towards a Credible Environmental Ethics for Africa: A Tanzanian Perspective*", Nairobi: CUEA Publications, 2007.

Msafiri, Aidan G. "*New Challenges and Hopes: A Tanzanian Perspective*" (Vatican: Urbanian University Press, 2009)

Msafiri, Aidan G. (2014) "*Thinking Beyond Climate Change Consequences For The East African Community: A Post COP 19 Value-Based Assessment And Paradigm Shift in EAC*" (Konrad Adenauer Stiftung – EAC/KAS) Dar es Salaam.

Msafiri Aidan G., (2013) "*Investing in Human Capital: A Prerequisite for Sustainable Development and Poverty Eradication in Tanzania*" in Elizabeth Nduku and Christoph Stueckelberger (Eds)

African Contextual Ethics, Geneva Globethics.net, Focus 13.

Mukandara, Rwekaza S. Unpublished paper by UDSM- Redet Workshop Jan. 2015.

Peeters, Marguerite A. *The Globalization Of The Western Cultural Revolution*, (Institute for Intercultural Dialogue Dynamics, asbl)

Pope Francis, Evangelii Gaudium (EG) No. 167.

Sachs, Jeffrey D. *The Price of Civilization: Economics And Ethics After The Fall* (London: The Bodley Head 2011)

Wantian Cui, et. Al. (2014) "Christian Faith and Values", Geneva: Globethics.net, China Christian I.

12

MORALITY WITHOUT RELIGION: ARGUMENT FROM THE AUTONOMY OF REASON

Crispin Ong'era Isaboke

Introduction

The question of whether morality can exist without religion is a critical one. It is critical question because it is somehow difficult to draw the distinction between the two.[101] This is a question of whether religion precedes ethics or ethics precedes religion. It has everything to do with whether reason is independent and autonomous or not. For some people the two are inseparable, like Muslims and followers of some other religions. Moralists, however, would argue that the two are not the same. We are then left at a cross-road because there are many ways in which religion has been seen to be identical with ethics to the extent that you cannot teach or talk of ethics outside religion nor can you teach or talk of religion without making reference to ethics. The aim of this paper is to explore the two concepts in close relation to mainstream world

---

[101]Crispin Ong'era Isaboke, Assistant Lecturer, Chuka University, Kenya.

religions with the view of resolving the conflict between ethics and religion. In other words, the question revolves around reason, ethics, and religion. Are they intertwined or not? Which order do they follow? The paper, therefore argues that religion is a product of reason while ethics is identical with reason.

The term "reason,"[102] on one hand, is used in this context to mean the "mind," which is the rational faculty by virtue of which man is different from other animals; he is an intelligent being. By reason, therefore, man is a knower and a doer. Mind is divided into two other faculties; the *intellect*, by which man searches and attains intellective or universal knowledge, and the (free) *will*, by which man puts knowledge into action. Nyasani argues that the intellect "[…] is the capacity […] of the mind whose task it is to understand, think and reason […] It also happens to be the faculty from which the will flows."[103] This implies that action, which is a function of the free will, proceeds from knowledge, which is a function of the intellect. The two faculties, in other words, work, and have to work, in harmony for the perfection of man. Moreover, this is the reason why to act according to reason is to act rightly; and one achieves that by conforming his free actions to knowledge; that is to say that there is an "ought" (to be done), a moral obligation to which any rational being must conform their actions. This is a dictate of the human nature and how it functions.

Religion, on the other hand, is a term used to refer to everything that has to do with belief and involves worship of a god or deities, ritual and a moral code. It is "[…] an institutionalized system of beliefs and values shared by a group and grounded in faith and the worship of a Supreme

---

[102] The word "reason" in this context also means "the moral law" which dictates that good ought to be done and evil avoided.

[103] Joseph M. Nyasani, Metaphysical Psychology: Rational Psychology (Nairobi: Consolata Institute of Philosophy Press, 2013) p. 27.

transcendent being (s)."[104] Thus, religious beliefs are normally communal and an expression of worship. Religion is moreover ritualistic in that those beliefs are enacted and made operational through ceremonies. An ethical code is also central and pivotal to religious life whereby rules about human behaviour are established and they define how followers ought to conduct themselves to constitute themselves as good persons.

Furthermore, ethics is a term derived from the Greek words *ethos* or *ethikos* which translates to character. Its Latin equivalent is *mores*, which in this case would mean *customs* or *habits of a person*. Ethics or Moral Philosophy, therefore, deals with human behaviour, that is, how we ought to conduct ourselves as human (rational) beings. It examines human acts or conduct from the aspect of their rightness or wrongness. In other words, conduct has the quality of being good or bad, right or wrong.

With the above understanding, it is now incumbent on the writer to argue our case on the relation between religion and ethics. This cannot be achieved without looking at the two in relation to culture, given that both are aspects of culture.

Religion and Culture

Culture can be defined as "the sum total of what a given group of people think (beliefs, values), what they do (behaviour) and what they produce (rituals and symbols)."[105] It means all that a people practice and how they practice them. Culture in this sense embraces the entire world-

---

[104] Judith A. Boss, *Ethics for Life: A Text with Readings,* Third Edition, (New York: McGraw Hill, 2004) p. 145.

[105] John Lukwata, *Integrated African Liturgy*, Revised Edition (Eldoret: AMECEA Gaba Publications, 2011) p.20.

view of a people; that is, a people's way of life, a *weltachaung.* [106] A culture defines and gives people their true identities. It is inconceivable to think of a human being without a culture. "[…] culture signifies that totality of customs, techniques, and values that distinguish a social group, a tribe, a people, a nation […]"[107]

In addition, cultures are characterized with languages that bear the meaning and expression of those specific cultures. In point of fact, there cannot be culture without language. It is within the confines of language that traditions, histories, and values of a specific culture, commonly known as heritage, are preserved and passed from one generation to another. Yet in Africa alone there are "a great diversity of peoples, cultures, religious systems and languages in close confines."[108] What this means is that different cultures practice different religious beliefs relative to their culture. The *Abagusii,*[109] therefore, would worship a god who resides in the Sun[110] and who is the provider of everything by dedicating a new day to him at sunrise while facing it; apparently asking for blessings for the day. The *Agikuyu* would face Mt. Kenya and express their gesture of worship to a god who also provides for all their needs but resides at the mountain. This is why all the water that nourishes their lives and crops comes, or is believed to come, from the mountain. It must be accepted therefore, that religion must be influenced and conditioned by the intrinsic organization of each specific culture and

---

[106] *Weltachaung* is a Germany word that means the totality of a people's way of life, which can be equated to what we call in English *world-view.*

[107] Battista Mondin, Philosophical Anthropology (Rome: Urbaniana University Press, 1991) p. 146.

[108] Lukwata. p. 21.

[109] *Abagusii* refers to a Bantu speaking group that resides in the Western part of Kenya bordering Luos, Kurias, Kipsigis and Maasais while *Gikuyu* is another Bantu speaking group around the Mt. Kenya region.

[110] *Sun* is the English translation of the *Ekegusii* term *Erioba* in which the god of the *Abagusii*, known as *Engoro*, resides.

that the differences of religions are due to that fact. Given that no culture is exactly identical with the other, religious beliefs would essentially be different depending on the perception of each culture as well as what they hold dear, meaning that even their ethics would be limited by that perception: "All cultures have distinctions between what they consider good and what they consider bad; what they consider right and what they judge to be wrong."[111] But it must be borne in mind also that some of the things that some cultures hold as values are not held as values in other cultures, while those things held as vices are not necessarily vices in other cultures. Thus, one culture cannot hold as vice what others hold as virtue and the converse is also true. Understood in this manner, right and wrong is destroyed since we cannot talk of the "ought to be done" by all human beings; that is to say that the moral obligation does not exist according to which all human beings have to act by conforming their actual acts to it in order for them to act virtuously while failure to conform their actions to it would make their actions evil and therefore hold them responsible of them. Religion in this sense reduces ethics to what it considers right and wrong; making it subservient to it.

Looking at virtuous acts from a religious perspective would only imply that acting virtuously or doing the good is acting according to the dictates of one's religion (not reason). Conversely, acting against the teachings of religion would mean doing evil. Good and evil would in this sense be reduced to what is religious. Yet with numerous religions and even denominations among the same religion which do not however hold same teachings, it would be impossible to think of acts that are good in themselves and which therefore ought to be done; acts that are universally accepted by any human being. In truth, it would as well be defeatist in such circumstances to argue that there is good and evil; what

---

[111] Brian Cronin, *Value Ethics: A Lonergan Perspective* (Nairobi: Consolata Institute of Philosophy Press, 2006) p. 133.

would be the meaning of a certain good for a Catholic to a Seventh Day Adventist who holds a different view on the same? For instance, it is an undeniable fact that for the Seventh Day Adventist, [112] Saturday is the Sabbath Day, in keeping with the Jewish traditions, that must be held holy by all their faithful. Yet for the Catholics and a number other Christian denominations, Sunday is the day of the Resurrection of the Lord without which Christianity would be non-existent; the critical question is which the appropriate day of worship is? What sense does this make to a Muslim who does not recognize any of the two days but rather carries his holy activities on Fridays? What about a non-believer? Or must every person subscribe to a religion?

The Inseparability of Religion and Ethics

Those thinkers who see religion as natural argue that religion is one and the same thing with ethics. In his book, *Value Ethics: A Lonergan Perspective,* Brian Cronin argues that "many who espouse religious values do not see the need for a defence of distinct moral values."[113] In other words, they identify their religion with an ethical code identical to, and inseparable from, it. Yet every religion has an ethical code different from those of other religions. So, however identical a religion is going to be with its ethical code, this view reduces ethics to relativism given that that ethical code will only apply and be sensible to that religion alone. Any other practices that do not respect that ethical code are, by virtue of that, evil and sinful. This essentially means that religion cannot be separated from ethical values; a perspective that would be interpreting right and wrong in accordance to a people's religious beliefs but not in

---

[112] Seventh Day Adventists is a Christian denomination that worships on Saturday.

[113] Brian Cronin, *Value Ethics: A Lonergan Perspective,* (Nairobi: Consolata Institute of Philosophy Press, 2006) p. 8.

accordance to reason. What this means is that followers of any one religion would definitely consider as superior their ethical code and in turn look down on, and treat with contempt, those who hold different views. Yet reason is what makes a person human, not religion. If religion were to make one human, then it would logically follow that all human beings would not only belong to one homogeneous religion but would also be necessarily religious, which unfortunately is not the case.

Cronin adds that Religious groups normally teach moral values as part of their religious way of life and they provide powerful motives to live well, to condemn immoral behaviour, to promote virtue and curb vices.[114] It is a fact that every religion teaches her followers on how to live well, and they connect living well with reward of a certain kind in a later life. It also relates not living well to some form of punishment in an equally later life. This explains why Christians, for instance, talk of heaven and hell; those Christians who live according to their ethical-religious ideals shall inherit the kingdom of heaven while those who do not (sinners) shall perish eternally in hell. Moreover, "generally, I considerate (*sic*) true that religious values trump moral values. A religious perspective is more comprehensive, more ultimate, and more profound, than a moral perspective."[115] In addition, "for a religious man, nature is never only 'natural'; it is always fraught with a religious value [...] for the cosmos is a divine creation; coming from the hands of the gods, the world is impregnated with sacredness."[116] Therefore, Cronin sees religion as something necessary for man.

On the contrary, I must argue without fear of doubt that motivating people to act as they ought would be as unethical as it would be

---

[114] *ibid.*

[115] *ibid.*

[116] Mircea Eliade, *The Sacred and the Profane: The Nature of Religion* (New York: Harcourt, Brace & World, Inc., 1959) p. 117.

threatening them. It is evil to persuade or be persuaded, influence or be influenced, threaten be threatened to act in accordance to reason. Instead, acting rationally is a duty of our human nature and we do not need to be persuaded, motivated or even threatened to do so. I, therefore, differ, and reasonably so, with my one time professor of philosophy, Rev. Fr. Brian Cronin, when he argues that a religious perspective is more comprehensive than a moral one. Alternatively, even where the universe could be a divine creation, as Cronin says, what is critical is the purpose of creation. It is my strong conviction that if God created man, he must have created him for a purpose. Having created him rational, God must have intended that man be rational, and therefore, moral; not to be religious. In this sense, to act rightly is to act in accordance to reason and one has no choice to act otherwise. That being the case, why would anybody want to looks at everything from a religious point of view rather than from the rational point of view? Is reason not universal and autonomous while religion can be subjected to it? Is reason not sufficient in determining the morality of an act and the subsequent implementation of moral decisions?

We know for fact that when people worship, they praise that which in their thinking has the highest worth or value: "God is worshipped because God represents perfect goodness."[117] In point of fact, religion is faith based whereby a man of faith in God believes that there is a God and that that God is all-powerful in whom everything is possible. Again, this is the reason why people believe in prayers. But, the question of whether religion precedes ethics or *vice versa* is a question of whether religion is natural or artificial. Is the moral natural or conventional? If both the moral and the religious are natural; does that imply that both are inseparable with reason? These are the critical questions in this discussion. The obvious implications of this, though, are that if religion is natural, then every human being would be necessarily religious or at

---

[117] Boss p. 145.

least potentially so; and if ethics or the moral is natural, then everyone would be moral or potentially so. Moreover, if the moral is conventional, then that would imply that one need to be moral.

We are first human beings before we are religious. Think of any religious organization, one is not born a religious but one acquires the religious values and traditions through socialization. We are victims of the religions that are dominant in the places we are born and bred. Hardly can one be a Christian, for instance, if they are born in Zanzibar; while it is equally almost impossible for one to be a Muslim if they are born in Rome. That is to say that most people belong to their religions not by choice but by circumstances; not by design but fortuitously.

Had religion come prior to ethics, as we have observed above, there would be only one universal religion for all human beings, given that every human being would have been born religious. Morality would then be a product of religion whereby only one religion would exist with one universal morality identical with it. But it defeats the principles of logic to argue so since it would mean that religion existed long before we were born; but how is that possible and where could it have been? The multi-religious groupings, therefore, evident in our society today, are the clearest indication that religion is rather acquired than natural. That which is natural is always present and inseparable with humanity, and that is not the case with religion. The problem gets even compounded when different faiths embark on a mission to win converts to their faiths, making it more evident that religion is something of a later development. Religion could not have been simultaneous with rationality, and therefore cannot be identical ethics.

Religion puts boundaries to ethics; it sets limits for reason so that the latter has to exercise its activity within those limits of religion. It limits and commands that followers of that particular religion act in accordance with the dictates or teachings of that religion, which can loosely be called her morals; and any act to the contrary is perceived as evil. It therefore limits reason yet the only limit to reason in conduct should, as we have already said, and must, be the good. What this essentially means is that man should act freely within the limits of that which is good. In any case, religions are different and if each religion looks at morality from her point of view that would reduce morality to relativism and in the end deny and destroy it. That would be equally subjecting reason to religion yet reason is independent and autonomous. The further inference would be that there exists as many gods as there are religions, which is not only ridiculous but also illogical. The reason for this is that if what is good is relative to religion that would be tantamount to saying that there is no good and evil; the two would depend on which religion one belongs and subscribes to.

In point of fact, the difficulties of separating religion from ethics are live on the grounds that many people look to their clergy both as religious authorities as well as moral ones: "people come to the clergy with ethical problems such as marital problems and personal conflicts."[118] Every religion, therefore, has an intrinsic connectedness with its ethics. And this makes it difficult for its followers to look beyond their religions to discover the true worth of the human person to be found in reason alone. In addition, "the concept of God in the major world religions – Judaism, Christianity, Hinduism, and Islam – is so intimately connected to the concept of moral goodness that the moral code is incorporated right into the doctrine of these religions."[119] This further explains why for Christians, for instance, the study of sacred scriptures is important, in part, because it teaches how to distinguish right from wrong. Yet in many Muslim countries such as Saudi Arabia and Morocco, the law of the sacred texts – the Qur'an – is the law of the

---

[118] Boss p.145.

[119] *ibid.* p. 146.

land and applies to everyone living in that country.[120] In spite of that fact, that alone does not and cannot mean that scripture is the only source of moral guidance or that morality is relative. Muslims belief that the Qur'an does the same and every other religion but all that can be implied from the fact that religion cannot be identical with ethics. It only demonstrates that religious ethical teachings are subservient to ethics itself, thus the latter precedes the former.

It must be noted, nevertheless, that in the Jewish religion, Roman Catholicism, and mainstream Protestant religions, the independence of religion from ethics is characterized by the fact that basic moral principles are also held to be universal and discoverable through other means such as the use of reason or intuition.[121] But when it comes to Muslims (though not all), ethics is viewed as inseparable from religion but is rather built entirely on it. For them, an action is right only if, and for the reason that, God commands it: "Religion informs not only the Muslim's personal life but also the basis of public policy."[122] According to them, human beings are not expected to discern right from wrong but to unquestionably submit to the will of God.

In addition, whereas a number of religions are monotheistic, quite a number are not equally polytheistic nor do all (religions) regard God as a divine entity with whom human beings can have a personal relationship. A section of the Hindu, for instance, believes that there is no God but truth. This is the reason why Gandhi maintained that we must learn to love and respect even the lowest of living beings.

> "Budhism and Jainism, which developed out of Hinduism, also had a major influence on Gandhi's moral philosophy. Neither Budhism nor Jainism is strictly speaking a religion because belief

[120] *ibid.*

[121] *ibid.*

[122] *ibid.*

in God or a transcendent being is not part of either worldview."123

In light of the above, we can safely say that the relationship between religion and morality may be looked at from two different angles; the divine command perspective and the natural law perspective. According to the former, morality is relative to God's commands and, therefore, subject to change from time to time or person to person; while in accordance to the latter, morality is based on universal, unchanging principles and that God commands or approves something because it is right prior to the command. Moreover, for the former, there are no universal moral standards by which to judge God's commands. No other justification is necessary for an action to be right other than that God commanded it. God's reasons are ultimately unknowable to humans, and for that same reason, God's commands must be accepted on faith: to question God's commands or to demand independent nonreligious reasons for accepting a divine command shows lack of faith. When Abraham was asked to offer his son Isaac as a sacrifice, he didn't object but obliged without question and that is how a man of faith should behave or conduct himself.

But for the latter, God commands an action because it is moral beforehand and independently of God's commanding it at that moment. In essence, therefore, morality is grounded in the rational nature of man rather than being relative to divine command, human feelings, and cultural norms. "By 'nature' they mean human nature unlike physical nature, human nature is seen as nonmaterial and rational [....] Human nature is free and autonomous."[124] By being free therefore, man is capable of acting in accordance to his rational nature or against it, although he also knows naturally of the moral law that he is under obligation to obey. In essence, the moral obligation according to which

[123] *ibid.*

[124] *ibid.*

'good ought to be done' and 'evil ought to be avoided' is a true expression and a reflection of the rational nature of man, given that conscience connects the will, which is essentially free, with this moral order. What that substantially means is that through conscience, which is a practical judgment of reason, we are commanded at that moment we want to act, to do good and refrain from evil. Thus, conscience acts as a guide to our future actions and always commands that we do the good; it does not lie.

> "Conscience has its own power and autonomy. It functions: judging us [...] but conscience speaks with a voice that is not easily silenced. Deep down inside the person, it still makes itself audible [....] It is conscience that does the shaking, and it is we whom it tries to punch into shape."[125]

Conscience, therefore, will always come back to judge and haunt us when we disobey it. It will punish us by denying us the so desired peace of mind or tranquillity by always reminding us that it was wrong of us not to obey it. It will reward us for giving us happiness for obeying it and thereby acting virtuously. This should not, nevertheless, be understood to mean that we act virtuously so that we may be happy. We act virtuously simply due to the fact that it is the right thing to do. Yet, happiness is a necessary outcome of virtue.

That is why Thomas Aquinas argues to the effect that moral law was created by God as part of God's divine plan for the universe, while Aristotle holds the view that natural law has always existed as part of the natural order. That notwithstanding, all natural law theorists agree that it lies outside cultural norms and laws and that the moral laws embedded

---

[125] Cormac Burke, *Man and values: A Personalist Anthropology* (Limuru: Kolbe Press, 2007) p. 72.

in our nature as humans take the form of a universal code that we all ought to follow. What about ethics and culture?

Ethics and Culture

Evidently, just like religion, ethics is also a component of culture alongside language, traditions and history as well as taboos, commonly known as the dos and *don'ts*. While religion focuses on ways of worship and relating with a deity or god, ethics deals with conduct, or particularly human acts.[126] It takes cognizance of the fact that human acts have the quality of being good or evil by either conforming to reason or not. That is to say that on their own, human acts can be right or wrong, good or bad.

Therefore, it is true, and absolutely so, that to act virtuously (ethically) has no direct relation with religion. Outside religion there is the moral obligation that dictates to us that good ought to be done. As a rational being, therefore, man has the duty to act in accordance to reason, not in order to achieve anything in return, but simply because it is good and rational to do so; it is the right thing to do. For this reason, the good can be defined as that which is in accord with reason. That is to say, good or virtue is that act which conforms to the moral law according to which knowing the good implies free response of the will to it (the good). This further means that to be free is to do the good without failure or exception.

Consequently, to act responsibly is to act according to reason; to do the "ought" to be done since this is a rational duty. Man cannot be said to be free where freedom means ability to do whatever one wants,

---

[126] *Human acts* are those acts that are in man's control so that he can choose to do or not do them. They are voluntary and deliberate and thus man is responsible for them. They are free acts as opposed to conditioned one, technically known as acts of man which man shares with animals.

whether good or evil. Man is not free to do evil since this will be going against his nature. The reason for this is that man acts for a purpose and happiness is the highest good that man attains only by virtuous acts. Thus, man must always act in such a way as to direct himself to his last end, which is happiness, by only doing the good. Acting contrary, therefore, signifies acting against reason by either doing the "ought not" or not doing the "ought." This would deny man his last end which is undesirable due to the fact that man naturally desires happiness. It is natural of him to seek happiness and find satisfaction in it. Yet this cannot be achieved except by acting in strict adherence to the moral law. It would be against man's nature to do evil. In view of this, evil is acting without reason while good is acting, at least, not without reason. From this, we can aver that there is no freedom in doing evil since there is no alternative route or shortcut to happiness.

Pope Francis I[127] maintains that "even those who do not believe in God can ascend to heaven if they lead good and honourable lives."[128] He goes on to emphasize that "the Lord has redeemed all of us, all of us, with the blood of Christ, all of us, not just Catholics. Everyone!"[129] My interest on what the Pope is saying is not whether atheists will go to heaven if they acted rightly, rather that even they[130] can make good moral decisions. It, therefore, means that one need not be religious to know the good and do it. With or without religion, by his rational nature, man is capable of knowing and distinguishing good and evil. Consequently, man can make a free decision to act morally (the only

---

[127] Pope Francis I is the World leader of the Roman Catholic Church and Bishop of Rome.

[128] www.straitstimes.com/world/pope-says-atheists-can-take-moral-decisions-like-catholics/ retrieved on April 25, 2018.

[129] www.straitstimes.com/world/pope-says-atheists-can-take-moral-decisions-like-catholics/ retrieved on April 25, 2018.

[130] Them refers to "those who do not believe in the existence of God," atheists.

reason why the Pope says they can also go to heaven). The point of the Pope is that regardless of whether or not one is religious, it is imperative that they be moral by practicing virtue or acting according to the dictates of reason. It is my conviction that religion is relevant inasmuch as it guides man in morals, not morals guiding man to be religious. Put in another way, one could not be religious if one were not rational. Yet morality constitutes a necessary part of being rational. Morality cannot be separated from rationality, religion can. This is the reason why we have human beings (rational and therefore potentially moral) but who are at the same time atheists. We cannot have people who are religious without being potentially moral. The fact that religion is separable from reason while ethics is not answers our leading question in this paper: can there be morality without religion? This question therefore can be answered in the affirmative – it is possible to be moral without being religious. The Pope correctly adds that "the question for people who do not believe in God is to listen to their consciences. Also for those without faith, sin is going against your conscience."[131]

On this, the Pope recognizes the central role that conscience plays in moral decisions and actions; that of guiding man in his actions by commanding that he does the good and refrains from doing evil in particular instances. He adds that "listening to it and obeying it means making up one's mind about what is good and evil."[132] This signifies that what is *sinful* in religious circles can somehow be equated with *moral evil*. This means that acting against the teachings of one's religion leads to sin while acting against reason or conscience leads to moral evil. This should not however be construed to mean that the two are identical in nature. It is possible to act morally without acting religiously

[131]www.straitstimes.com/world/pope-says-atheists-can-take-moral-decisions-like-catholics/ retrieved on April 25, 2018.

[132]www.straitstimes.com/world/pope-says-atheists-can-take-moral-decisions-like-catholics

and it is also possible to act religiously without acting morally. Furthermore, acting in the dictates of conscience conforms our acts to the moral law (reason) and they by that fact become good but disobeying conscience goes against the moral law and by that fact results in evil.

All known cultures have this kind of moral consciousness and this implies that this is naturally known by man. It is irrefutable that action proceeds from the intellect after the process of deliberation and decision making. In other words, to act is to put knowledge into use. Nyasani states:

> "[…] the intellect is the capacity (faculty) of the mind whose task it is to understand, think and reason…it may translate into mind or intelligence having the potential or capacity to conduct mental and rational activities lurking all the while in the state of potency in the human consciousness. It also happens to be the faculty from which the will flows."[133]

From Nyasani's observation, it can be inferred that action flows from knowledge. We act on the knowledge that we have, and particularly in ethics, knowledge of good and evil. Man therefore has the potentiality as a rational being to know good and evil; he is also capable of doing good and avoiding evil yet he is equally under obligation to do good and avoid evil at all times. Wherefore, when he conforms his free acts to knowledge he acts rightly and when he does not conform his free acts to knowledge he acts wrongly. Furthermore, Nyasani sees the will as:

> [...] the faculty of conscious and deliberate choice of action. It is the faculty of human volition which, in its functionality, must necessarily entail actions which are freely willed and which, in

---

[133] Joseph M. Nyasani, *Metaphysical Psychology: Rational Psychology* (Nairobi: Consolata Institute of Philosophy Press, 2014.

moral education, are referred to as voluntary actions. All human acts as opposed to acts of man are voluntary, deliberated and consciously undertaken. They take place as a result of some conscious and voluntarily willed decision and hence create unshakeable moral, legal and social responsibility for an individual.[134]

Moreover:

"[...] a conscious decision and deliberation, must, ipso facto, flow and emanate from the intellect. The intellect, therefore, is always behind the acts of the will explicitly or implicitly, or, in other words, the will must always involve the intellect in producing its own effects, unless it chooses to exceed or disobey the dictates and specifications of the intellect."[135]

From the above we can infer that human acts are free acts and are done without coercion or pressure of any kind, but also that one cannot act without knowledge. It is in the search for knowledge of the rightness or wrongness of human acts that deliberation is a *sine qua non* condition.

Hence, even where the two, *religion* and *ethics*, are components of culture, ethics embraces all ways of a people's behaviour or conduct (from the Greek *ethos*) while religion does not. In essence, there is always a good way to act religiously but there cannot be a religious way to act ethically. Religion, in other words, is practiced within the morals of a culture. Be that what it may, culture is not universal, hence religion too; since people of different cultures practice and cherish different religious beliefs. By that fact, religion is culture-specific; it is one of the components of any culture. It is part of what a people hold dear and cherish as their values. In other words, religion is a cultural value.

---

[134] *ibid.* p. 31.

[135] *ibid.*

Religion is particular; for instance, Christianity is a borrowed religion from a borrowed Western culture, which replaces a people's cultural beliefs and practices as a superior religion. Nevertheless, it is not universal but ethics transcends and permeates all cultures and is *ipso facto* universal since it applies to all human beings. On the same wavelength, Islam is a borrowed religion from the Arab culture neither is it universal; it only applies to a specific group of people, precisely those who have accepted the Arab culture. But all cultures are rational and therefore are founded on morality; man is social by nature.

What transpires from the above is that ethics is not culture-specific as religion is. Every culture recognizes the fact that there is a difference between good and evil but also that good ought to be done and evil ought to be avoided, what the good or evil is notwithstanding. Thus, ethics, by virtue of that, goes beyond culture, is universal and cannot be reduced to religion. Instead, Religious beliefs can at best hinder free will and freedom, both of which should only be limited by the good because of the rational (moral) obligation to do that which is good; in other words, for man to be free, he must do anything insofar as it is good.

However, by virtue of the fact that man is a rational being, blessed with the faculties of the intellect and the will; he is naturally an ethical being. This is so for the reason that the freedom of the will makes it possible for man to be held responsible for his actions, and *ipso facto*, a moral being. Morality cannot be separated from reason and the two together define man as a rational being. For what could a human being be without reason? Could he have been any better than a mere animal? Still, could there have been religion? Religion is a product of reason. Animals do not have reason and therefore do not practice religion. Effectively, any argument that religion is prior to ethics is defeatist for then even animals could be religious though not rational. Yet man alone practices religion.

Conclusion

In conclusion, therefore, ethics is enshrined in the very rational nature of man and is inseparable with it while religion is a product of reason and separable from it. For this reason, we can strongly affirm that ethics without religion is possible but religion without ethics is impossible. Accordingly, religion and ethics are neither identical nor does religion precede ethics; rather, morality constitutes a part of the rational nature of man and is identical with it while religion is a product of the two. The moral instincts are natural, and therefore, simultaneous with reason while religion is not.

References

Boss, Judith A. *Ethics for Life: A Text with Readings*. Third Edition. New York: McGraw-Hill, 2004.

Burke, Cormac. *Man and values: A Personalist Anthropology*. Limuru: Kolbe Press, 2007.

Cronin, Brian. *Value Ethics: A Lonergan Perspective*. Nairobi: Consolata Institute of Philosophy Press, 2006.

Eliade, Mircea. *The Sacred and the Profane: The Nature of Religion*. New York: Harcourt, Brace & World, Inc., 1959.

Lukwata, John. *Integrated African Liturgy*. Revised Edition. Eldoret: AMECEA Gaba Publications, 2011.

Mondin, Battista. *Philosophical Anthropology.* Rome: Urbaniana University Press, 1991.

Nyasani, Joseph M. *Metaphysical Psychology: Rational Psychology*. Nairobi: Consolata Institute of Philosophy Press, 2014.

www.straitstimes.com/world/pope-says-atheists-can-take-moral-decisions-like-catholics/ retrieved on Aril 25, 2018.

13

CURRENT DEBATES ABOUT COLONIALISM, SLAVERY AND BLACK LIVES MATTER

ETHICAL PERSPECTIVES ON CHRISTIAN MISSIONARY ACTIVITIES IN AFRICA REVISITED

Obiora Ike

"The refusal to take sides on great moral issues is itself a decision; it is a silent acquiescence to evil."
Ven Fulton J. Sheen (1895 -1979,
American Bishop of The Catholic Church

Introduction

The Recent Trigger for the Debates on Recalling Past History

On May 25 2020, the brutal and outrageous murder of a black American citizen under the hands of the United States of America white police officer Derek Chauvin who pinned the life out of him spread virally on video recording.[136] Seemingly protected by State power, under socially tolerated traditions and legal institutions over centuries, these

---

[136] Obiora Ike, Executive Director, Globethics.net.

historically atrocious and racially based injustices have continued unabated in that country, and as is widely known, in many other parts of the world.

The *#BlackLivesMatter* 2020 protests forced governments and other entities across the world to reckon with oppressive histories including slavery, colonialism and racism. It emboldened activists globally and boosted a new sense of humanity, solidarity and empathy and thus galvanized a new awakening of people to stand up everywhere with moral courage and demand that they "*want to breathe*". The last words of George Floyd *"I can't breathe"* implies a re-visit of the many dark shades of human history, especially the chapters covering slavery, colonialism and racism which calls for the purification of memories in the present through recalling the horrible injustices of the past. To understand the political, cultural, economic and social tempers, we see on streets happening in every continent, - drawing crowds of inter-generational, inter-racial, inter-religious and multicultural activists globally - it is necessary to have some knowledge of the preceding period in order to correct them.

It is precisely because of the centrifugal racial, sectarian, ethnic, and religious strife that plagues our world that we need to expose, analyse, and morally evaluate the dark sides of history. By exposing such historical injustices that continue to victimize, marginalize, and embitter people in the present, we find true liberation using the call of Emeritus *Pope Benedict XVI* to proclaim Truth in Charity, published in the Encyclical letter *"Veritas in Caritate"* (2009). Recently, the Holy Father *Pope Francis* writing a preface to the new book of Cardinal Walter Kaspar found these words to make the point about some oppressive practices of history, which continue into our time. *"We must be shaken by global injustice to be able to wake up and hear the cry of the poor and of our very gravely sick planet," (Preface to the new book by Cardinal Walter Kasper on Hope and Communion, July 2020).*

Nothing will minimise the injustices and brutality neither embedded in the practice of slavery and colonialism perpetrated on African peoples (and in some cases of Africans within themselves) nor diminish the culpability of the invaders and impostors of these systems. As has been noted elsewhere, "*colonialism throughout the world has always been an essentially violent phenomenon. It was imposed by violence and maintained by its potential capacity for violence*" (Elizabeth Isichei, A history of Igboland, p.9). For Christians, the challenge is to hold to its principal teaching of standing for Life in dignity (Joh 10:10) and to take a stand on issues that bother on the promotion and protection of life of every life and at all times.

Arguments against Re-visiting History and its Rebuttal

There are some who would wish that these conversations were not opened at all. The intent is on shutting down corrective, constructive, and revisionist conversations about past historical injustices and their injurious and traumatizing resonance in the present. They even invoke diversionary registers to try to engineer a backlash or blunt the momentum towards reckoning and corrective healing. These are dangers of silencing history and making pretensions about its revisit.

The first major argument is that talking about past racism, slavery, conquest, colonialism, exploitation; slave raiding, injustices, and myriad oppressions will fray the social fabric, exacerbate societal tensions, and activate the impulse of revenge.

The second argument is that we should consider historical injustices and crimes such as slavery and racial terror and those who perpetrated them in their temporal context, in the spirit of the times in which those crimes occurred. We should not apply today's moral standards on the past.

There is a third argument that interrogates the issue by asking: "If you start revising the past and tearing down past monuments of racists, violent colonizers, slavers, and other historical criminals, where do you draw the line"?

A short response to these three and possibly other arguments is that these forms of emotional blackmail should be ignored by people of conscience. *John Lewis*, who died a few weeks after George Floyd had witnessed these discriminations based on slavery, colonialism and racial injustices in the United States. His response to historical silencing is apt: "*When you see something that is not right, not just, not fair, you have a moral obligation to say something, to do something.*" (US Congressman & Civil Rights Activist). The task for Christians is found in the mission to preach the Gospel of Love and Justice in Jesus Christ to all creation (Mathew 28 20).

One fact we know is that history cannot be easily divided into watertight compartments. Indeed, there are no clean breaks in history for the events of one era have their origins in the past and their influence upon the years to come. This essentially means that we need to know of past wrongs, correct them and heal social relations in the present. This makes the healing of memory possible and enables an authentic Truth and Reconciliation filtering of history so that society be fundamentally rebuilt from the bottom up. Africa's failure is essentially a European experiment that failed, not African. In order to understand how we got to where we are, we need to connect the dots and face uncomfortable truths.

Right now, the world is already in turmoil, so where is the peace or harmony to be preserved by suppressing historical truth-telling and the sincere, good-faith airing of historical grievances? The focus on placing Christian missionary activities carried out during the 19th and 20th

centuries era of colonial rule over Africa raises heavy challenges that compel facing our own history as Christians. It also provides us with a moment to "*say something*" and "*do something*" so that truth, justice and peace may lead to authentic reconciliation. This paper shall focus on three broad outlines namely:

- What should mission look like today, given the colonial history of the Church?
- How should the accusation that Christianity in Africa is the religion of white people be dealt with?
- How do we deal with the history of colonialism and 'cancel cultures'?

Examining Christian Mission Today in the Face of the Past Colonial History of the Church

The question concerning how Christian missionary activity would be best continued and transmitted to the people of Africa today was already the topic and subject of the First *Special Assembly for Africa for the Synod of Bishops* convoked by Pope John Paul II and held in Rome in 1994. The focus was on "*The Church in Africa and her evangelising mission – You shall be my witnesses* (Acts 1:8). The summary of the contents of that Synod was given in the Post Synodal Apostolic Exhortation in Rome which approved the famous document *Ecclesia in Africa of Pope John Paul II in 1994.*

No other activity affecting the life of the entire Church in Africa since the time of the historical Jesus had such an impact, interest and worldwide attention as the Africa Synod of 1994. It took five years to prepare (1989 to 1994). It was attended by 40 percent of the 497 Bishops in Africa who were present at the Synod; 242 members, 46 observers, 20 experts and 7 fraternal delegates added to another 30 assistants of the Vatican Synod Secretariat. By choosing the topic *"Church as family"* the Synod touched the essential point of the question: What should mission look like today, given the colonial history of the church? Father Albert Nolan, Dominican priest had a response to this namely:

> "We speak about hope and about motivation and about challenge and about what Jesus said in the past, but we have no News for the people, let alone Good News. If the Gospel is Good News, then it is not a message about hope and about challenge and about the past but it the kind of news about our times that must be a news for our times that will create hope and energise people as Jesus did in his time" (Nolan, A; God in South Africa, CIIR, 1988, p. 9 – 11).

The Berlin Conference of 1884/1885 divided an entire continent, its peoples, ethnic lineages, territorial boundaries and cultural legacies for the purposes of European interests. This colonial conquest of African nations deepened the already inflected wounds of the slave trade that separated families and peoples and lasted for over three hundred years. It was followed with yet another onslaught of near 100 years of colonialism which method and interest was brigandage and power for economic profit, resources exploitation, cultural degradation, political hegemony and the total degradation of a people, often without any qualms and even justified under religious, cultural and philosophical theories of the time.

Whereas Christian missionary activity had other motives for their entry into Africa, namely the salvation of souls for the Kingdom proclaimed by Jesus Christ (Luke 4:16), their arrival into the scene concurred with that of the political, colonial and commercial dealers, making it difficult for the local natives to easily differentiate or distinguish the foreign groups and their distinctive aims. They were all Europeans and they came as colonialists, traders, or preachers. It was often difficult for the natives to make any distinction between colonialist and Missionary, the Flag and the Cross-, Preacher and Trader. In many parts of Africa, the three letters of C's representing Colonization, Commercialization and Christianization happened concurrently all in the name of Civilization.

The arrival of Christian missionaries from Europe in the 19th century coincided with the period of the abolition of slavery and its replacement with colonial conquest and commercial exploitation of natural resources described as "*legitimate trade*". In annexure, an old European maritime maps, the West African coastline from *'Ouidah'* (in Benin Republic today) to *'Old Calabar Port'* (in Nigeria today) was called *Slave Coast*.

The missionaries introduced a new approach that leveraged formal education and Christian faith, built health centres and saved many lives of persons who otherwise died of incurable diseases. They introduced social centres for people to learn new skills and trades for self-sustenance. Many Christian missionaries identified with the local people based on equality of all persons in dignity before God and entire creation. Yet, in some cases, their methods questioned and contradicted this respect of accepting the authentic socio- cultural and belief systems of the people.

Today we know better that these histories have unleashed changes, divided the entire African space into countries without consultation, will or consent of the indigenous peoples but solely at the whims and caprices of the colonials Lords and masters. . These colonial divisions remain primarily responsible for the continued war, instability, disunity and divisions within that continent until today. Colonial boundaries arbitrarily created, separated peoples previously united into new amorphous boundaries and territories for the sake of the coloniser. It truncated the unity of clans and kindred with their relations and languages with disruptions that have until current times completely affected the ways people lived earlier. The consequences have been largely negative, even though some have found some positive elements in the colonial intrusion into Africa.

The arrival of the Christian missionaries at the heat of this unfortunate colonial episode made them also share some of the persistent ignorance concerning Africa and its peoples. It was a period of Eurocentric dominant worldview, with pejorative prejudices against others, making historians describe the 19th century Christian mission as "*European cultural export*".

As is now largely known and acknowledged, much of what is known or written about Africa and Africans in the past and present has been done by non-Africans, mostly Europeans and much of it are incorrect, false and cheap blackmail. One general tendency has been '*to look down'* on Africa and the Africans as people inhabiting the "*continent of hunger, Lions, scorpions, reptiles and monstrous animals"; "the land of black people with black souls as dark as the devil and destined to be the wretched of the earth; uncivilised and primitive".* Thus whatever is bad is termed black. They include *"Black magic, black slaves, black market, black money, black devil, black religion and black is bad" (*Obiora Ike, Freedom is more than a Word – Towards a Theology of Empowerment, 1998, p.19 ff.*)*

The core of the African Synod of 1994 and the decisions of the Synod Assembly focused on a New Era of Evangelisation, which is new in zeal, new in method and new in expression. Described as the Synod of Hope, Pope John Paul II himself had these words to say:

> "The Church which is in Africa celebrated with joy and hope its faith in the Risen Christ during four weeks of the Special Assembly for Africa of the Synod of Bishops. Memories of this event are still fresh in the midst of the whole Ecclesial Community. Faithful to the tradition of the first centuries of Christianity in Africa, the pastors of this continent, in

communion with the successor of the Apostle Peter and members of the Episcopal college from other parts of the world, held a Synod which was intended to be an occasion of hope and resurrection, at the very moment when human events seemed to be tempting Africa to discouragement and despair" (John Paul II: Post Synodal Apostolic Exhortation, Ecclesia in Africa, no 1).

The theme of the Synod, with focus for Africa on the topic "*Church as Family*" - evaluates and makes very relevant the pathway for the Christian Mission in Africa to follow during these circumstances of our historical re-evaluation and revisiting. By expanding the meaning and language of Evangelization to include an integral dimension, Catholic Christian Mission in Africa is poised to move from the Synod Talk to Synod Action. There are five pillars for this agenda:

- Proclamation of the Incarnate Word, Jesus Christ made flesh as the saviour.
- Enculturation of the Gospel on African soil as Family in all its dimensions.
- Dialogue within the levels of Church and also with other religions and society.
- Justice and Peace as practical response to serve the poor with good governance, poverty eradication, rule of law and human rights protection.
- The Means of Social Communication which is the technical engagement of proclamation with images, visual, audio, telematics and other methods imbued with Gospel values.

The incarnation of Christianity on independent Africa already started since Vatican II (1962-1965) with the focus on "aggiornamento" was the great fruit and initiative of the Africa Synod. It carried a new image and model of the *Church as Family*. This image corresponds best to the many belief systems and cultures on this continent, thus making Christians the family of God in Africa. Indeed, this model is full of implications starting with the Bishop. It shall no longer be "His Lordship" but an understanding and compassionate Father.

The Laity Women, especially should find their rightful place in the Church: from being fully consulted in matters concerning them and sharing in the lay ministries, to leading Sunday services and even cooperating in the formation of future priests as teachers and advisors. "*The quality of the Church as Family also depends on the quality of our women folk, be they married or members of institute of the consecrated life*" (Exhortation, no. 121). In this sense, the whole church considered as a "Home", gives a sense of belonging to all, since it is a community "from which absolutely nobody is excluded". Such a community gives a welcome access to the family meal, the holy Eucharist. Moreover, this African Church is an extended family with a diversity of tasks and ministries, governed by principles of solidarity and subsidiarity and kept working by dialogue. Such dialogue relates to its own members and with other Churches and religions (cf. John Bauer, 2000 years of Christianity in Africa, 1994, p.510).

The central question of the Synod was *inculturation*. This is best described as

> "a marriage of professed faith and concrete life harmony between faith and culture. One must be a Christian and an African without split of personality. The basis of Inculturation is the Incarnation (John 1:14). If Inculturation is faithfully carried out, the African Church would be more mature. Inculturation therefore, understood as integral evangelization, takes into account every aspect of life – intellectual, cultural, social, economic, political, religious and technical (Michel Eneja, Bishop of Enugu, Towards an Indigenous African Church – post Synodal theological review, 1996, p.16 -17).

It is for this reason that the Synod called the Inculturation of the faith

> "one of the greatest challenges for the church on the continent on the eve of the Third Millennium. It includes the whole life of the Church and the whole process of Evangelization". Therefore "our local Churches must be involved in the process of Enculturation in an ongoing manner, respecting the two following criteria. Compatibility with the Christian message and communion with the Universal Church" (Propositions at the Synod, 31 – 33; John Paul II Papal Exhortation, 1994, nos. 59 – 62).

The fact that the theme of *justice and peace* attracted the highest number of Episcopal interventions is symptomatic of the fact that it touched the most burning issues of present-Africa and the Bishops deep concern about them. With eloquence, they demanded more justice between the Northern industrialised countries and the south. They denounced unjust corruptions of world trade and called the selling or arms and ammunitions to belligerent African factions a crime. The Synod called for a generous solution to the debt problems and gratefully mentioned the support of the European Bishops Synod in these issues (message no. 32, 40 – 42). Their criticism at the Synod of the local corrupt practices within African nations and at all levels was strong.

Pope John Paul II himself who participated at the Synod joined in this criticism and declared in the exhortation

> "Africa's economic problems are all compounded by the dishonesty of corrupt government leaders who, in connivance with domestic or foreign interests, divert national resources for their own profit and transfer public funs to private accounts in foreign banks. This is plain theft, whatever the legal camouflage may be. I earnestly hope that the international bodies and people of integrity in Africa and elsewhere will be able to investigate

suitable legal ways of having these embezzled funds returned" (Exhortation, 113; see also Concilium 1996/2 p. 139).

At the beginning of the Christian history, there stood out of African soil the figures of the great Church Fathers as a challenge to our theologians to fructify once more the universal Church. When Tertullian formulated the famous principle of the *anima naturaliter christiana*" – "*the human soul is by nature Christian*", he deduced it from the pious African *people of* his time. In the new Africa, their number is ever increasing but calls for guidance – a challenge to African sisterhood and brotherhood, and a call for a spirituality lived by those who believe globally – founded on our common humanity.

From the many dark centuries that led from Antiquity to our modern Christianity as historian John Baur writes,

> "there surfaces out of bush, savannah and desert sand the image of the African slave, deported, degraded, exploited, suffering and crying, but overcoming it with a song and a laughter and a prayer in their heart".

The hope for a Christian future may be justified by the words of Archbishop Tchidimbo who writing from prison said: "*Christianity is above all a religion of the future. There lies the secret of its youth, its eternal youth*". This future belongs to Christ and to those who trust in him, for Christ is the Lord of history.

Examining the Critique that Christianity in Africa is a Religion of the White Man

There was a time - the year 256 AD – when an African Bishop, St Cyprian of Carthage, sent an inquiry to Rome on introducing some innovations around Enculturation in the local Church. He received this response from the officials of the Church: "*Nothing should be innovated except what was handed down" (Nihil innovetur nisi quod traditum est).*

St Cyprian felt offended that the Church in Rome was not ready for discussion on a matter concerning his diocese and territory, which needed action but asked for conformity with Roman tradition. Looking at ancient North Africa, the country of the great St Cyprian, St Athanasius, St Clement of Alexandria and St Augustine of Hippo, we may well rejoice that these saints were the great teachers of the Christian West – that part of Europe which later sent its missionaries to Africa. However, filled with sadness we remember that the Church spread throughout North Africa failed to translate the Bible and the liturgy into the language of the local Berbers.

We now know that lack of enculturation left many of them not evangelized on time; and then, left alone when the Church leaders had fled to Europe for fear of the conquering Arabs, they succumbed to Islam. Moreover, we cannot forget that one of the main causes of this failure was the inner division due to the trending differences in faith understanding of the time in the Church in North Africa into Catholics and Donatists. The Donatists could be likened to the being the first independent African Church movement, that protested against the official rich and not-holy-enough Church (Cf. John Baur, Christianity in Africa, p. 515).

Coming to the period between the 15th and 18th centuries, when the European missionaries, under the Portuguese Kings came to Africa, south of the Sahara, many African ancestors accepted the Christian faith with great devotion and wonder, especially in the Kingdom of Kongo and in Warri and Benin. Historical records show that the missionaries failed to build a Church that could be sustainable and outlive their absence. Dissensions with the Portuguese government prevented the formation of a sufficient clergy. The lay catechists were dis-allowed from baptizing catechumens even in the absence of clergy. The Bible was not to be translated into local languages, the faithful could not participate in the management of Church affairs and the faith could not linger on when the Europeans left. This is the story of the Benin Mission, the Delta and Warri and the Kongo missionary enterprise in Africa. A new experiment had to be done in the 19th century – but this- at the height of the colonial era. .

The observation and constant accusation of a white man's Church designating Christianity in Africa was actually in many places. During the 1960's – a period of anti-colonial struggles for the liberation and independence of colonies it reached its peak.

The African peoples wished to take over political, economic, social and even religious control and power from the white people who had held sway and dominated the destinies of the people in their own space and territories. .Locals did not easily distinguish between the Crown, the Cross and the Flag. The trader, colonialist and missionary are lumped together in the propaganda to gain independence. But since the 1980's, things have indeed changed and locals in most African countries are to some extent, at least externally, in control of their countries and destinies.

Demographic changes in the 20th and 21st centuries' made it possible for ageing European missionaries to go home and there were no replacements. The novel policies of population and birth control introduced in their home countries to increase prosperity led to a diminishing youth population, with consequent less priestly vocations.

Since the 1980,s African missionaries have become missionaries to their own people. The local churches had at last come of age and were already taking over control of their own Church affairs with many good vocations. Yet, the faces may have become blacks but the mind, practices, thinking and mentality still European dominated. This explains the background for the growth and spread of African independent Christian churches and the Pentecostals movements. Their rise has given the traditional Christian dominant missionary churches both competition and challenge

The first African country that accepted the Christian message was Egypt, alongside the Kingdom of Ethiopia. Christianity flourished and sustained its life and presence on those territories, because it was enculturated and allowed the Bible much early in their history to be to be translated into the local vernacular languages around the year 300 AD. They also developed their own Coptic liturgy. Egypt is the country that first developed and introduced Christian monasticism into the religious life of the Church, an idealism which inspired many to apply the Gospel literally by leaving everything and following Christ. The four pillars of the Bible and the Liturgy, Nuns and Monks made the Egyptian Church withstand the pressures of the Islamic occupation of their land that has lasted well over one thousand years. Because Christianity was well incarnated in these cultures becoming part and parcel of their language, clothing, ethics, prayer lifestyle, dance and music, entire cultures, indeed, their national Copts heritage, it has continued to survive all the aggressions of Islamisation from within and outside. These churches still stand out as authentic witnessing Churches within Africa and seen globally as they remain heroic in suffering and triumphant people in the hope its people.

The philosophical background for a white Church, dominated and run by Europeans and centralised in Europe with their other inventions had indeed some background. The middle ages and new times delivered the ideologies of European dominant and racist superior understanding of the world.

An example of this philosophical thinking was Leonardo da Vinci's "Vitruvian Man". - It was the iconic image that most powerfully expressed the European-centred universalised assumption about what it means to be human in 'modern times' (even though his enormous lifetime oeuvre [1452-1519] made him the first holistic systems thinker (see Capra, 2008)). *Vitruvian Man defined what it meant to be human as someone who is male, white, rational, alone, perfectly proportioned, disconnected from nature and free of any hierarchy (either social or cosmological).* Hegel the German philosopher of the 19th century had shared the same prejudices as many of them did. The numbers are many in philosophy as well as in anthropology, sociology, theology and the sciences. We mention but a few including Leo Frobenius, Karl Marx, Immanuel Kant and many of the known British, French, Italian and philosophers of the time.

Following Braidotti (2013), everything and everyone else was '*othered*': woman via sexualisation, people of colour via racialisation and nature via naturalisation. Complementing this image of the disconnected male self, we have the relentless quest of Rene Descartes to find out what defines him as human. He concluded: *"I think, therefore I am.*" This ultimate foundational statement from the dawn of contemporary Western culture established binary thinking as the ultimate way of knowing – because A is Not A, A cannot be A, and 'not-A' at the same time (Nicolescu, 2002). Hence, we have the mind-body binary, but also the other disconnects that follow: self and other, self and nature, self and things.

Peter Singer, the Australian philosopher and ethicist of our times put it this way.

> *"In an earlier stage of our development most human groups held* to a tribal ethic. Members of the tribe were protected, but people of other tribes could be robbed or killed as one pleased. Gradually the circle of protection expanded, but as recently as 150 years ago we did not include blacks. So African human beings could be captured, shipped to America, and sold. In Australia white settlers regarded Aborigines as a pest and hunted them down, much as kangaroos are hunted down today. Just as

> we have progressed beyond the blatantly racist ethic of the era of slavery and colonialism, so we must now progress beyond the specific ethic of the era of factory farming, of the use of animals as mere research tools, of whaling, seal hunting, kangaroo slaughter, and the destruction of wilderness. We must take the final step in expanding the circle of ethics". (Peter Singer, philosopher and professor of bioethics (b. 6 Jul 1946).

Colonial governance brought with it, the forceful imposition of foreign rule against the compete will of the people and against their interests and entire destiny. Have reparations been paid? Colonialism imposed the exploitative economies of the 19th and 20th centuries which continue to affect the current problems of disruptions in Africa at all levels. Some of these include the African identity and personality, which were forced or made to follow foreign cultures. Many Africans stretch to become Europeans, and fail neither being Caucasian or real black – a cultural limbo.

To the extent that all history is about standing in the present and looking backwards into the actions of past actors, the historian, whether they acknowledge it or not, is applying the moral and ethical and professional standards of their time to whatever past era they are studying. This is the gist of historians' critique of positivist history, the pretentious 19th century notion of history that has since been discredited. Perhaps the most cited of these critiques of positivist history is Gabrielle Spiegel's book "The Task of the Historian". In that piece, Spiegel also argues correctly in defence of histories of minorities and historically marginalized groups, histories that had been excluded from the dominant archives and canons of the profession, and that demand the moral judgments and analytical interventions that privileged and conceited advocates of positivist history and silencing disapprove of.

To actually do an "objective" history and reconstruct history without the biases and moral conventions of the present, which is what the advocates for silencing history are advancing, the historian would have to time-travel to the past and inhabit the temporal and spatial universe of the particular time and place that they are studying, which is impossible. Alternatively, they would have to write a "history" of their time, of the present. But that would not be history but journalism, and even at that, no journalism manual or theory will tell you that journalism is free of biases or that journalists do not bring their perspectives, moral commitments, predilections, socializations, and their employers' editorial bents to bear on their stories.

Unfortunately, racial supremacy is not an impression that can be corrected by wiping off the names of colonial masters and beneficiaries of the slave trade. Racism is a structure, and its pillars uphold our modern world. It is a mistake to think you can touch the formidability of its structure by renaming streets. By the time society starts to build a monument to a certain cultural practice or the person that embodies it, it means its norms have calcified. You can pull down statues, and rename streets and neighbourhoods, but the world that slave trade/colonialism built will remain intact.

Examining the History of Colonialism in the Context of the Movement "Cancel Cultures"

Quite well, #BlackLivesMatter has opened the floodgates for a re-visit of the past in the present and with a passion not seen for a long time. It should not end in America. This wave of uncomfortable historical conversations with a minefield of many unresolved historical questions should travel from Europe via Australia to Asia and the Middle East and revert to Africa. These questions have for far too long been denied or swept aside in a misguided and failed effort to foster and maintain a façade. What is needed is a new approach of holistic and sincere historical reckoning and accountability. In addressing the history of colonialism and slavery, we have the advantage of learning from the past and not repeating the same mistakes.

It is important to state that an agenda or call it the ideology that seeks to deal with past colonial history by calling for a call to *"cancel cultures*" is surely the wrong way to go.

Culture is sway of thinking, feeling, believing and living. It is the accumulated experience, knowledge, and wisdom of one social groups stored, for future use, in the memories of people, in books, in objects" (Okere, T, 1974).

Our age is confronted with questions that previous generations did not really have to face. The fact is that many people have rejected the traditional sources of ethical illumination. Today, the old certainties are virtually gone. Shame is seemingly gone. Truth is somehow not fashionable. Integrity and credibility are strange words. Dignity and decency are not seen to be very clear and living in deceit and debauchery happen to be relatively fashionable, albeit for just a short period. This is because the old truths and its search are unquenchable to the human soul and psyche, no matter what pretensions any persons may try to make of it.

One of the great ethical questions that generations of thinkers across all world systems of thought have posed over the ages is this: "what does it mean to be human"? Today, the question becomes: now that we are a geo-physical force of nature with extra-ordinary informational powers, what does it mean to be human in the Anthropocene? To answer this question, we need to bring Sub-Saharan African philosophy into conversation with the 'post-humanist turn' in Western social science.

In an earlier paper I wrote, I mentioned that

> "today, we cannot remain unconcerned by the debate that is going on around us on culture, on our cultural heritage; on the

Church and culture and the adaptation of Christianity to indigenous cultures; on the relationship between religion, cultures and civilizations; on whether or not Christianity as we got it from Europe is trans-culturally viable; and on whether or not missionary work as have known it is still justifiable (Ike, Applied Ethics to culture and Development, 2020).

Let me begin with some analysis and interpretation of the philosophical hermeneutics concerning the concept of culture. In his "*Notes towards the Definition of Culture*", the Nobel prize winning poet and literary critic T. S. Eliot asserts that the term culture has three different associations according to whether we have in mind the development of an individual, of a social class or of a whole society. Understood in the meaning of cultural anthropologists, culture refers to the entire way of life of a people. It includes the sum total of the mannerisms, beliefs, music, clothing, religions languages, behavioural patterns, food, housing, agricultural methods, as well as their traditional behaviour in a broad sense, including their ideas arts and artefacts. It is the social heritage which an individual acquires from his or her group and which heritage classifies a people belonging to a group (Ike, Reflections on Culture and Development, 2020).

Culture makes it possible for us to distinguish between a Chinese, Briton, Jew, Arab, Indian, Swede, Russian, Arab, Igbo, Yoruba, Fuji, Papua New Guinean, Frenchman and German to mention but a few of the many cultural groups under the sun.

Culture "*denotes a historically transmitted pattern of meaning embodied in symbols of inherited conceptions expressed in symbolic forms by means of which people communicate, perpetuate and develop their knowledge about and attitudes towards life"* (C,. *Geeertz: Religion as a Cultural System, in ''Anthropological Approach to the Study of religion'*).

Culture in contra-distinction from nature is that part of his or her milieu which people themselves created. Why we must eat in order to survive is a question of nature. Why the Igbo fulfils this with "Ukwa" and Okwuru" and the English with "Bread and Tea" are matters of culture. That man and woman enter into marriage is altogether natural. But that an Englishman thinks monogamy the only legally acceptable type of marriage forbidding bigamy, and that a Yoruba person considers polygamy just as reasonable and normal within the norms of that society is matters of culture, which always means: This is the way they have been brought up.

The interconnected relational nature of all reality sits at the very centre of the world-view expressed in both the Christian and African systems of thought. This, in turn, has major implications for our understanding of what it means to be human in the Anthropocene. In short, it results in the replacement of "*Vitruvian Man*" with a relational self that does not depend on the 'othering' of anyone or anything. In the words of Rosi Braidotti, one of the chief exponents of the Western post-human turn that is infusing many natural and social sciences:

Sub-Saharan African philosophy has always emphasized *'relatedness'* between all things (animate and inanimate) and beings (humans and non-humans). The underlying science that substantiated the nature-culture binary is questioned across many disciplines. An alternative is offered by the notion of '*complex adaptive systems'* (CAS) (see Preiser, Biggs, De Vos and Folke, 2017).

The other factors are the social and economic practices, political systems, cultural patterns where there are failed attempts to imitate the west in its manifold development models. All these failed.

The concept of *Ubuntu* is that one cannot be a complete human being without the reciprocal affirmation of other human beings—*umuntu ngumtu ngabantu*. The Igbo of modern Nigeria would say "*Onye nwere madu kariri onye nwere ego"* and Akan of Ghana would say: *onipa na oma onipa ye onipa* still expressing the same reality- "*it is a human being who makes another person a human being.*"

Cancel cultures does not fit into the global understanding of culture and what it stands for. The often quoted "*I am because we are*" is pregnant with the profound meaning of the generative essence of being human:

- We are endowed with a divine spark that never dies because it is connected to the source of all life. 'The dead are never dead.' Our ancestors are forever part of us; they are the link between past, present and future.
- Humans are social beings. We are wired to be with others, to nurture and shape who we are, and to make sense of our world with one another.
- Our personalities are shaped by what those close to us affirm or sanction. We are whole and endowed with the potential for right and wrong. We are choice-making beings who are socialized to seek what is right.
- We have the capacity to express compassion, reciprocity, dignity, self-respect, and respect for others inherent in us that defines our human beingness.
- Harmonious relations within family, community, and society are expressions of character beyond an individual person. The individual is both shaped by and shapes relationships with others to sustain life beyond the self.
- Our human connectedness goes beyond present relationships. We are inextricably related to our ancestors, who continue to live in present generations as guiding spirits. We stand as bridges to future generations who may still be carried as seeds in our bodies or are children born into this unending web of intergenerational connectedness.

- The interconnectedness of all life makes our being possible and demands we contribute to its sustainability. African people are totemic in that they affirm their connections to nature by identifying with an animal and/or a plant that best reflects our clan identities. (For example, the Ramphele's are Bakwena, Kwena (crocodile) is our totem animal. We also have the willow tree as our totem tree. Our clan's history is associated with water and crossing rivers with the help of our totem animal and tree.)
- We have an ecological commitment to conserve and enrich. Our capacity to empathize is the core of our being and essential for the sustenance of life itself. The intimate totemic relationships with plants and animals reinforce our reverence for nature of which we are a part. For many Sub-Saharan African writers, this relatedness to everything (people, nature and ancestors) is central.

Conclusion

The Challenge to Ethical Integration in Thought and Action

Doing a general but also introspective conclusion to this reflection around current debates on slavery, colonialism and Black lives mater, a few words addressed to the victims and oppressors likewise bring this reflection to a conclusion. Through their actions and moral failings, some African leaders feed the machinery of racial supremacy. Modern Africans and even those in positions of power underplay the enormous implications of racism/slave-trade/colonialism or their consequences in confronting issues that emanate from these discussions towards a new rebirth for their own countries. In this regard, reading the essay by the historian, Moses Ochonu, *Looking for Race: Pigmented Pasts and Colonial Mentality in "Non* Racial Africa", where he eloquently demonstrates how the vestiges of racism and colonialism have been deeply sublimated into our socio-political culture and currently manifest through the tropes of class, social differentiation and daily cultural encounters. Or the essay by the ethicist, Nimi Wariboko, *Colonialism, Christianity and Personhood*, to understand how the ideologies of race, colonialism, and Christianity configured us both as a subject of the empire and as a consumer.

Africans must also admit their own culpability right from the days of slavery and ongoing neo-colonialism. African peoples have been accursed with bad leaders who have in the course of history dehumanised their own peoples. They need historical lessons on the long-lasting impacts of slavery/colonialism and racism. They also need to understand how they have been contributing resources to its insidious effects. Until they learn that as members of the political elite and leadership class, they are still not different from what they were in the days of slavery, we have not started. They have to acknowledge that they are still as greedy, brutal, violent, and utterly selfish as they have always been. Until we understand how our forefathers got carried away by the shiny objects of capitalism, we have culpability in the moral vacuum we accuse others of and must decide once again with determination to take a stand against racism. Saying we should teach our children languages and ideologies of black supremacy only demonstrates that we are locked in our bad behaviour. Are we ready to ask ourselves the questions that will set us free?

The African economies are dependent mostly on extraction caused by colonial vestiges as they are not manufacturing. Leaders know this. What they do to stop it? The continent exports crude oil and natural resources but imports the final product from abroad. Colonialism created this structure. Why is it impossible to stop and change? Is anyone surprised that Chinese miners are being caught in African jungles illegally digging up resources now that the future of oil is uncertain? What else would have given a foreigner the gumption to do that if not that the local leaders are hugely incompetent, corrupt and participating in the rape of their own people? The little revenue realised from selling those raw materials still end up abroad.

Many social, political and economic leaders take most of the hard earned national resources to overseas, to shop for better education, health facilities, pleasure tourism, and even a breath of fresh air that they deny millions of their people at home. In the political and economic game plans of many nations today, the repetition of such brutal behaviour including internal colonialism still defines many people's lives. There is the case of largest populated country in Africa namely Nigeria with more than 200 million people and 400 languages. Like Nigerians who correlate racism with their home-grown tribal differences, the supposed racial superiority could be cured by promoting African values and culture as a counter. Second is how, in their critique of race, they exhibited a massive blind spot on how they – as African leaders – contribute to the impression that black people are innately inferior. As happened recently in that country, lawmakers of a certain State recently admitted their wives spent N80m to travel to Dubai on a frivolous educational trip. How do they justify such an expense? If their wives truly wanted an education, why did they not sit through secondary examinations like normal people? No, they had to go all the way to Dubai at the public's expense even while Lagos schools lie comatose. Why did they not spend the N80m to renovate schools and equip them with functional libraries? Even if your wives needed a seminar for whatever reasons, why not have it in Lagos? You cannot even keep Lagos as clean as it was in the colonial era, but your priority is renaming streets to correct racist/colonial impressions.

Has it ever occurred to these people that they contribute to the myth of black inferiority through their culture of wanton consumption? Do they not know that Dubai people see Africans arrive in their country and wonder what kind of people these are? The roads that lead to our overpriced housing estates get badly flooded every year, but rather than come up with a solution, we just steal enough money to gape at spectacles in Dubai and elsewhere. These are not problems that are resolvable by doing the easy work of changing labels. People have to change habits wholly. This is the ethical challenge, of doing right because it is right to do so. It corresponds also to the Golden rule that commands that we love others, as we would want others to love us.

There is a challenge here. It corresponds to the Christian teaching about dignity and common good. While it is impressive that the debates about Black Lives Matter goes on, and indeed all lives matter, black transnational solidarity would need far more complex thinking. Until people understand how our present and past bad habits of unquestioned tolerance of everything including consumption patterns and exchange patterns of commodities as established, one would not fully know racial supremacy enough to challenge it. What good does it do to pull down the visual vestiges of colonialism and slave trade while its psychological infrastructure remains lodged in the heads of those who should lead? As the philosopher Socrates of old did say: *"The unexamined life is not worth living"*. It is time for both introspection and renewal. Black lives Matter is one moment for this much-needed momentum to gather. It is hoped that its reverberations shall continue and an admission by the oppressors that evils committed in the past are condemnable even in the present and need reparations.

Refrences

Baur, John. 2000 years of Christianity in Africa: An African history 62-1992. Paulines Publ. 1994.

Benedykt, X. V. I. "Caritas in veritate." Wydawnictwo AA, Kraków (2009).

Braidotti, Rosi. Metamorphoses: Towards a materialist theory of becoming. John Wiley & Sons, 2013.

Ike, Obiora. "Current debates about Colonialism, Slavery and Black Lives Matter: Christian Missionary Activities in Africa revisited." (2020).

Ike, Obiora F. Freedom is more than a word: towards a theology of empowerment. Catholic Institute for Development Justice and Peace (CIDJAP), 1998.

Isichei, Elizabeth. A History of the Igbo People. Palgrave Macmillan, 1976.

Preise, Rika, et al. "Social-ecological systems as complex adaptive systems: organizing principles for advancing research methods and approaches." (2018).

Okere, Theophilus. Culture and Religion. Black Academy Press, 1974.

14

THE STORY AND THE MORAL: THE ETHICAL DIMENSION OF AFRICAN LITERATURE

Selline Oketch

Introduction

A significant role of Higher Education is to inculcate ethical living. [137] Literature plays a vital role in affirming society's moral principles. It is an art that seeks to understand human action and to suggest ways of behavior that promote good human relations. Storytelling is an integral element of literature designed as a moralizing strategy. This paper examines the significance of literature in fostering thoughts about moral issues and ethical obligations. In traditional Africa, the family was the first institution that taught children concepts of good and bad. Older members transmitted knowledge and values to children to mould them into responsible and humane individuals. One vital tool in this socialization process was oral literature. The fictional characters in the stories portrayed moral and ethical dilemmas which children drew lessons from. However, with the advent of colonialism and the introduction of formal education, the home gradually abdicated this educational role. Colonialism subjected Africans to political domination,

---

[137] Selline Oketch, Lecturer, Literature and Communication in the Department of Languages, Catholic University of Eastern Africa.

economic exploitation and social degradation, acts that far from raising moral questions also necessitated the freedom struggle spanning about seventy years before the first African countries gained independence. Most leaders of the new African nations, while promising to improve the welfare of their citizens, ironically continued to plunder the economies of their countries. Bad governance ensued as most nations plunged into political turmoil, civil wars, corruption, and violations of human rights resulting in massive deaths. These are ethical issues that can be addressed through multidisciplinary approaches. My discussion focuses on storytelling strategy and Francis Imbuga's play, *The Return of Mgofu* which condemns impunity in the African society. Anchored on the transformative role of literature, the paper explores regeneration strategies in the play and argues that the present societies can draw moral lessons from the traditional African value system. It concludes that literature can project values that can establish peaceful co-existence among people. It recommends the play's vision as a model for ethical living in the modern African world.

Literature, as a programme of study in higher education, plays a vital role in affirming society's moral principles. Literature can be used to document human activities, beliefs and knowledge. To mainstream ethics in literature, classroom discussions can entail ethical criticism to examine the moral and ethical nature of the work. Literature uses the narrative framework to imaginatively retrieve experiences and present them through various aesthetic modes. Characters in a literary text are mimetic of human beings and hold a mirror to us to reflect on our own actions. African writers use various discourses to portray the realities of their societies. One such discourse is storytelling that functions in a tripartite context of the storyteller, the tale and the audience. In traditional Africa, stories were created and handed down to children over generations to help them understand their world and to inculcate positive learn values.

The term traditional in reference to Africa is essentially understood in relation to the advent of the Europeans in Africa that set the stage for both colonization and missionary activities, including establishing mission schools and hospitals to modernize the Africans whose value system they viewed seen as backward. The Europeans imposed their own systems in Africa thus indoctrinating Africans to disregard their own traditional institutions that had shaped their lives; an important one being the family. Pre-colonial African society had beliefs, practices and moral values that governed the people's ways of life. The traditional African structure placed the family on a high pedestal as the basic institution that imparted values to the child.

The concept of family can be understood as a system whereby 'everybody is linked with all other members living or dead, through a complex network of spiritual relationship into a kind of mystical body.'[138]In traditional Africa, the family assumed a broader context to include grandfather, grandmother, father, mother, children, uncles and aunts. Older members were responsible for education through an informal process involving children's observation, imitation and prolonged interaction with the adults. Children would naturally acquire norms, values and knowledge that helped them fit in the community as responsible and morally upright members. Storytelling played a major role in this socialization process that also taught children their history and general way of life as well as proper conduct.

---

[138] Ogbonmwan 2008 cited in Madukwe, Isaac C. and Madukwe H.N., African Value Systems and the Impact of Westernization: A Critical Analysis in International Journal of Research in Arts and Social Sciences Vol. 2 www.academicexellencesociety.com/africa_value_system_and_the_impact_of_westernization.pdf 2010:264-274 accessed 2 September 2018

This paper examines the role of African literature in transmitting ethical values that individuals need in order to exist harmoniously with their fellow human beings. This is significant especially after the spirited struggle by the African peoples to break the colonial yoke. It is more than half a century of African political independence yet the continent continues to experience perennial political turmoil, impunity, negative ethnicity, and intolerance, gross violations of human rights, destructions and massive deaths of innocent individuals.

Ethics is the 'establishment of right and wrong founded on sound reason sound moral judgment and the free choice of a rational mind.'[139] This paper argues for a re-think of the role of literature as a vehicle for fostering ethical values in the contemporary African world. It advocates an ethical criticism of literary works to examine their moral and ethical nature. Focusing on Imbuga's *The Return of Mgofu*[140], the paper reiterates that literature demonstrates what is good or bad for individuals and the society. Literature provides a forum to remind us about the importance of inculcating values that nurture tolerance and peaceful co-existence. For instance, the experiences of Kenyan general elections of 2007, 2013, the primaries ahead of 8 August, 2017 election and those after the actual 2017 election tell the tale of the youth who have imbibed violence as followers of leaders with ogre-like traits that the play depicts. Increasingly the youth lack the kind of role models espoused by the African narratives.

---

[139] Ike, Obiora, Ethics in Higher Education as a Tool for Discovering our Ultimate Destiny in Ethics in Higher Education: values-driven Leaders for the Future pdf_1550.pdf 2017:17-30

[140] Francis Imbuga, The *Return of Mgofu.* Longhorn Publishers. Nairobi, Kenya, 2011.

Storytelling Framework

Storytelling is an integral element of literature designed as a moralizing strategy. Stories were told both to entertain and to educate. Storytelling functions as a mode of ethical inquiry.[141] The storyteller recreates history to respond to contemporary realities. The story does not just bear witness to the past, it actively re-examines the existing realities of the society ostensibly to offer certain lessons to individuals. For many people around the world, the transmission of oral literature from one generation to the next lies at the heart of culture and memory.[142] The first point of interaction for the child is in the 'family which then becomes the cradle of human society and the nursery ground for moral values'.[143] In the traditional African context, stories were not just told for entertainment but they were used as channels for transmitting culture and education. Older family members used stories from their memory bank to teach the young the cultural values of their society and to impart thoughts about moral issues and ethical obligations to children and young adults.

---

[141] Meretoja, Hanna, Ethics of storytelling. Narrative Hermeneutics, History and Possible. Oxford Scholarship Online.http://www.oxfordscholarship.com/view/10.1093/oso/9780190649364.001.0001/oso-9780190649364 2017 accessed 3 September 2018.

[142] Turin, Mark, foreword to Finnegan, Ruth. *Oral Literature in Africa.* World Oral Literature Series: Volume 1. 2012:xviii http://ia701204.us.archive.org/27/items/OralLiteratureInAfrica/OralLiteratureInAfrica.pdf accessed 10 August 2018.

[143]Madukwe, Isaac C. and Madukwe H.N., African Value Systems and the Impact of Westernization: A Critical Analysis in International Journal of Research in Arts and Social Sciences Vol. 2 www.academic exellencesociety.com/africa_value_system_and_the_impact_of_westernization.pdf 2010:264-274 accessed 2 September 2018.

The term value can be attributed to the belief system that governs positive and acceptable behaviour of members of a given society or culture. The concept of good behaviour is generally based on the universal principles such as obedience, honesty, kindness, respect, love and hospitality. The essence of this value system in traditional African society is that children belonged to the community and everyone was responsible for their proper upbringing. But this African value system was adversely disrupted by colonialism. This paper explores two functions of storytelling: that of promoting values and transmitting a people's history. Originally this discourse belonged purely to the oral realm but it has evolved to be fused into both the print and digital media. In this paper the terms story, tale and narrative will be used interchangeably.

Storytelling is a powerful tool for preserving the past as well as for social change. Stories are ways of passing down the beliefs and values of a culture in the hope that the new generations will treasure them and pass the story down further.[144] Smith further argues that the 'story and the storyteller both serve to connect the past with the future, one generation with the other, the land with the people and the people with the story.'[145] Achebe outlines the significance of story and memory through the parable of the anthills of the savannah.[146] In other words, it is through storytelling that a new generation learns about and from the past. In the novel, Old Man reiterates that only the story can continue

---

[144]Smith, Linda T. *Decolonizing Methodologies: Research and Indigenous Peoples*. (2nd Ed.). New York: Zed Books, University of Otago Press, 2012:145

[145] Ibid, 146.

[146]The title of the novel Anthills of the Savannah is based on the parable that implies that anthills survive the drought to tell the new grass of the savannah about the previous year's brush fires.

beyond the war and the warrior and that the story is our escort into the future.[147]

Many African tales have animals and human beings as main characters where each animal symbolizes virtues or vices known to specific communities. These characters play mimetic roles understandable in the present context in which they are told. Children were told stories that celebrated values such as respect, honesty, tolerance, hospitality, sharing, forgiveness, obedience and responsibility. Other stories discouraged vices such as greed, disrespect, theft and intolerance. In one such story, the animals were invited for a feast in the sky and they agree to send birds as representatives for their ability to fly. Tortoise became jealous and begged to accompany them. The birds showed compassion and donated a feather each to help their friend acquire wings. Before they left, tortoise advised them to choose names to use once they reached their destination. Tortoise's new name was 'all of you'. Each time their hosts brought refreshments and meals, Tortoise sought clarification that the food was meant for and the hosts promptly replied "for all of you". He then consumed everything telling the birds to wait for their turn. Starving and realizing that they had been tricked, the birds reclaimed their feathers and flew back to earth. One of them accepted to convey tortoise's message to his wife to spread out soft materials for him to land on. However, the bird distorted the message and directed lady tortoise to spread tough substances and as tortoise landed, he cracked his shell.[148]

The characters in the story play an aesthetic role as an indirect strategy for ethical commentary. Apart from explaining why tortoise has

---

[147] Achebe, Chinua, *Anthills of the Savannah*. Nairobi: Heinemann Kenya Ltd 1987:124.

[148] The story appears in various versions in different communities and in different anthologies of Oral Literature.

cracked shell, the story also teaches virtues such as compassion, kindness and sharing expressed by the birds while discouraging vices like greed and grabbing shown by tortoise. The story upholds the principle of natural justice[149] where good behaviour is rewarded and bad punished. Protagonists such as Ananse the spider, in the folktales of the Akan of Ghana, *Ijapa* the tortoise and Frog in the Yoruba and the Luo stories respectively, and many other animal characters provide good role models to children in their behaviour. Frog in Luo narratives even transforms into an old woman to rescue children in danger.

Children display greed through simple activities like demanding larger shares of foodstuffs or even eating faster to consume more than others. Yet in adult life greed has the potential to beget corruption, impunity and other vices that afflict African countries. Literature strives to eradicate greed by presenting stories set even in modern family contexts through the medium of digital technology. In the animated story of 'The Goose that Laid the Golden Eggs,'[150] Tia cautions her younger brother Tofu against eating greedily lest he becomes like the poor couple who lost their treasure because of greed. Tofu learns from the story and promises to discard that habit.

Children were also told stories about the ogres, monsters and dragons. In the folktales, the ogre is a weird and evil creature that is capable of disfiguring itself in several ways to cause destruction and to devour human beings. It has features of a giant usually with certain abnormalities and can camouflage its nature instantly. Girls were particularly cautioned to beware of the ogre's capability to transform into a handsome suitor only to devour its bride later on. Children left on their own had to be careful and vigilant because the ogre could easily imitate a mother's voice and devour a child who carelessly unbolted the

---

[149]See Jean Piaget's *Theory of Cognitive Development*

[150]T-Series Kids Hut, *The Goose that Laid Golden Eggs* 2014 https://www.youtube.com/watch?v=5zznLdp5fRM accessed 5 September 2018

door to him. The ogre continues to be a significant symbolic character and metaphor in literary texts, including *The Return of Mgofu* where it represents forces of destruction.

In the written form, African literature continues to exploit the rich heritage of the oral tradition as one of its distinctive features. For instance, the story about a visit to the sky above is also adapted in Achebe's *Things Fall Apart* for the relevance of its moral function. Other authors use storytelling strategy to recount the history and socio-political developments of the African nations that they depict.[151] Beah develops his memoir through a series of stories and refers to many storytellers including his grandmother who had an influence on his childhood. He presents the history of his country Sierra Leone revealing the traumatic experiences of the civil war and its effects on him and other children as child soldiers. Beah's story exposes how conscripting children into the army violates their rights and negates ethical values.

Storytelling is therefore an indigenous resource[152] that can be harnessed to foster ethical values that would help individuals resist the temptation to harm or kill fellow human beings. The political climate in some African countries, indeed in Kenya, is volatile and highly ethicised particularly during campaign periods to the extent that there are numerous cases of extra judicial and other random killings of innocent citizens on account of different affiliations. Often the youth are victims or perpetrators used by older individuals for selfish gains. Such people have abdicated their role as models to the youth as was envisioned in the African oral tradition. Re-thinking the functional role of literature in

---

[151] This includes writers like Achebe 1987, 2009; Ngugi 2010; Beah 2007, 2014.

[152] Olojode, Funlola, *Storytelling as an Indigenous Resource in the interpretation of Old Testament Ethics and Religion* Pdf 2014:1-9 Accessed on 8 August 2018

fostering ethical values stresses the rendition of stories with moral values in homes and schools through various media.

The Writer as Storyteller

African writers utilize literature as a tool that interrogates the dynamics of society through the devices of memory and narration. In this endeavour, the writers infuse oral literature techniques into the written mode to respond to contemporary realities of the African continent in its different historical phases. They narrate the story of the traditional African society highlighting its value system and the cultures of the African peoples. The literary texts present the story of the African people's struggle for independence and their expectations and aspirations of freedom. African literature narrates the onset of neo-colonialism, bad governance, political turmoil, civil wars, ethnic violence, displacements, massacres, genocide and various other forms of injustices. All these are indications of erosion of moral values and the writer becomes the conscience reminding readers and the society of the high cultural ethos that must be upheld.[153] This paper calls for rethinking of the role of literature in fostering moral values and nurturing positive attitudes that our torn apart African societies need in the healing process. In this restoration and healing process, Imbuga's plays indict African regimes that thrive on excessive lust for power, corruption, injustice and gross violations of human rights. The Return of Mgofu advocates the reclamation of the moral order of traditional African society as a framework for remoulding the present and the future African society.

---

[153]Ojaide, Tanure, Modern African Literature and Cultural Identity in African Studies Review Vol.35 No.3 1992:43-47. Modern_african_literature_and_cultural_identity.pdf Accessed on 4 September, 2018

Imbuga's first political play, Betrayal in the City dramatizes African dictatorship and intimidation of the citizens. It depicts a society characterized by vices such as betrayal, oppression, corruption, nepotism, inefficiency, bad governance, numerous injustices including murders of innocent citizens. Man of Kafira reiterates these injustices and disregard for the value of human life. Game of Silence reminds ordinary citizens that they have a role to change their own destiny by revolting against the political elite.

In these three plays, the writer underscores the negation of moral values. The characters in Betrayal in the City exhibit tendencies similar to those of the tortoise in the story above. Tumbo has amassed wealth through corrupt means while Mulili kills Kabito over the award of the milk tender. Thus, the play demonstrates that the pursuit of material wealth and power has brought forth human beings who possess undesirable traits. In The Successor, Imbuga depicts succession wrangles where one kills in order to ascend to power. Imbuga introduces and deploys elements of the traditional African belief system such as diviners to redeem the society represented by Masero. Diviners serve as agents of unveiling mysteries of human life who also perform medical and priestly functions.[154] In Imbuga's play, See Through is a prophet with powers to predict the future and plays the fundamental role of steering Masero back on a moral course through his steadfastness in championing the truth.

In his later texts, the playwright is concerned that society should be redeemed and demonstrates that this can only be done through a return to the values of the traditional African society. Imbuga presents the family as the best socializing institution from where human values such as respect and hospitality are inculcated. His subsequent works present the home as the foundation for nurturing values and attitudes that

---

[154]Mbiti, John, *African Religions and Philosophy*. Oxford: Heinemann1990:172

individuals need to foster peaceful relations in the society. The works are set in the homes and use the relationships between family members as a prism to explore broader relationships in the society. In Aminata, the girl child Aminata learns from her father that the vices that have created male domination and marginalization of women should be eliminated. She can be seen as the epitome of a girl empowered by her father to fight for her rights. Conscious of the need to safeguard the African family values, Imbuga continues to explore more diversified strategies through the novel as a genre of literature.

His two novels are set in homes that offer proper and supportive environments for the children's growth to help boost their self- esteem and positively shape their world-view. Shrine of Tears, Headmaster reiterates that all adults should take part in the positive formation of children. The families in this novel and in Miracle of Remera display positive relationships, mutual understanding and creates opportunities for dialogue between children and their parents. The writer's vision is that these values and positive attitudes that are nurtured in the family should be replicated in the wider society.

Shrine of Tears also concretizes loss of moral values as a consequence of modernity. As Fanon states, as a sign of prosperity, a nation needs to elevate and enlighten the consciousness of its younger generation.[155] The novel depicts girls as victims of the loss of moral values in the contemporary African society. Silverspoon, a white sailor and Gaylord sexually undermine and exploit girls at Hell's Gate Bar and Restaurant. The girls have lost sense of the value of going to school. They have even lost their own dignity as they pose nude for photographs

---

[155] Fanon, Frantz/Philcox, Richard. *The Wretched of the Earth / Frantz Fanon; translated from the French by Richard Philcox*. New York: Grove Press. Original: 1961. *Les damnes de la Terre*. Paris: Francois Maspero, 2004:141

in exchange for money.[156] In Miracle of Remera, Imbuga depicts moral decadence in the sense that girls drop out of school and enter into early marriages while others are raped and infected with the dreaded HIV/AIDS. In all this, the writer as storyteller is optimistic that the contemporary society is still able to learn from its mistakes and reclaim its lost glory. Pedophiles here can be regarded as the modern ogres that the society should get rid of.

These negative traits emphasize the need to re-think the functional role of storytelling in the family. In Shrine of Tears, Headmaster and his wife begin to mentor and inspire the youth of Kilima by instilling in them a sense of determination and commitment during the production of the play, "Farewell to Ogres". At the end of the novel, the youth seem to have a clearer vision of their identity as useful young members of the society. Boge too confronts fellow men molesting girls asserting that he considers all Kiliman girls his sisters and has a duty to protect them from such evil men.

The writer as storyteller reminds the contemporary society of the importance of family values that we seem to have overlooked as individuals develop undesirable behaviours that are detrimental to their fellow human beings. Imbuga argues that modern writer has a similar duty to that of the traditional artists who educated evil doers in society without making them feel uncomfortable but secure with the knowledge that if they reformed, they would be reintegrated into the society.[157]

Evidently, in presenting the socio- political dynamics of contemporary Africa, the writer also creates a parallel theme of the traditional African set up. A return to the past seems to be the writer's

---

[156] Imbuga, Francis, *Shrine of Tears.* Nairobi: Masterpiece Series. Longman Kenya, 1993:175-190.

[157] Ruganda, John, *Telling the Truth Laughingly: The Politics of Francis Imbuga's Drama.* Nairobi: East African Educational Publishers, 1992: xxi

regeneration strategy to restore moral order in the fictional society to accentuate the significance of the moral fibre of the African nations. Folktales taught individuals moral lessons that helped them to live in harmony with fellow members of the community. What is pivotal in all these works by Imbuga is the writer's emphasis on the loss of family values as principles that shape the behaviour of African peoples. Instead, people have imbibed alien traits based on individualism and pursuit of power and material wealth. A host of African countries have experienced different forms of violence and massive deaths. McIsaacs acknowledges that the African continent is characterized by a shared history of colonial, political and economic domination, and problems such as political instability, corruption, high rates of crime, insecurity and interethnic conflicts. She argues that oral narratives can be used to reject these vices and as a potential tool in the moral and character formation of the African child.[158]

The Return of Mgofu: Confronting Ethical Issues in the Nation's Past

The *Return of Mgofu* is set in a fictional African country called Mndika that has emerged from the traumatic effects of politically/ethnically instigated genocide. It attempts to redeem society as it condemns the recurrent ethnic animosity and intolerance that continue to plague most African countries. Through narrative strategy, the play provides vital information about the nation's past and affirms the significance of memory in understanding the present and contemplating the future. Imbuga uses characters as witnesses of history

---

[158] McIsaac, Elizabeth, 'Oral Narrative as a Site of Resistance: Indigenous Knowledge, Colonialism and Western Discourse' in Del, G.J /Hall B.D (Eds.) *Indigenous Knowledge in Global Contexts*, Toronto: University of Toronto pdf 2018:89-101. Accessed 11July, 2018

to tell their story from their personal memory which reflects the collective reality. Thori and Thoriwa, a couple from the world of spirits, return to tell Mndika's story as they remember it. Their story brings healing to a society in the process of regaining its identity. They narrate how ethnic violence suddenly erupted and how their neighbor's burnt many of them in their local shrine; how Mgofu's wisdom guided him to seek refuge in Nderema to save his expectant wife; how priestess Kadesa, a Mndikan exile from an earlier violence, welcomed Nora in her shrine and refugee camp where the younger Mgofu was born making Nderema the new home of Mgofu and other exiles from Mndika.

The play opens up a forum for conversation on reconsidering the contribution of moral values to the well-being of the human person. It calls for introspection into historical injustices in the African countries. The narration of violence transcends condemnation and stresses on redemption and reconciliation. The questions to paused are: how is it that people who have co-existed in harmony suddenly turn against one another, killing innocent people and burning homes, churches and property? How does such a society regain sustainable peace? The dead characters have undergone a healing process and return with a message of forgiveness, peace and reconciliation. This technique of omnipotent presence enhances their authoritative voice as the custodians of the nation's master narrative. The writer experiments with literary strategies that improvise a context of Truth, Justice and Reconciliation (TJR) on the occasion of the Remembrance Day celebrated at the end of the play. This is a significant national day in which the citizens of Mndika commemorate those who died in the genocide as well as those in exile. Their leader Mhando leads them to recognize the futility of violence and the need for forgiveness and reconciliation. The day becomes more important as it marks the return of Mgofu, the embodiment of that significant past and the beginning of the nation building process anchored on human values.

Redeeming Society through Moral Values

The title of Imbuga's play has a multiplicity of meaning: it draws attention to the significance of Mgofu as an allegorical figure, a symbol of Mndika's history and well-being. It also refers to the reincarnation of Mgofu, the great half blind seer of Mndika, through the birth of his son named after him. Priestess Kadesa is knowledgeable in her people's history and offers hospitality and spiritual guidance to the refugees. Mhando displays human values and adopts an inclusive leadership style presented as a model for the African political leaders. *The Return of Mgofu* reinforces the role of African traditions in enhancing peaceful relations between people. The victims of genocide display reconciliatory attitude accentuating the play's overall theme of respect for fellow human beings. Mgofu is both a character and an ideology. As an ideology, Mgofu implies old age, wisdom, goodness, orderliness, harmony, perfection and other virtues of African oral tradition. In the play, the ancestors return to restore moral order hence the reunion of the ancestors with the living to re-establish peace and tranquillity in the society.

The virtues expressed in the play parallel the African philosophy of Ubuntu.[159] Fox cites Archbishop Tutu's explanation of Ubuntu as 'humanness, the very essence of being human'. He elaborates that Ubuntu 'remembers past generations and ancestors drawing on the

---

[159]Ubuntu was the guiding principle in the South African Truth and Reconciliation Commission (TRC) chaired by Archbishop Desmond Tutu. Tutu outlined that Ubuntu is an African worldview based on human values of respect, compassion, kindness, hospitality.

memory of their lived experiences[160]...' and that those who possess the virtues of Ubuntu live in harmony with fellow human beings. Ubuntu can thus be summarized as an African world view based on human values that include respect, compassion, kindness, hospitality. Achebe emphasizes the need to recognize one another's presence and the ability to accord human respect to all people. [161] Mandela's asserts that no one is born hating another person because of the colour of his skin or his background or his religion therefor if people can learn to hate they can be taught to love because love comes more naturally to the human heart than its opposite.[162]

In the play, these virtues of Ubuntu are displayed in the wisdom of Mgofu, and the humaneness of ideal characters like Mgofu, Mhando, Kadesa and Nora. The play conveys an optimistic message about respect for humankind and harmonious relationships. Kadesa's shrine is symbolically referred to as 'Farewell to Ogres', a sign that these characters have rejected the impunity and intolerance that befell their home country. This is the context in which we should understand the playwright's concept of 'alternative slice of reality'. Its overriding message is contained in the virtues of respect for fellow human beings, tolerance and forgiveness. Mgofu condemns aspects of tradition that sanction women's oppression and upholds people's capacity to create peaceful relations between themselves, irrespective of their gender.

---

[160] Fox, Graham. 2011. "Remembering Ubuntu: Memory, Sovereignty and Reconciliation in Post-Apartheid South Africa." *Platforum*. journals.uvic.ca/…hp/platforum/article/download/….: 105-107 accessed 10 August, 2018.

[161] Achebe, Chinua, *The education of a British-protected child: essays*. New York: Alfred A. Knopf, 2009:123, 166.

[162] *Long Walk to Freedom: The Autobiography of Nelson Mandela*. South Africa: Macdonald Purnell, 1995:542

Conclusion

Mainstreaming ethics in African literature should entail classroom interactions on moral issues depicted in oral literature, children's literature, literary theory and practical criticism of texts. Imbuga's play proposes that impunity and intolerance in contemporary African nations can be resolved when people rethink the place of moral values in their lives. Those governed by moral values are hospitable, respectful and live harmoniously with others. The play's ideal characters are entrusted with spearheading the process of rebuilding their nation. In mainstreaming ethics in higher Education, a play like *The Return of Mgofu* can be subjected to ethical critical reading for its relevance to the African society. It can used to educate various communities across the African continent on issues like consequences of negative ethnicity, national dialogue and cohesion and the need to confront historical injustices that have created instability in various nations. After three decades of indicting African political leaders for betraying the hopes and aspirations of their people, Imbuga uses storytelling in *The Return of Mgofu, to* underscore the role of human values of the African traditions in providing a basis for the restoration of peace and harmony in the contemporary African society.

References

Achebe, Chinua. *Anthills of the Savannah*. Nairobi: Heinemann Kenya Ltd, 1987.

Achebe, Chinua. *The education of a British-protected child : essays*. New York: Alfred A. Knopf, 2009.

Apartheid South Africa." *Platforum*. journals.uvic.ca/…hp/ platforum/article/download/... Accessed 10 August 2018.

Beah, Ishmael (2007). *A long way gone: memoirs of a boy soldier*. New York: Farrar, Straus and Giroux.

Fanon, Frantz & Philcox, Richard. *The wretched of the earth / Frantz Fanon; translated from the French by Richard Philcox.* Paris: Francois Maspero, 2004.

Finnegan, Ruth. *Oral Literature in Africa.* World Oral Literature Series: Vol. 1 http://ia701204.us.archive.org/27/items/OralLiteratureInAfrica/OralLiteratureInAfrica.pdf, 2012, accessed 10 August 2018.

Fox, Graham. 2011. "Remembering Ubuntu: Memory, Sovereignty and Reconciliation in Post-

Ike, Obiora,' Ethics in Higher Education as a Tool for Discovering our Ultimate Destiny' in *Ethics in Higher Education: Values-driven Leaders for the Future*, Geneva: Globethics.net, 2017:17-30.

Imbuga Francis, *Betrayal in the City* Nairobi: East African Publishing House, 1976.

______*Game of Science* Nairobi: Heinemann Educational Books, 1977.

______*The Successor* Nairobi: Heinemann Educational Books, 1979.

______*Man of Kafira.* Nairobi: Heinemann Educational Books, 1984.

Aminata. Nairobi: Heinemann Educational Books, 1988.

The Burning of Rags Nairobi: Heinemann Educational Books, 1989.

Shrine of Tears Nairobi: Longman Kenya, 1993.

Miracle of Remera Nairobi: Africa Wide Network, 2004.

The Return of Mgofu Nairobi: Longhorn, 2011.

Madukwe, Isaac C. and Madukwe H.N., 'African Value Systems and the Impact of Westernization: A Critical Analysis' in *International Journal of Research in Arts and Social Sciences* Vol. 2 www.academicexellencesociety.com/africa_value_system_and_the_impact_of_westernization.pdf 2010:264-274 accessed 2 September 2018.

Mandela, Nelson, Long *Walk to Freedom: The Autobiography of Nelson Mandela*. South Africa: Macdonald Purnell, 1995:542

Mbiti, John *African Religions and Philosophy*. Oxford: Heinemann, 1990.

McIsaac, Elizabeth, 'Oral Narrative as a Site of Resistance: Indigenous Knowledge, Colonialism and Western Discourse' in Del, G.J /Hall B.D (Eds.) *Indigenous Knowledge in Global Contexts*, Toronto: University of Toronto pdf 2018:89-101Accessed 11July, 2018.

Meretoja, Hanna, Ethics of storytelling. Narrative Hermeneutics, History and Possible. Oxford Scholarship. Online./www.oxfordscholarship.com/view/10.1093/oso/9780190649364.001.0001/oso-9780190649364 2017. Accessed 3 September 2018.

Modern_african_literature_and_cultural_identity.pdf Accessed on 4 September, 2018

Ojaide, Tanure, 'Modern African Literature and Cultural Identity' in *African Studies Review* Vol.35 No.3 1992:43-47

Olojode, Funlola, *Storytelling as an Indigenous Resource in the interpretation of Old Testament Ethics and Religion* Pdf 2014:1-9 Accessed on 8 August 2018.

Ruganda, John, *Telling the Truth Laughingly: The Politics of Francis Imbuga's Drama*. Nairobi: East African Educational Publishers, 1992

Smith, Linda T. 2012. *Decolonizing Methodologies: Research and Indigenous Peoples*. London & New York: Zed Books.

T-Series Kids Hut, *The Goose that Laid Golden Eggs*, YouTube 2014 https://www.youtube.com/watch?v=5zznLdp5fRM accessed 5 September 2018

15

THE ROLE OF RELIGION AND MORALITY IN SOCIAL CONTROL

THE CASE OF PRE-COLONIAL IGBO CONTEMPORARY SOCIAL ILLS

Samuel C. Nwankwo

Introduction

Many anthropologists, historians, political scientists and sociologists, even ethnographers have at one point or the other written differently on various aspects of the Africa people.[163] Unfortunately, the traditional systems of social control and policing of the various ethnic groups in Africa drew little attention, especially, those of Igbo land. It is worthy of note to reiterate that the unique and sometimes traumatizing methods of offender apprehension and disposal in many of Africa, remain hidden to scholars in various regions of Africa as well as scholars from outside of Africa. This study succinctly, used historical/phenomenological approach, and secondary sources of data collection, to examining majorly what were considered offenses, the seriousness of such offences in Igbo land, the agents of social control and methods of offences disposal. It was discovered that the Igbo people had stringent methods of controlling deviant behaviours in the society and recommended that

[163] Samuel C. Nwankwo, Department of Theology at Wesley University, Ondo, Nigeria.

while the modern judiciary system has not actually solved the menace of societal evils; that traditional methods should be re-considered.

Africans and especially, the Igbo people have continued to witness breakdown of law and order in the society. This society has witnessed constant threat to human lives and property due to the culture of moral poverty which infiltrated our society; making most people not to have values for human life. No human society ever flourished in a state of chaos and anarchy, instead, societies tend to progress in an atmosphere of peace, love, tranquillity, brotherliness and care for one another. Where these traits are missing in any society of human person, what follows is retrogression occasioned by myriads of social breakdown, incoherence, unrest, abominable acts and all manner of evils. This is the case with many societies in the past and in the present. Deviance is a ubiquitous phenomenon. It is found in every society. [164]

However, the pre-colonial Igbo society has a well-defined and culturally enshrined customary standard of conduct and negative sanctions for any breach. They have usually fashioned a way through which they controlled their people even before the advent of the Europeans. These methods of social control, no doubt curbed the menace of social breakdown to the barest minimum during the period under review. The fear of being publicly ridiculed, sanctioned, ostracized, being struck down by the god of thunder and other deities, kept people's behaviour and activities in check.

This is not the case today. In our society today, we have various modern means of check-mating moral decadence, yet, evil snowballs on daily bases. We have the police, the military, civil defence, agencies for corrupt practices, prison yards and other forms of tracking offenders like kidnappers and armed robbers; yet, the problem of crime shows no sign

---

[164] Nwankwo, S.C (2017). *Understanding Religious Ethics: An Exercise in Afrocentric Ethicalism.* Aba: Rainbow Printing Press, p.61

of abating. Many have argued that the society is better with the pre-colonial and traditional methods of social control than the modern methods; and have advocated for a return to the traditional means, which is the crux of this research.

Historical Phenomenological approach which according to Ituma refers to "the method which insists that no religious phenomena can be understood outside of their history" [165] shall be used in this research. It is a study of historical fact or event in nature (or society) as it appears or is experienced by the senses. Historical phenomenological method deals with the true nature of the theme from inside. It examines the historical, cultural and socio-economic contexts of the event. It will be applied in this work to enable the researcher uncover historically, how the Igbo people in the pre-colonial era were able to handle social issues that troubled them during their time and thus maintained peace and security in the society. The work shall equally make use of the secondary sources of data collection. This is basically the use of related and relevant literature in the libraries.

The research among other things will aim at understanding what constituted offences in the pre-colonial Igbo society. It will as well examine how the people during the period were able to dispose of these offences in other to maintain peace and tranquillity. The agents/agencies that specialized in offences disposal at the time shall be considered; as well as relevance of those agencies in curbing social ills today. Finally, the research will suggest ways through which religion and morality can help in the maintenance of peace and order in the society.

---

[165] Ituma, E.A (2015). *Basic Research Guide for Humanities and Social Sciences*. Nsukka: Timex , p.38

Conceptual Analysis of Religion, Morality and Social Control

A concise understanding of what religion is will be very necessary. Ayodeji, defines the term religion as "faith in a divinely created order of the world, agreement with which is the means of salvation of a community and thus for each individual who has a role in that community." [166] Furthermore, Obilor conceptualized religion to mean, "The whole *complexus* of attitudes, beliefs, practices, gestures, rituals, emotions, convictions, and institutions through which we express our deep fundamental relationship with reality, and not excluding the created order." [167]

We shall deduce that, religion is a strong ideology and conviction which may seem difficult to resist once conceived. It encompasses the totality of human person and explains the deep fundamental questions bordering on reality, essence and existence. Man in religion tries to reach out beyond self to God or whatever is considered supreme, the wholly other. It is equally a social phenomenon. No definition of religion will be adequate if it fails to consider its God-ward and man-ward relationship. Man has a duty or role towards God and towards his fellow man.

The term 'morality' according to Okere is defined as "that quality of human life by which it can be described as good or bad, good in the sense that it must be done, or bad or evil in the sense that it must be avoided." [168] Morality is a spiritual dimension of human action. Animals

---

[166] Ayodeji, O.S (2013). "Religious Values and Corruption in Nigeria: a Dislocated Relationship. *Journal of Educational and Social Research. Italy: Vo.4 No.3. MCSER Pub,* p.523.

[167] Obilor, J.I (2010). *Many Religions one God.* Owerri: Matts Books Publishers, p.317.

[168] Okere, T (2006). "Religion, Morality and Governance in Nigeria." Lecture Delivered at Owerri: Multi Purpose Hall, p.38.

have no morality. Iroegbu and Echekwube understood 'morality' to mean "the conventionally approved rules of behaviour in the society." [169]

'Morality' in the words of Obaje, in Kudadjie (ed.), "is usually considered as ways of regulating the conduct of individuals in communities."[170] In other words, human conduct must be guided in order to avoid chaos in the society. Morality is further defined as "the quality of conforming to the principles of good conduct, moral or virtuous conduct." This boils down to the fact that morality covers good or bad, right or wrong principles of human behaviour. That is why we can say some of human actions are bad, some are morally good, and some are immoral.

Social control in the words of Chukwu (eds.) refers to "the techniques and strategies for preventing deviant human behaviour in any society." [171] This is a concept usually applied in sociology, history and other social sciences. It equally, could be referred to as social order. It is a set of linked social structures, social institutions and social practices which conserve, maintain and enforce "normal" ways of relating and behaving[172]. Obi accentuated that, "a social order is a relatively persistent system of institutions, patterns of interactions and customs, capable of continually reproducing at least those facts of society which

---

[169] Iroegbu, P and Echekwube, A. (2005). *"What is Ethics?"* In *Kpim of Morality: Ethics General, Special and Professional*. Ibadan: Heinemann Educational Books (Nigeria) Plc., p.32.

[170] Obaje, Y.A (2002). "Religion and Morality as Instrument of Transformationm in West African Society." In Kudadjie (ed.) (2002). Religion, Morality and West African Society. Accra: Wesley Printing Press, p .22

[171] Chukwu, C.C, Okonkwo, G.A and Kalu, E.O (2013). *The History and Culture of Old Bend and the Emergence of Umunna.* Lagos: Serenity Publishers p.234.

[172] Wikipedia, Social order, http://en. wikipedia.org/wiki/social order. Retrieved on April 28, 2016.

remain relatively constant over time." [173] These conditions could include property, exchange and power relations, cultural forms, communication relations and ideological systems of values. Whenever, these conditions experience friction, the result is usually, unpalatable. There is always chaos in the society.

Delineating Crime Rates in Modern Society

The threat and fear of crime are constant concerns that impact many people in modern society. In societies like Nigeria and other African states, many contemporary social problems have emerged which are against the norms, morals and ethics of the society and of course make life very uncomfortable. The challenge lies majorly on the rate at which it snowballs compared to what we have during the pre-colonial period.

George and Ukpong articulated such problems today to include "the deviant behaviour toward the commandments of God, cultural norms and stipulations and moral principles as in the struggle for the control of available scarce resources wrongly and violently. This in turn creates problems in the society that affect all and sundry." [174]

One major cause of crime increase in the modern society is the problem occasioned by science and technology and the breakdown of family value system in Africa.

George and Ukpong further enumerated the many woes of science and technology by noting that:

---

[173] Obi, C.A (2013). "Religion as basis of Social Order." In Kpim of Social Order. Edited by Ukagba, G.U, Obi, D.O and Nwankwor, I.K. U.S.A: Xlibris Corporation, p.437

[174] George, I.N and Ukpong, D.E. (2013). "Contemporary Social Problems in Nigeria and its Impact on National Development: Implication for Guidance and Counselling Services." *Journal of Educational and Social Research. Uyo:* Vol. 3 (2) May 2013 p.167.

"though a blessing seems to be a curse to man and humanity over time. It is a two way traffic affair. Although it is the mother of inventions, a breakthrough in modern business, facilitator of qualitative education and the controller or pivot of the modern day economy, expanding and covering larger frontiers of the universe in each new day, yet it is not without its own evil intentions. It has been responsible for the alarming rate of crimes, injustice, killing and robbery, kidnapping and many other social disasters. Among other negative impacts of science and technology are the hi-tech business crimes e.g. credit cards and internet robbery and theft, hooking on to false business links and contacts on the internet; cyber crimes which promote all forms of examination malpractice for example the use of phone for cheating in examination, pornographic shots and films which lure our youths to unhealthy and indiscriminate sexual activities, access to ungodly websites also known as (satan.com), juvenile robbery clips, unauthorized and destructive clips showing crimes, shooting and sexual lawlessness. Others are building of nuclear and sophisticated weapons of crime and warfare which are used by reckless youths and criminals e.g. suicide bombers for crimes against humanity. These and many more are readily available on the internets, home videos, crimes novels, journals and other publications etc. These negative impacts of science and technology threaten to destroy the modern society and also serve as spring boards for the proliferation of small and large scale crimes that result in total breakdown of law and order in the society." [175]

---

[175] George, I.N and Ukpong, D.E. p.167.

The erosion of African family value system is another strong reason why social ills are on the increase in modern society. Today the institution of marriage has received myriads of attacks. Homes are broken and single parenting on the increase. Children are constantly exposed to violence because of what they watch and learn from peers. Home training has been left in the hands of people who do not understand family values and thus the morals of the young people are jeopardized. The result is obvious: lack of respect for constituted authority, cultism, lack of respect for human lives, kidnapping, promiscuity, pre-marital sex, abortion, emphasis on western values and the relegation of African values, homosexuality and in fact total breakdown of the moral system of the society. [176] Other reasons for crime rate in modern time include: poverty, unemployment, population explosion, political and economic problem in the society. The difference between crime rate now and in the pre-colonial period is that the pace at which crime increases now cannot be compared to what obtains in the past.

Offences Constituent and Social Disorder in Pre-Colonial Africa

There are acts which are considered religiously unethical; when they are committed, Africans frown at them and apply various methods in doing away with them. The researcher shall examine further in this discussion those acts that constitute offences in Africa.

There is clear cut definition of offences in pre-colonial Igbo land, though offences are categorized based on their degrees and scholars like Onyeozili, Ebbe,[177] Chukwu, Okonkwo and Kalu[178] agreed that the

---

[176] Nwankwo, S.C., pp.262-263.

[177] Onyeozili, E.C and Ebbe, O.N.I (2002). "Social Control in Pre-colonial Igbo land of Nigeria." *African Journal of Criminology and Justice Studies: AJCJS, Vol.6, Nos.1 &2* November, pp.32-35.

concept of crime does not apply in pre-colonial Africa. However, Onyeozili tried to distinguish two types of offences which are: abominations (public offences) otherwise called *aru* or something that earth abhors and delicts called *mmehie* (private offences). In general terms, when acts are abhorred, terrifying and indecent, they become offences; because, they are not incorporated in the values and mores of the land. When moral values are broken the society sees such acts cherished by every society which stipulates the strong ideas of right and wrong and approves certain acts while gravely forbid others.

According to Onyeozili offences as murder of brother, sister or kinsmen, incest (that is a son having sexual coitus with one's sister or one of his father's wives when his father is still alive); killing or eating a domestic animal dedicated to the gods (totem), or any other offence against the gods are considered as abomination. [179] On the other hand offences such as burglary, fighting, quarrelling, stealing (not of yam) is considered as delicts or *mmehie*. Such offences do not receive grave penalty in most African societies. But when the stealing involves yam produce, it becomes an abomination in Igbo land.

An intentional breach of any various social norms, law and order (*iwu*), cultural taboos (*nso ala*), or abominations (*aru*), disrupts the inter and intra-harmony existing among God, the deities, ancestors, man, and nature attracts fugitive measures as retribution, deferent, rectification or restitution. A process of ritual cleansing or purification as in the case of adultery, may accompany this.

In some communities of Igbo land and Africa in general due to the relationship between religion, ethics and law; some pieces of lands, rivers, trees, forest and some week days were defined as sacred. For the sacred pieces of land, certain days were set apart on which no farming

---

[178] Chukwu, C.C, Okonkwo, G.A and Kalu, E.O, p.238.

[179] Onyeozili, E.C Ed. p.32.

activity of any kind was done on them. It was a taboo for anyone to catch and eat fish from a sacred river. It was forbidden for anybody to cut down a tree among the forbidden or sacred trees as *uboldia* (*umune* or *ogirish*, *anunu ebe* and *ngwu*) among some Igbo communities.

Most communities in Igbo land had certain days in the four-day Igbo week (*Afo, Nkwo, Eke, Orie*) when nobody were allowed to work or any form of ceremony like marriage or funeral was allowed to hold. If anybody violated any of the above sacred rules, he/she must provide all the prescribed items for ritual cleansing to appease the gods.

Adeyemo agreed with other African scholars that wrong deeds are graded in terms of heavy and light offences. He states that "in Yoruba land, the heavy offences are termed *ese nla* or major sin while the minor sins are called *ese kekere*." [180] He reveals that witchcraft ranks very high among the abominations. That the violation of the tribal taboos also ranks very high. To reveal the secrets of a cult to the non-initiate is also a great crime.

Awolawu and Dopamu noted that, "it is a great disaster for any person to be guilty of abominable acts. It is a disaster not only for him or her, but for other members of the family; sometimes, the whole community." [181] That is why it is abomination. This is because these acts constitute the pollution of the land. Such acts in Igbo land include patricide, incest, stealing especially of yams, killing of totem animals and a woman climbing a palm tree.

Ajah observed that, "traditional Africans believed that when there is an upset in natural and normal system of life, it is believed that someone

---

[180] Adeyemo, T (1979). *Salvation in African Traditional Religion*. Nairobi: Evangel Publishing House, pp.54-55.

[181] Awolawu, J.O and Dopamu, P.A (1979). *West African Traditional Religion*. Ibadan: Onibonje Press and Book Industries Ltd, p.217.

has broken the rule and offended the gods". [182] If nothing is done at this time, terror will be unleashed in the community.

Anigbo noted that, "there are also *nso ani* which are considered very outrageous and to which people are expected to react to spontaneously. The most known is *itikpo isi monwu* (to shatter the head of the mask dancer)." [183] The expression is however figurative for it means 'an action or actions designed to pass information about the nature of the mask dancer to woman or to the uninitiated male.' This is a serious disrespect shown for the masking spirit and is considered grave and summarily dealt with.

At this juncture, the research would consider thematically grave offences and how they are done away with in Igbo land.

Cardinal Offences and Methods of Disposal in Igbo Land

Chukwu (eds) and other scholars like Iroebgu, discussed in detail some of the offences that were and are still considered abomination in Africa and especially Igbo land. We have touched them briefly but now shall consider them thematically.

Homicide

Mores require that human life be kept sacred. Homicide or *igbu ochu* or murder was the greatest abominations. Iroegbu said, "to kill a kith or

---

[182] Ajah, P.O (2007). *African Traditional Religion*. Uburu: Truth and Life Publication Ltd, p.289.

[183] Anigbo, O.A.C (1992). *Igbo Elite and Western Europe*. Onitsha: Africana-Feb Publishers Limited, p.51

kin or any member of one's community merited either capital punishment or total banishment from the community." [184]

Chukwu, Okonkwo and Kalu asserted that, "homicide is seriously frowned upon, even when it is unintentional; so much that an attempted or a demonstrated threat menace to inflict a machete cut on someone is forbidden. The sharp or a pointed end of the machete must be struck on the ground to douse or tamper the hot blood of anger." [185]

In Bende, when homicide is committed, the murderer's family often pleaded with the victim's family to spare the life of the culprit and in earlier times, usually offered one of their children as substitute (*ikura ochu*) for the deceased. In most cases, homicide culprit fled the town to avoid the wrath of the community and the gods whose norms he had flagrantly violated. In any case, he must be banished from the community. This was the case with Okonkwo in Achebe's Things Fall Apart. In this story Achebe noted that "the only course open to Okonkwo who mistakenly killed the son of the deceased Ezulu during his funeral was to flee from the clan. It was a crime against the earth goddess to kill a clan's man and a man who committed it must flee from the land." [186] Not only did Okonkwo flee into exile, his houses were burnt down and he must spend seven years in exile before returning to his homeland.

All these need to be done in order to cleanse the land (*iju ala*) to appease the offended gods, ancestors and the innocent blood that had been shed.

---

[184] Iroegbu, P (1994). *Enwisdomization and African Philosophy*. Owerri: International Universities Press, p. 91

[185] Chukwu, C.C, Okonkwo, G.A and Kalu, E.O, p.237.

[186] Achebe, C. (1958). *Things Fall Apart*. London: Heinemann, p.99.

Stealing

Iwuagwu said,

> "stealing is a serious offence in the traditional society which was treated according to the gravity of the offence. It is a mark of bad characters. In the pre-colonial African setting, the notorious thief was either heavily fined or openly disgraced, or sold into slavery or killed. There was no sympathy whatsoever for the thief." [187]

On the other hand Okafor noted that "stealing of seedlings and other kinds of theft like removing a property on which a sample of earth is placed to indicate ownership are regarded as *aru* or *nso ala* (abominaton)[188]." This kind of theft was regarded as fundamental break of the law.

When a thief (*onye oshi*) is caught and eventually with the stolen object or objects say yam seedlings or any other item, he is given a public beating, bald-shaven, stripped naked, draped with itchy weed and compelled to dance along the villages and sometimes around the market square with his loot and empty snail shells hung around his neck as a public odium and a powerful deterrent measure. People shunned the culprit and would at the slightest provocation spite him with the experience.

Suicide

This is a crime against humanity. It is an act by which one decided to take owns life, either by hanging or poisoning oneself. Life is sacrosanct

---

[187] Iwuagwu, A.O (1998). *African Traditional Religion: Students' Handbook.* Owerri: Ager Publishers, p.157.

[188] Okafor, F.U (1992). *Igbo Philosophy of Law*. Enugu: Fourth Dimension Pub, p.42.

and must not be treated with levity. Africans and especially, the Igbo love their lives and value it. It is an offence not just for the offender but to the entire community. It is an abomination. Suicide victims are denied a decent burial to serve as a deterrent to those contemplating the action. Having desecrated the land and denied mankind his valuable contributions to life, he does not deserve a burial or mourning.

In Achebe's work when Okonkwo took his life for fear of being manhandled by the white man, having killed one of them and discovered that his people were not ready to go to war against the white man, he took his life. This was a taboo in the land. The people cannot even touch his body not to talk of bringing him down from the tree. Achebe noted, "It is an abomination for a man to take his own life. It is an offence against the earth, and a man who commits it will not be buried by his clansman. His body is evil, and only strangers may touch it." [189] Okonkwo, despite being a great man, died a disgraceful death and must be buried like a dog.

In some communities in Igbo land such victims are not buried at all. Their bodies are thrown into the evil forest- *ajo ohia* and are devoured by wild beats and birds, as a sign of penalty and atonement for the heinous crime. Such people are neither received by the ancestors, nor do they have the ability to reincarnate. They usually transform into evil spirits, terrorizing their communities.

Sorcery

Sorcery (*igwo nsi*) is a heinous crime in Igbo land and Africa in general. This is a situation where somebody indulges in killing other people in the community through sorcery or poisoning. When somebody is suspected to be a sorcerer (*onye nsi*) such a person is taken to the

[189] Achebe, C, p.165.

shrine and concoctions are given him/her by the chief priest or the *dibia*. If the person is guilty, he/she will start to confess (*isa n'ire*). The person will mention those he killed through poisoning and those he intends to kill.

In some communities, such a person is treated the way criminals are treated. They are stripped naked, shaved with broken bottle, dragged through the community with people singing around him, flogging and spiting at him and is finally dragged out of the village into exile for a number of years. When the years of exile expire, the person returns home and pays the fine that will be given him and engages in a ritual feast of reunion known as *oriko*. It is only after this that such a person can now be reintegrated into the community, having ascertained that such evil act will not be practiced again. [190]

Other forms of Offences Disposal for Inclusive Social Control in the Past and Present

There was no system of imprisonment during the period under consideration. When an abomination was committed as we have variously noted, depending on the gravity of the offence like murder; the offenders were sent to exile or may be perpetually dedicated to the gods. Such a person becomes (*osu*) outcast. In some communities, the length of time one spends in exile depends on the offence. Other forms offences disposals include ostracism or excommunication and public shaming.

Ostracism is a socio-economic embargo that prohibits economic and social interactions with a blacklisted culprit. Nobody buys from, sells to and renders assistance to or interacts with him/her. It may be so total that nobody takes a burning coals from his/her fire place to stoke one's

---

[190] Nwankwo, S.C., p.67

stove and he/she cannot take from anybody‘s either. [191] Onyozili and Ebbe noted that, “a person excommunicated in pre-colonial Igbo land was lost in the crowd.” [192] Such a person will have neighbours but will always be lonely. Even when he/she is in need, nobody will help him/her. It is also believed that in death, he/she would neither be able to transmigrate nor reincarnate. It is in fact the fear of communal sanction, the thought of non-reincarnation, and non-transmigration after death that keeps members’ behaviours in check.

Ostracism servers the organic link of the culprit with the society and he/she ceases to exist as a living entity in their minds. His/her presence is considered *putrescence ad spat at.* No one greets or acknowledges greeting from him/her. Ostracism declares the culprit a *persona non grata*. It is a form of isolationism that inflicts psychological torture on the victim, meant to teach the lesson that an individual cannot be greater than the community (*otu onye anaghi aka oha*) and enforce compliance with the public norm by streamlining individual’s interest with that of the community for the common good. In fact in Africa, the individual apart from the community is not anything real, non-existent.

On the other hand, public shaming is another stringent method of disposing of offences in Igbo land. Crimes in Africa are punished by satire in the form of caricaturing songs that make jest of the repulsive and repugnant conduct of the culprit, sometimes for a crime that had already been punished. This method of bringing a culprit to social opprobrium is frequently employed during certain annual festivals. It is a social prick on the conscience of the culprit and his/her family. The aim is to correct and deter by condemning vices and upholding the positive norms and values of the society. Its efficiency lies in

---

[191] Chukwu, C.C, Okonkwo, G.A and Kalu, E.O, p.36.

[192] Onyeozili, E.C ed., p.36.

psychology. The substance of the satire lies in truth; they were not defamatory in content.

Agents of Social Control in Pre-Colonial Igbo Land

It has already been noted that there was no law court as we have it now where people are formally reported and proceedings carried out for proper adjudication of offences. There were however, institutions and agents that were consigned with matters that contradict social order, whose responsibility, it was to intervene and administer appropriate punishment to offenders. Most of the times justice in traditional African society was never delayed, offenders were promptly judged and punishment or penalty meted out without delay to douse the anger of the gods and those who were offended. In pre-colonial Africa such responsibilities were vested into the hands of the divinities, ancestors, masquerades, the use of *ofo* and *ogu* symbols, through oaths and covenants and other institutions like men and women organizations. In what follows, we shall examine few of these agents in detail.

Divinities

The divinities play intermediary roles between the supreme God and the people. Sacrifices are and prayers made to them are directed to the supreme God. They are powerful agents when it comes to social control. Some of the divinities that existed in pre-colonial Africa especially in Igbo land were: the mother Earth- *Ala*, the *Amadioha*, thunder divinity and the sun god *Anyanwu*. These were powerful agents of the *Chukwu*-Supreme Being. The Supreme Being vested on these divinities the powers to dispense justice and restore peace and order in the communities of Igbo land where they operate.

Iwuagwu said, "Sometimes God may be asked to arbitrate in land cases, or to destroy a thing in order to establish justice or to remove charm or poison planted by an enemy." [193] Uchendu described the cult of divinities as the highest "court of appeal" in Igbo judiciary system in pre-colonial times. [194] It was known as the "oracle." The most famous oracles in traditional Igbo land were the *Agbala* of Awka, the *Ibini Ukpabi* of Arochukwu (the long Juju) and the *Haba* of Agulu among others. The common characteristics of the oracles and their operators were shrouded in a strict code of secrecy and an institutionalized intelligence service.

The Ancestral Spirits

The ancestors are the past heroes of Africa traditional religious practitioners. They are the guardians of morality. Ifesieh described the ancestors as:

> Those highly honoured, great, gentle, wise, faithful influential respected as Dibuno/Dibiuno, Ndichie and by virtue of their children (begotten) and their activities became fathers of clans, villages and towns but have undergone a physical change (death) in their good matured and ripe ages but then are still living and are still 'members' of their respective families whose ide/pillars they were and are ...[195]

The ancestors do not only guard morality, they equally enforce morality in African communities. The cult of the ancestors is thus a model for evaluating human behaviour. To this end, the ancestors help

---

[193] Iwuagwu, A.O, p.113

[194] Uchendu, V.C (1965). *The Igbo of South Eastern Nigeria*. Chicago: Holt, Rinchart and Winston.

[195] Ifesieh, E.I (1976). "The Igbo Family in a Changing Society." Ph.D Dissertation, University of Salzburg, p.129.

to enforce morality by encouraging or rewarding the living with prosperity and punishing the immoral and unjust in the society.

Ugwu carefully observed that, "it is palpable that the ancestors detest adultery, fornication, incest, suppression, gossip and witch-hunting." [196] In some cases an accused person is summoned to the ancestral shrine before the council of elders and ordered to pick a lobe of kola-nut from the ancestral altar and eat. If the accused is guilty but out of sheer boldness or instigation eats the kola-nut, he faces instant death. If on the contrary, the accused is innocent, provable only by surviving the oath after one full month of twenty-eight days (*izu assa*).

Masquerade Institutions

The masquerade institutions or organizations or secret societies also help in the enforcement of morality in Africa. Orji, Awolawu and Dopamu argued that masquerades have a great responsibility of standing out for justice and fair play by helping to enforce the laws of the land. Orji observed that, "masquerade was successfully used for the maintenance of peace and enforcement of laws and regulations." [197]

Awolalu and Dopamu noted that:

> "Originally the secret societies were instituted for the purpose of self-preservation and for the preservation of the community. They enforced and maintained traditions, customs and regulated

---

[196] Ugwu, C.O (2002). "Sources and Enforcement of Morality in Igbo Traditional Society." In Religion, Morality and West African Society. Accra: Wesley Printing Press, p.122.

[197] Orji, O.M (1999). *The History and Culture of Igbo People before the Advent of the White Man*. Nkpor: Jet Publishers, p.156..

> attitudes. In this way, they became the 'power' of the community where they functioned. "[198]

Describing the roles of masquerades in Arondizuogu of Imo State, Nwankwo citing Obioha articulated some of the reasons for the institution of masquerade in Igbo land and especially in Arondizuogu. He said, "the institution of *mmonwu* serves three-fold functions namely: entertainment, arm of government and a corrective instrument." [199] Masquerades serve as institution that dispenses justice, the last hope of the common man in Arondizuogu; through their roles the people usually experience peace and unity.

Okafor observed that, "there were no specialized courts as such entrusted with judicial matters. Judicial methods may at times appear informal, but they follow recognized if diverse lines. These include among other institutions, the *mmonwu* (masquerade) society." [200] This corroborates with the observation made by Ilogu on the functions of masquerades in Igbo land. He said, "The *otu muo* (masquerade society) members also perform some political duties; they guard the village against thieves, collect fines from people pronounced guilty of offences and help in seeing that *aru* (abominations) are not hidden. They stand out for justice and fair play by helping to enforce laws of the land." [201]

Similarly, Onunwa accentuated the above new points when he wrote that:

> "Offenders of public morality (thieves, adulterers, witches) are mercilessly beaten or flogged by masquerades. The maskers of

---

[198] Awolawu and Dopamu, p.220.

[199] Nwankwo, S.C (2014). A Socio-religious and Ethical Roles of Igbo Women in Nation Building. An Unpublished Ph.D Dissertation Submitted to Imo State University Owerri, p.131.

[200] Okafor, F.U p.7.

[201] Ilogu, E. (1974). *Christianity and Igbo Culture*. New York: Nok Publishers, p.102.

these secret clubs are used to enforce the ruling or decisions of the council of elders of the village by the way they display uncontrolled power just like the Muo (Spirits)."[202]

Masquerade as enforcers of morality as the plenipotentiary agents of the deities or spirits. They have full powers to punish any immoral conduct and restoring peace and harmony in the community.

Council of Elders in the Village

This is one of institutions that dispensed justice during the period under discussion. Council of elders is a conglomerate of elderly men who are family heads in the community. Each village was made up of people who were united by ties of consanguinity. The cases that reach the village or community council were inter-family, civil and criminal victimizations. Civil matters were settled amicably but criminal matters had double barreled penalty. The convicted offender had to pay back whatever he took away from the victim by restitution or compensation. If the person becomes a notorious offender, other stringent measures may be applied, some of which we have discussed before. However, this may vary from community to community. [203]

Daughters of the Family (*Umuada*)

Nwankwo said that, *Umuada* play both social, religious, ethical and political roles in Igbo land. The roles of *umuada* as peace builders and conflict mediators within and outside their traditional maiden homes are

---

[202] Onunwa, U (1990). *Studies in Igbo Traditional Religion*. Obosi: Pacific Publishers, p.29.

[203] Nwankwo, S.C. (2017), p.82.

well pronounced. *Umuada* are known as peace builders and conflict mediators."[204]

Onunwa writing on the roles of *umuada* in Igbo land said:

> "Umuada acting through their leaders exercise such moral powers that no one questions within the community. They act as the last court of appeal in traditional and unduplicated Igbo society. At times they are often invited to settle family disputes that deity the orders of the elders or in modern times, the law court."[205]

When a person is accused of murder or sorcery, *umuada* in Arondizuogu would resort to administering oath when the matter is brought to them. The parties involved would be required to swear an oath using *ekwu nji igwe* (three legged cooking stand) or *akpa aka umuada* and *ekwe oha* (hand bags belonging to *umuada* and the community wooden gong). It is very dangerous to attempt swearing an oath with these objects if one's hands are not clean. The bags are believed to contain some traditional items which can hurt anyone guilty of the offence he/she is being accused of.

Obi commenting on the functions of *Umuada* in Igbo land said:

> The institution of Umuada (married daughters) is highly respected in Igbo land. They can hold the community to ransom for various moral reasons. They discipline erring women with various sanctions, support married women in any wise decision taken for the progress of the community maintain peace between husband and wife, family and family, community and

---

[204] Nwankwo, S.C (2014), p.101.

[205] Onunwa, U p.136.

community. They checkmate and balance their dual roles as married daughters and wives. [206]

Onyike said "women are important peace makers in their ancestral villages as *Umuada* (daughter born in the village or town). In traditional Igbo culture, *umuada* are usually invited to resolve conflicts that men and ndinyom (women married into the town) were not able to resolve. In this case, their decision is final." [207] In some Igbo communities, they were seen as the last court of appeal. They sanction, penalize and enthrone sanity among family which constituted their maiden homes.

According to Quacoopome "besides the men and women groups, the traditional religious leaders namely: the traditional priests, the medicine men, diviners, seers, mediums and prophets and prophetesses are seen as servants of divinities and repositories of national customs among the Igbo. They engage in such duties as praying, healing, proffering solutions to human problems, using divination objects to find out hidden or mysterious things, discovering human problems through prophecy and ecstatic uplift." [208] These functions or contributions are all geared towards the optimistic goals of ensuring and maintaining a morally just society. Their lifestyles are exemplary and the members of the society emulate them, thereby building a virile, morally sanctions Africa/Igbo society.

---

[206] Obi, D. (2010). "The Role of African Women in Nation Building". In *Kpim of Feminism Issues and Women in a Changing World.* Eds. Ukagba, G.U, Obioma, D.O and Nwankwor, I.J, Canada: Tranford Publishing, pp.174-175.

[207] Onyike, N.B (2009). "Women as Peace Makers at Home and Outer Society." Aba: Government Press, p.7.

[208] Quarcoopome, T.N.O (1987). *West African Traditional Religion*: Ibadan:AUP, p.74

Religion and Morality as Panacea to Contemporary Social Ills

The role of religion in the society when rightly applied includes the maintenance of social order or control; thus giving cohesion, meaning and purpose to life and the social construction of the sacred. Religion and morality or ethics correlate. African is notoriously religious according to Mbiti. [209] The importance of religion and morality in ensuring social control in Africa cannot be over emphasized. In fact throughout human history the positive values of religion have been adjudged to have outweighed it dysfunctional role. [210]

Religion is however, good in itself. Through religion and ethics based social control, Africa have promoted social solidarity by reinforcing social values and principles that made the society then a habitable place for all. Obi, citing Durkheim noted that "Religion promotes social cohesion, uniting the members of the society through shared values and norms. Social life is impossible without shared values and moral beliefs that form the collective conscience. In their absence, there would be no social order, social control, and social solidarity." [211] Religion and ethics promote solidarity among members of the society through shared values and norms. Religious and moral values like, respect for human dignity and sanctity of life, respect for cultural and customary norms and constituted authorities, truth-telling, honesty, love for one another, empathy, innocence and hardworking, justice and fair play, are all enshrined in the religious and moral principles of a given

---

[209] Mbiti, J.S (1969). *African Religions and Philosophy*. London: Heinemann, p.1 Quarcoopome, T.N.O (1987). *West African Traditional Religion*: Ibadan:AUP, p.74

[210] Manus, C.U (2006), "Religion and Politics in a Multi-Ethnic Society," Orita: Ibadan Journal of Religious Studies XXVIII (June-December).

[211] Obi, C, A (2013), "Religion as basis of Social Order" in Kpim of Social of Social Order. U.S.A: Xlibris Corperation, p. 437.

society; written or unwritten. Any form of breach in the flow of the system through acts contrary to the statutory code of conduct will be detrimental to both the individual and the society at large.

In other words the people are supposed to be taught the tenets of religion, ethics and culture from the cradle. This will serve as a check to constant flagrant abuses of constituted authority and lack of respect to human life and worth prevalent in our society today.

Conclusion

We started this research by identifying the place of religion and morality in ensuring a stable society. The work uncovered various behaviours and practices that could be categorized under serious offenses whose consequences are detrimental not to just the offender but to the entire community. There were various means of disposing offenses in pre-colonial African societies, especially, those of Igbo land. The work further noted various agents involved in social control. Through these agents, African people were able to dispense justice, restore peace, order and tranquility to the society.

Recommendations

The researcher recommends the following, based on the work's findings:

- That both the elderly people and the young ones be educated on the core moral values of their respective societies and as well made to know the consequences of their evil actions to both themselves and the entire society.
- That some of the stringent measures used in disposing of offences and ensuring peace and tranquil atmosphere during the

period under study, be re-introduced. Such measures like public shaming and ostracism. This could reduce the rate at which evil and social ills snowball in our society today.

- That the roles of elders in council and women groups in restoring order in the society be heightened. That their judgment be recognised by the government.
- That masquerade societies be elevated as law enforcement agents in communities where they are, to aid the police in the fight against indiscipline and social menace.

References

Achebe, C. (1958). *Things Fall Apart*. London: Heinemann.

Adeyemo, T (1979). *Salvation in African Traditional Religion*. Nairobi: Evangel Publishing House.

Ajah, P.O (2007). *African Traditional Religion*. Uburu: Truth and Life Publication Ltd, p.289

Anigbo, O.A.C (1992). *Igbo Elite and Western Europe*. Onitsha: Africana-Feb Publishers Limited.

Awolawu, J.O and Dopamu, P.A (1979). *West African Traditional Religion*. Ibadan: Onibonje Press and Book Industries Ltd.

Ayodeji, O.S (2013). "Religious Values and Corruption in Nigeria: a Dislocated Relationship. *Journal of Educational and Social Research*. Italy: Vo. 4 No.3. MCSER Pub.

Chukwu, C.C, Okonkwo, G.A and Kalu, E.O (2013). *The History and Culture of Old Bend and the Emergence of Umunna*. Lagos: Serenity Publishers.

"Crime and the Impact on Modern Society," retrieved from https://www.ukessays.com/essays/crimonolgy/crime-and-the-impact-on-modern-society-criminology-essay.php?ref=1

George, I.N and Ukpong, D.E. (2013). "Contemporary Social Problems in Nigeria and its Impact on National Development: Implication for Guidance and Counselling Services." *Journal of Educational and Social Research.* Uyo: Vol. 3 (2) May 2013.

Ifesieh, E.I (1976). "The Igbo Family in a Changing Society." Ph.D Dissertation, University of Salzburg.

Ilogu, E. (1974). *Christianity and Igbo Culture*. New York: Nok Publishers.

Iroegbu, P (1994). *Enwisdomization and African Philosophy*. Owerri: International Universities Press.

Iroegbu, P and Echekwube, A. (2005). *"What is Ethics?"* In *Kpim of Morality: Ethics General, Special and Professional*. Ibadan: Heinemann Educational Books (Nigeria) Plc.

Ituma, E.A (2015). *Basic Research Guide for Humanities and Social Sciences*. Nsukka: Timex.

Iwuagwu, A.O (1998). *African Traditional Religion: Students' Handbook*. Owerri: Ager Publishers.

Manus, C.U (2006), "Religion and Politics in a Multi-Ethnic Society," Orita: Ibadan Journal of Religious Studies XXVIII (June-December).

Mbiti, J.S (1969). *African Religions and Philosophy*. London: Heinemann, p.1

Nwankwo, S.C (2014). A Socio-religious and Ethical Roles of Igbo Women in Nation Building. An Unpublished Ph.D Dissertation Submitted to Imo State University Owerri.

Nwankwo, S.C (2017). *Understanding Religious Ethics: An Exercise in Afrocentric Ethicalism.* Aba: Rainbow Printing Press.

Obaje, Y.A (2002). "Religion and Morality as Instrument of Transformationm in West African Society." In Kudadjie (ed.) (2002). Religion, Morality and West African Society. Accra: Wesley Printing Press.

Obi, C.A (2013). "Religion as basis of Social Order." In Kpim of Social Order. Edited by Ukagba, G.U, Obi, D.O and Nwankwor, I.K. U.S.A: Xlibris Corporation.

Obi, D. (2010). "The Role of African Women in Nation Building". In Kpim of Feminism Issues and Women in a Changing World. Eds. Ukagba, G.U, Obioma, D.O and Nwankwor, I.J, Canada: Tranford Publishing.

Obilor, J.I (2010). *Many Religions one God.* Owerri: Matts Books Publishers.

Okafor, F.U (1992). *Igbo Philosophy of Law*. Enugu: Fourth Dimension Pub.

Okere, T (2006). "Religion, Morality and Governance in Nigeria." Lecture Delivered at Owerri: Multi Purpose Hall.

Onunwa, U (1990). *Studies in Igbo Traditional Religion*. Obosi: Pacific Publishers.

Onyeozili, E.C and Ebbe, O.N.I (2002). "Social Control in Pre-colonial Igbo land of Nigeria." *African Journal of Criminology and Justice Studies: AJCJS, Vol.6, Nos.1 &2* November.

Onyike, N.B (2009). "Women as Peace Makers at Home and Outer Society." Aba: Government Press.

Orji, O.M (1999). *The History and Culture of Igbo People before the Advent of the White Man*. Nkpor: Jet Publishers.

Quarcoopome, T.N.O (1987). *West African Traditional Religion*: Ibadan: AUP.

Uchendu, V.C (1965). *The Igbo of South Eastern Nigeria*. Chicago: Holt, Rinchart and Winston

Ugwu, C.O (2002). "Sources and Enforcement of Morality in Igbo Traditional Society." In Religion, Morality and West African Society. Accra: Wesley Printing Press.

Wikipedia: The Free Encyclopedia. http://en. wikipedia.org/wiki/social order. Retrieved on April 28, 2016.

16

WITCHCRAFT AND MAGICOLOGY AS A HUMAN RIGHTS PHENOMENON: IN SEARCH OF ETHICAL SPIRITUAL INTEGRITY

Clement Majawa

Introduction

'Witchcraft' is a broad and complex term. It refers to 'the use of magic', whilst magic itself can be defined as 'manipulation and coercion' of hidden powers in nature in order to benefit or harm people.[212] *Witchcraft* and *magic* are often used interchangeably creating abuse of the concept. Philosophically witchcraft refers to the cunning, manipulative and skilful use of wisdom to benefit a person or community progressively or destructively. In ethnographic studies, magic has both positive and negative impact. Some researchers in Global North have a biased presentation of magic and witchcraft in Africa. Others consider it as manifestation of ignorance, primitive, underdevelopment or limitation of thought. There is need to reveal the truth about the generic magic and 'witchcraft' and its contribution to better understanding of the African philosophy, mysteries and cosmology. The paper employs the *Theory of Witchcraft Stigmatization* as an Issue of Human Rights Abuse in need of integrated sensitization approach by Church and State, and *Ethical Psycho-Spiritual Integrity.*

---

[212]Clement Majawa, Professor, Catholic University of Eastern Africa.

Africa and international community should uphold the complexity of magic and witchcraft which has to be addressed with a multidimensional approach leading to transformational common good.

Complex Concept

Social anthropologist and historian, Donald Mcphearson (2003) observed that the concepts of *'magic'* and *'witchcraft'* are very complex and controversial because many people use them interchangeably and often they are misunderstood in meaning and functionality. Many scientific researches worldwide done by anthropologists, sociologists, educationists, theologians, philosophers, historians psycho-analysts, psychologists, medical doctors, psycho-therapists, spiritual counsellors, exorcists, politicians, professors of religions, government and religious leaders etc. conclude with statistical verification that the reality of magic and witchcraft creates superstitious fear, hinders personal transformation and disturbs many social institutions.[213] Judy Ann Nock (2018) cites further that another complexity is observed in the fact that there is a diversity of Magic: magic of goodness and magic of evil; magic of wisdom and magic of 'error'; magic of science and magic of witchcraft.[214]

Experiences of superstition, magic and witchcraft are real in the world. Pope Benedict XVI said when he visited Angola in Southern Africa, on March 21, 2009: "Witchcraft is real in Africa, as elsewhere in the world. It is a complex reality needing a profound strategic approach to address it. Pastoral experience shows that destructive magic and witchcraft are one of the great conversional challenges today needing a

---

[213] D. Macphearson The Contemporary Understanding of Witchcraft and Sorcery, Manchester: Burns & Hills Publications, 2003. 11-17.

[214] Judy A. Nock The Modern Witchcraft: Book of Natural Magick, New York: Adams Media Publishers, 2018, 33-38.

multidimensional consulted awareness, research, discussion, engagement and solution by all people of God (both in Church/religions and society) for effective evangelization and sustainable progress in a nation."[215]

Methodology

The study used *Convergent Parallel Mixed Method Research Design* which enabled the use of concurrent procedures and merged quantitative and qualitative intellectual and experiential data as provided by various sources in order to provide a comprehensive analysis of the challenge or problem in question (Creswell, 2003).[216] This was complemented by and contextualized with the *Patristic 'Paideia' Methodological Approach* which explores the values from all cultures and institutions, and elevate them to high standards in the light of Christ's prophetic message for the highest common good. This design focuses on the true knowledge, beliefs and practices from various contexts, and when elevated by the Divine Wisdom, becomes an ethical standard for doing and enriching human and society activities. Every human being needs authentic epistemological and ethical rooting and routing to become a true person before God, humanity and nature: *Cosmo-thea-ndrian.*[217] (Majawa, 2014)[218] Thus, the study used oral, written and experiential wisdom from various local and international sources.

---

[215] Pope Benedict XVI, Pastoral Visit to Angola o 21st March, 2009.

[216] John W. Creswell, Research Design: Qualitative, Quantitative and Mixed Approaches, London: Sage Publications, 2003.

[217] Clement of Alexandria, Stromata, 1, 18, 18, 90, 1: SC 30.

[218] Clement Majawa, Patristic Education, Nairobi: Kijabe Publications, 2014.

Magic in Historical Wicca

In history, magic and witchcraft were defined by different scholars in various ways; some definitions are clear and others not. The definitions explicate some of the following insights:

- the wise or cunning use of intelligence and experience to influence society
- the use of various types of mysterious magical or mystical powers
- the practice of magic or sorcery by those outside the religious mainstream of a society.
- the practice of sorcery, enchantments and intercourse with spirits the use of certain kinds of supernatural or magical powers
- a diabolical conspiracy against religion or Christianity
- a cultural ideology which explains human misfortune by blaming it either on a supernatural entity or an evil person in the community
- .mysterious practices, generally dealing with spirits or deities, the afterlife, magic rituals
- a pantheistic, nature-based religion with possible pre-Christian roots
- teaching or explanation of mysterious events and negative experiences of life: diseases, famine, death, misfortunes, fear. [219]

Witchcraft has historically been applied to any action or influence on another person's mind, spirit, psychic, emotion, body or property against his or her will of social or religious order. Throughout history, witchcraft has been confused with magic. However, it should be stressed that the practice of magicology is not necessarily associated with evil or the infliction of harm, nor with diabolism. Magic was associated with

---

[219] Rosemary Ellen Guiley, *The Encyclopedia of Witches and Witchcraft,* New York: Facts On File, 1999.

wisdom and intelligence to explain mysteries of life and do things correctly and righteously for the common good. These wise people were referred to as Wiccans; the wise ones or righteous ones or societal or religious leaders. Because of their high intellectual acumen and wisdom many of them were advisors, counsellors, healers, mathematicians, astrologers, scientists, dream interpreters, businessmen, etc. Modern magic or Witchcraft is manipulation positively or negatively of the mind, spirit, psychic, emotion, five senses to create light or darkness, joy or fear, construction or destruction in society accompanied by mystic or mysterious powers or rituals or 'psychic technologies' Many witches do not believe in spirits, and most if them reject belief in a literal Devil or demons. Thus, simplistic understanding of magic or witchcraft needs scientific research and investigation.[220]

Magic are practices that call upon supernatural, mysterious and unseen forces to impact life positively or negatively. The positive use of such forces is 'Wicca'. Witchcraft is the use of these forces for negative ends and to extort evil. Witchcraft (black magic) has been found to exist in all cultures, religions and societies of the world. It is no coincidence that during the Enlightenment, witch hunts in Europe and North America became common. The aim was to cleanse, purify and rid society of evil people who practiced evil magic, regarded as unreasonable and dangerous. Witchcraft is said to be the most widespread cultural phenomenon in existence in the past, today, and throughout history. The belief in magic and witchcraft refuses to die. Even those who shun the ideas of witchcraft cannot discount the similarities and it prevalence in stories and events in the world.

---

[220] Kardia Zoe, Living Wicca Today, Pagan Holidays and Earth Magic: A Beginners Guide to traditions and Practices, London, 2014.

Witchcraft, its ideas and practice have spread across racial, religious, and language barriers from Asia to Africa to America.[221]

Brooks Alexander (2004) an expert on the occult and counterculture, gives a summary of certain distinctions between the terms *Wicca, witchcraft,* and *Neo-Paganism.* The socio-historical religious term *Wicca* evolved in history in reference to intellectual wisdom, analytical common sense, the art, the craft, the skill or the practice of secretive magic which manipulates human and world mystic forces to produce a new reality which can be beneficial or destructive in society. The word "wicca" is originally an Old English (Anglo-Saxon) word, meaning *"wise one" or 'wise trickster' or wise magician or a 'societal genius'*. It has Germanic root "wic" meaning to "bend" or to "turn". Those who followed the path of the magic-wisdom of numbers, stars, medicine, geometry, entertainment, science, logics and rationalism, etc. to reveal hidden truth about complex reality were called *Magicians.*[222] Rodney Weeds (1976) calls these wicca-magicians with a wise title: *Scientists* because they made intensive study, research and experiments with hidden or secret theories, figures, tricks and methodology or rituals to produce miraculous results. In the old days the wicca or wise magicians were in tune with the forces of nature, atmosphere, earth, secrets of the air, earth, water, atmosphere, forests, vegetation, human-cycle, etc. and were often seen as respected philosophers, healers, leaders and advisers in society because they understood the complexity of life and how to work with natural energies and social instincts in order to analyse, affect, heal, protect and promote everyday life.[223]

---

221 *Patrick Howard, The Philosophy and Functions of Wicca and Witchcraft, New York: Arts Publications, 1965, 202.*

222 Alexander Brooks, A. Witchcraft Goes Mainstream: Uncovering its Impact on You and Your Family, Eugene, OR: Harvest House Publishers, 2004, 56-60.

223 Rodney Weeds, *Wicca Magicians and Contemporary Scientists*, New York: Scribner Publications, 1976, 42-44.

Many wise wiccans were philosophers, mathematicians and scientists who honour and respect the earth, the atmosphere, and all its inhabitants, and we treat every soil, plant, animal and human as an aspect of the Divine. When we perform wise magic with intelligence and compassionate we do so with the utmost respect to the origin of divine wisdom (Supreme Being) and with the intention to harm none. Later the historical development of Wicca show that the concept of Wicca was often misunderstood, compromised and misinterpreted. Some Wicca used their intelligence, wisdom and experience for the common good; others used their wisdom to manipulate the vulnerable people and led them to fear, tension, pain and division for material or commercial gains. Wicca was neutral in function; it could be used to develop life and could be used to distort or destroy life.[224] It is important to note that not all Wiccans practice harmful magic, and not all who practice magic are Wiccan (*are the wise ones*) The good Biblical example of the ancient Wicca are the three Magi from the East; they are also referred to three Wise men (Wicca) or three kings, or three scientists of the heavenly bodies (astronomers) *(Luke 2:1-12).*

Greek Philosophy on Wisdom of Magic

Philosopher Pythagoras (580-500 BC) taught that the intellectual nature in a human being is superior to the sensual and physical nature, and founded a semi-religious order with rules and norms regulating behaviour and customs/rituals that demonstrated ethical beliefs. Pythagoras taught about a sharp dualism between mortal human bodies and immortal human souls. The human soul is linked to reason and supernatural wisdom which brings meaning and transformation to the society. Some people are endowed with more natural and supernatural

---

[224] Ibid.

wisdom to guide, protect and develop society. (Joe Jenkins, 1999). Thus, such category of people can use their wisdom to discern, teach, heal and sustain life. Such divine-humanistic wisdom evolved and later metamorphosed into '*Wicca' and 'White magic'*. It was construed to mean use of divinized-humanism to develop science, numeracy, geometry, astronomy, biology, legal integrity, artistic work, technological enterprise.[225]

Magicians, wise-craftologists or 'witches' of ancient Egypt, Greek, Romans, Sumeria, Babylonia and Mesopotamia invented an elaborate ideology and praxis of *constructive spirits* or *destructive spirits* or *Demonology*. They had a belief that the world was full of spirits and that most of these spirits were hostile. Each person was supposed to have their own spirit which would protect them from *Demons* and enemies, which could only be fought by the use of magic (including *amulets, incantations and exorcisms*). Wise witches in ancient Egypt purportedly used their wisdom and knowledge of geometry, numerology, astronomy, hydrological-cycle, amulets, spells, evil-eye, formulas and figures to bend the cosmic laws and powers to their purpose or that of their clients or society. The Greek's magic was close to their religion. It was called *Theurgy* the practice of rituals, magical in nature, performed secretly to invoke gods' beneficial action, and "*Mageia*", which often used poisonous substance or harmful objects to harm others.[226] Egpyt is considered by some scholars as the cradle of wise-magic (Wicca). St Clement of Alexandria (160-215) said: "Egypt is the mother of magicians". The Egyptian philosophy and religious wisdom, including the 'wicca' should be shared with the world community.[227]

---

[225] Joe Jenkins, *Ethics and Religion*, Oxford: Heinemann, 1999.

[226] Geraldine Pinch, Magic in Ancient Egypt, London: British Museum Press, 1994. 4-10.

[227] Clement of Alexandria, The Stromata or Miscellanies in Early Christian Writings, Book 2.

Magic and Witchcraft as Secret and Complex Reality

The complexity of the reality of black or destructive magic and witchcraft makes its definition and interpretation complex. Many scholars have given different definitions to fit different situations. While some are profound in content, others are too simplistic; yet some are conflictual in essence without systematic research parameters. Majawa (2017) has attempted to give a comprehensive definition and description:

> "Witchcraft is knowledge, belief, manifestation, practices and experience of controlled or uncontrolled mystic-psychosomatic (hidden) destructive evil power emanating from a person directly or indirectly due to the absence of Truth, and operates skilfully and secretly using various magical objects, rituals or medicines to manipulate vital forces of nature so as to deceive and mislead one while inflicting fear, superstition, faithfulness, hatred, suffering, illness, immorality and even destruction of life of a person, property or community, preventing the realization of the common good in the society".[228]

From this comprehensive definition come 14 categories and expressions of magic and witchcraft depending on their functionality in the society. (a) Contagious/ imitative magic (b) Homeopathic/Symbolic Magic (c) Hyper -active/Viagrasiosis Magic (d) Private/Evil Eyed magic (e) Innate/ generational/Family Magic (f) Egoistical/Passive /Silent Magic (g) Defensive and/Counteractive Magic (h)Religious sterilic Magic (i) Malapalavic Magic (j) Metamorphic Magic (k) Telecosmic Magic (l) Moral Destructive Magic (m) Bonding Accompanying Magic (n) Mortuary Magic (*Clement Majawa,2007).*

---

[228] Clement Majawa, Patristic Education, Nairobi: Kijabe Publishers, 2014, 30.

Human unearthed mysteries, secrets and hidden activities surround the reality of magic and witchcraft. These mystic phenomena have to be known in order to address them. John Mbiti (1969) cites that witchcraft is a term used more popularly to describe all sorts of evil employment of mystical power generally in a hidden and secret fashion. African peoples believe that there are individuals with evil intention who have access to mystical power which they employ secretly for destructive purpose in society.[229]

Derrick Alumbuwao (1998) cites that magic and witchcraft are essentially secretive and manipulative because they are religious, magical, mystical and mysterious in nature. Witchcraft uses hidden tricks, deceptive skills, mystic objects and its rituals are unknown to many.[230]

Does Magic and Witchcraft Exist?

Professor Robert Anderson (2013) research of Convergence and Divergence of Magic Today' revealed that beliefs, talks, studies, practices and impact of witchcraft is a reality that is not taken seriously in diverse contexts. It is greatly misunderstood and criticized by some, and greatly renounced, denounced, ridiculed, compromised and even rejected by others. Furthermore, the research showed that many people both literate and illiterate are ignorant about it, on the flip side the same groups of people including religious and non-religious alike embrace it seeking explanation and solution when encountered with challenges or mysteries of life.[231] Majawa in the book, *Borderline between*

---

[229] Clement Majawa, A Handbook of Borderline Between Christianity and Witchcraft, Nairobi: Kijabe Publications, 2017.

[230] Derrick Alumbuwao, Evolution of the Wisdom of Magic and Its Contribution to Civilization, London: Panaf Books, 1998, 103.

[231] Robert Anderson, Convergence and Divergence of Magic Today, London: Nelson Press, 2013.

Christianity and Witchcraft (2017) mentions that there are some who argue that 'magic' and 'witchcraft' do *Not* exist and are *Not* real, but are creation of ideological imagination, superstitious beliefs, cultural illusion, sub-conscious hallucination, manipulation of supernatural fantasy, or psycho-somatic primitive historical relics, etc. Thus, there is need to define 'existence'. Cambridge Advance Learners Dictionary (2003:424)[232] defines "exist" as to be real in visible or invisible dimensions. Alexander Pfeiffer (2010) explicates that existence follows the origin, identity, nature and destiny, nature and destiny of reality. He argues that reality exist as a human being perceives it.[233] It starts in the mind or thought or belief or idea or imagination, and then it exists in the heart, soul and spirit of a person. Then reality becomes sensual (5 senses) of a person: It exists in the Sight, Hearing, Smell, Taste and Touch. Patrick Robinson (1998) confirms that reality exists in nature or supernaturally in relation to human being who defines it.[234] These qualities apply to the reality of magic and witchcraft in various contexts.

Rudolf Otto's [1869-1937] Theory of Religion as a source of excitement, awe, fear and magic, cites, '*Imagination is the true foundation for magic and later witchcraft*'. On the other hand, a Scottish James Frazer [1854] developed a Theory that '*Magic is the Source of Religion*' and is applicable to all cultures. In the context of idea and magic, Majawa [2009] concludes his socio-anthropological and theological research with a statement that the reality of ideas, imagination, magic and witchcraft all begin in the mind, and so, controlling or curbing the vices of magic, sorcery or witchcraft has to

---

[232] Clement Majawa, A Handbook of Borderline Between Christianity and Witchcraft, Nairobi: Kijabe Publications, 2017, 22-27, 35-39.

[233] Alexander Pfeiffer, Human Consideration of Magic, Boston: Beacon Press, 2010. 89.

[234] Patrick Robinson, P. Natural and Supernatural Reality of the Invisible Powers, New York: Guild Press, 1998, 47-50.

begin with the mind. The mind should be educated, catechized, evangelized and transformed properly, if this socio-religious vice is to be properly addressed by the Church and State.

Thus Alyward Shorter (1990) asks a pertinent question, 'if magic and witchcraft is not real, why does it have significant impact in both Christian and non-Christian life, in the Church and secular life, among the educated and illiterate? Why is it refusing to die?' [*Shorter, 'Devil Worship in Kenya', The Tablet, 25/09/1999, 1290*] A Comboni Missionary, Fernando Domingues states 'Magic is real but morally neutral because it can be used either for good or for evil'; to construct or destruct life. In the world there are both: white magic and black magic [*Christ Our Healer, Nairobi, 2000, 22.* A leading African Moral Theologian Laurenti Magesa (2002) argues a step further to unveil the effects of fear and insecurity which leads many people to the beliefs and practices of witchcraft. He says, 'Most of the time, superstition, suffering, sickness, misfortune, destruction and death have their origin in 'witchcraft. As a psychosomatic reality, witchcraft hides under and uses religious power to convince and influence people negatively. Thus as witchcraft ideas, images and symbols penetrate human mind they become the personification on incarnation of all that is anti-life and therefore the ultimate enemy of life, evangelization and progress on earth.

Research on Nature, Causes and Impact of Witchcraft

Mkhatswa's Research in Southern Africa

Alexander Mkhwatswa from South Africa did research in 10 different South African countries including: South Africa, Namibia, Botswana, Swaziland, Lesotho, Zimbabwe, Zambia, Mozambique, Angola and Malawi. The findings were very informative. Magic and witchcraft are a result of the following 12 reasons: (a) Lack of Education; (b) Fear and Insecurity; (d) Ignorance of Christian Faith and

Identity; (d) Poverty and Underdevelopment; (e) Injustices and Exploitation; (f) Diseases and Sickness; (g) Oppressive Cultural Beliefs and Practices; (h) Struggle for Power, Dominance and Influence; (i) Emergence of Devil Worship and Satanism (j) Infiltration of materialistic and secular religions; (k) Negative influence of globalization (l) Abuse of human rights and institutional constitutionalism. Further researches show that many people engage in the practice of magic and 'witchcraft' for security, protection, health and healing, economic and political prosperity, spiritual and psychological wellbeing, sexual and marital fecundity, and social status (Majawa, 2017).[235]

Witchcraft's Detrimental Impact on Society

Many researches in Africa and global contexts reveal that issues of magic and witchcraft should be taken seriously because whether these phenomena are accepted or denied, they have great detrimental impact on personal life, culture, religion, government and societal existence. In a universal consideration, these socio-religious realities are: (a) Barrier to religious and Christianity transformation; (b) Jeopardizes sacramental, religious and marital lives; (c) Prevents socio-economic and political progress and development; (d) Limits the process of local, continental and universal globalization; (e) Advances the anti-life; anti-moral and atheistic agenda; (f) Promotes community tension, disorder, injustice and underdevelopment; (g) Perpetuate the culture of fear, suspicions and superstition; (h) Escalates the power of evil, unrighteousness, sin, Satanism and Devil worship; (i) Impedes the rule of law, justice and peace in organizations; (j) Contributes to global

[235] Majawa, Patristic Education, 2014.

warming, deforestation; environmental degradation and ecological crisis (k) Leads to ignorant, poverty and disease and social upheavals

Positive and Negative Magic in Society

White magic which is correct use of supernatural powers for good intention; and is often also referred to as "natural or constructive magic". Black Magic is the negative use of energies and powers for evil and selfish purposes in the community. Robert M. Place's 2009 book, Magic and Alchemy provides a broad modern definition of White magic and Black magic:

(i) White magic is also called "positive magic" or "high magic" or "constructive magic". The purpose of white magic is invoke 'good spirits' to "do good" or "to bring progress in society" "bring the practitioner to a higher spiritual state" of enlightenment or consciousness or transformation. *Good or white magic* is accepted and esteemed, used mainly by specialists such as medicine men, diviners and rainmakers. These practitioners use their knowledge, experience or tap into this power for the benefit of their community. Examples of beneficial use of magic power include, the treatment of diseases, counteracting misfortune, neutralizing or destroying evil power or witchcraft.[236] Later this beneficial magic was linked to supernatural powers above (God). These powers are acquired through prayer to the divine, intercession of religious leaders, or through intermediary of the living dead and spirits. Spiritual power is usually channelled through physical means, rituals and performances.

(ii) *Evil or black magic* involves belief in and practice of tapping malaise (evil) powers and using this destructive extraordinary power to harm human beings and their property. Belief here is largely based

---

[236] Robert Michael Place, Magic and Alchemy, New York: Infobase Publishers, 2009, 33-43.

on evil, ignorance, fear, suspicion, jealousy, malice, hatred, ignorance, sickness or false accusation. Such mystical power is termed black magic, evil magic or sorcery. Many African communities believe that all ills, misfortunes, sicknesses, accidents, tragedies, sorrows, dangers, unhappy mysteries, etc., are caused by evil mystical powers. Accidents, cases of barrenness, misfortunes or other unpleasant experiences are considered mystical experiences of a deeply religious nature. Black magic is manifested in society through sorcery, wizardry and witchcraft.[237]

Religious and Societal Leaders Acknowledge the Reality of Magic

Benedict XVI's Apostolic Exhortation: *Africae Munus* [19/11/2011] acknowledges the reality of magic and witchcraft on the African Continent as elsewhere in the world: destructive magic *and Witchcraft, which has some links with traditional religions, is currently experiencing a certain revival. Old fears and superstitions are re-surfacing and creating paralyzing bonds of subjection. Anxiety over health, well-being, children, the climate, and protection from evil spirits at times lead people to have recourse to practices of traditional African religions that are incompatible with Christian teaching (AM 93).*

Furthermore, the working document, *Instrumentum Laboris* of the Second Special Assembly of the Synod of African Bishops [*Benedict XVI June 2005*] made a serious remark on the existence of magic and witchcraft that "Some false beliefs and practices from African cultures demand special attention and research". It is an evidenced fact that superstitious magic and witchcraft is tearing villages and urban areas, These phenomena need thorough investigation by the Church, academia

---

[237] Ibid.

and government because they are a barrier to deeper evangelization and sustainable development (no.32). The Symposium of Episcopal Conferences of Africa and Madagscar (2009) made a prophetic challenge to the African continent: *"Each particular Church in Africa should embark on a serious campaign against fear and belief in magic or witchcraft, and other negative and harmful traditional practices" [SECAM: Input by the Pastoral Departments of SECAM: Justice and Peace. October 2009].*

Africa on a Socio-religious Crossroad: Christianity versus Witchcraft

Many scholars agree that the root cause of destructive magic and witchcraft is evil. In life, evil is real and accompanies all human activities. Magic and witchcraft are dangerous to religious belief and socio-moral-political integrity. Magic and Witchcraft are dangerous to one's Christian spiritual and moral life because it operates within the realm of the sins of *unbelief, idolatory and superstition.* The Catechism of the Church explains that "*superstition is a departure from the worship that we give to the true God.*" It is manifested in *idolatry*, as well as in various forms of divination and magic. Destructive magic and witchcraft leads people to the divinization of natural objects, agents, rituals and events. This breaks the first commandment of the Decalogue "You shall have no other gods except me". (Ex. 20:3; Dt. 5:7). In the final philosophical, socio–anthropological and theological analysis, witchcraft, as all other forms of superstition is *a sin against the virtue of religion.* Thus, it opposes Christianity and other religions. The crucial question today is, if Christian evangelization has been in Africa for three millennia, why is witchcraft still persistent? Why is it refusing to die? Three reasons are identified:

(a). A spiritual dilemma (crossroad) because of people's ignorance about *African philosophy, religion, ethos, life-force, communion-*

integrity and *worldview*, and how some of these values should be transformed and integrated in Christian life. (b). Lack of holistic educational policies, curricula, systems and renewed knowledge and experience of Christian *Teaching, Morality Spirituality and Witnessing*. Thus, the faith of many people is shallow, hollow, skin-deep and non-transformational. (c). Failure of Governments and pertinent socio-political structures to legislate laws to regulate this vice and teach the Truth about personal and communal liberation and transformation in schools and institutions of learning as a strategy to address the challenge of superstition, magic and witchcraft.[238]

When there is fear, panic, helplessness, emotional limitedness, sickness and insecure in people, they search for answers and solutions to these life challenges from traditional healers, herbalists, diviners, magicians (not necessarily witches or sorcerers) for social, psycho-spiritual healing and holistic protection in life. Clement MacLemon (2008) explains that Christians, followers of other religious faiths and many people are willing to go to anybody who has powers to heal their sicknesses, protect their families and property, attain various social status-quo, punish and avenge their enemies and transform their lives.[239]

A Cameroonian anthropologist James George Agasuguruso (2005) explains that '*all human beings are potential magicians, witches or sorcerers*' because they are inclined to do mysterious, communications and evil activities. This vice is experienced and shared by everybody directly or indirectly, actively or passively, consciously and unconsciously. Majawa (2017) explores that Magic then has three fold experiences: (a) *Mystico–infected experience*: it includes those who

---

[238] S. A. Tower, From the Craft to Christ: The Allure of Witchcraft and the Church's Response, San Francisco: Dwell Publishers, 2014, 4-29.

[239] Clement MacLemon, Christianity and Occult Religions, New York: Exposition Press, 2008, 33-37.

knowingly and wilfully accept and engage in its practices. (b) *Mystico–affected (indirectly) experience:* it includes those who acknowledge its existence and are affected by proxy, family members, neighbours and kin-relations (c).*Mystico–silently (passively) effected experience*: it includes those who deny magic existence but are still affected by it through communal existence since what touches the community influences all members. Thus, even those who deny its existence can't run away from its experience.[240]

Christian Teaching on Magic and Witchcraft

The Bible as the Word of God is the principle source of revelation. Scriptures give us the Will of God. It provides guidance. It teaches humanity on what to do and what not to do regarding the vices of superstition, magic and witchcraft. The belief and practices of witchcraft have existed in human culture since creation. In the Bible there are many texts which denounce and renounce the belief and practices of magic. In the Old Testament, prohibitions of magic appear in Ex.22:17; Lev.19:31; 20:27; Deut.18:10. The death penalty for witchcraft is explicit in Ex.12:17. In the New Testament, the Biblical teaching on magic is found in Act 13:6-11; 19:13-17; 19:18; Gal 5:20; Rev.13:6-11; 19:13-17, 19:18; 21:8; etc.

The Old Testament Teaching: Most of the condemnation against witchcraft and sorcery is found in the Book of Leviticus. One of the commandments given in the book is that people shouldn't engage in magical practices, witchcraft, evil spell and demonic rituals or anything related to it (Lev.20:27). Likewise, the Book of Law (Deuteronomy) teaches that no one among you should make his son or daughter a

---

[240] Clement Majawa, A Handbook on Borderline Between Christianity and Witchcraft: Foundations, Anthropology, Theories and Trends, Nairobi: Scroll Technologies, 2017, 108-109.

witch/wizard so to make him pass through fire or consult evil spirit (Deut 18: 10 – 12) Don't turn to magicians, mediums, sorceries or witches to seek for evil spirit for you will be defiled and defeated by them (Leviticus 18: 31) Lev. 19 contains a series of precepts to be observed by God's people because God, their creator is Holy while Satan who is the origin of witchcraft should always be abandoned because it can lead you astray. Those who have a covenant relationship with God are forbidden to do activities associated with witchcraft. 2 Chron, Deut 10: 10, Dan 2:2, Ex 11: Mic 7.

The New Testament Teaching: Jesus Christ came to fight the three protological enemies of *sin, death* and *Satan*. These three are the root cause of witchcraft. The N.T. prohibits involvement in witchcraft, sorcery and medium. They should not believe in *Belzebul = Prince of Devils* (Mt. 12:24, Lk. 22:31). Belzebul is the arch-enemy of Jesus Christ and he is the religious initiator of evil spell, evil magic and moribund witchcraft. Thus, Christ came to wage war against him and defeated him after the mystery of the resurrection. Jesus then gave his apostles authority to carry out the totality of his mission here on earth which included the fighting and expulsion of the devil, evil spirits, destructive magic through the power of the Holy Spirit (Mt. 28:18-20; Mk. 16:17). Throughout the public life of Christ, he was constantly engaged in the battle against evil spirits, spiritual enemies and sin. *(Mk 1:23-34; Lk 4:33-36; Mt 8:1-4; Lk 5:12-18; Mt 9:1-8; Mk 2:1-12; Mt 17:14-21; Jn. 10:1-21, Lk 13:10-17; Mt 20:29-34, Lk 9:1-2)*

The Church from its beginning has taught strongly against negative magic and witchcraft basing itself on the Gospel of Life of Jesus Christ. Throughout the Church History, when the doctrine, morality and discipline of the Church was threatened by vices or errors of magic and witchcraft, the Church convoked some Councils or proclaimed some Exhortations to condemn it and clarified the teaching of the Church on these issues. The Vatican II Council (1962-1965) stated categorically that Christ is Divine and the Universal Savior of humanity. He is the answer and Savior to all human challenges, fears, diabolic threats and aspirations (2 Co 5, 15; there is no other name under the heaven given to man by which it is fitting for him to be saved." (Acts 4,12) *The Catechism of the Catholic Church* (CCC) clearly states that *all practices of magic and sorcery are gravely contrary to the virtue of religion. These demonic practices are to be condemned* (CCC 2116).

New-age Witchcraft in Third Millennial Society

The reality of destructive magic and witchcraft is revolutionizing and metamorphosing itself into new realities of evil in society. The world today is facing many new-age emerging issues of socio-religious-political, economic or superstitious nature. Some phenomena are coming in forms of new-religion and new philosophy called 'New Age Witchcraft'. New Age Witchcraft is a religious secretive cultic beliefs and praxis which are blended with contemporary ideologies of relativism, secularism, materialism Scientism, etc. for unrighteous aim. Since the new age, magic addresses many modern challenges, many Christians and non-Christians, the educated and the illiterate alike find them appealing and refreshing. When investigating the phenomenon of modern or new age witchcraft, it does not take long to notice a range of terms associated with the practice: *The Craft, Wicca, Paganism, Neo-paganism, Mother-earth, Scientism, Neo-atheism, Illuminati, Black Knights, Luciferians, Devil Worship, Satanism, Couples of Satan*, and so on.[241]

Thus, 'new age' involves a number of things: a combination of spirituality and superstition, magic and life-force, about which the only thing certain is that it is not new. Although the term is abstract, it has

---

[241] Ibid,153-154.

been in use for a long time. Later, it took the form of *Occultism.* The occult (from the Latin word *occultus* "clandestine, hidden, secret") is "knowledge of the hidden wisdom". *Occult* often refers to "knowledge of the *paranormal*" as opposed to "knowledge of the measurable" usually referred to as science which must be kept hidden because it can threaten and cause harm in society. The occultism is increasingly accepted by many worldwide. It manifests itself in sorcery, witchcraft, magic, Wicca, Satanism, Devil worship, wizard, mediums, fortune-tellers, spiritualism, psychics, Scientism, Shamanism, and Paganism. The New Age Movement defines, promotes and popularizes some of these cultic movements.[242]

Many communities in global north are defining the relevance of Scientism, Worshipping Mother Earth, Devil worship, Satanism and witchcraft as a modern way of religions; of how human beings relate to religious powers. Such atheistic religions defend Satanism or Devil worship as in line with one's constitutional right to religious freedom. However, such religious ideologies and rights are a contributing phenomenon of magic and witchcraft to permanence in our society

Magic, Witchcraft and the Prosperity Gospel

Poverty, underdevelopment, sickness, disease, ignorance, protection, human infertility and desire for children, desire for quick richness and success, and shallow Christian/religious values are some of the major factors leading many people to the Prosperity Gospel. The emergence of the prosperity gospel and the popularity it has achieved are a major challenge facing the church in Africa today. Prosperity gospel teaches that God has met all human needs of health and wealth through the

---

[242] George Williamson, G. Addressing the Vice of Superstition and Magic for World Transformation, Ontario: Prentice-Hall INC, 2003, 27-33.

suffering and death of Christ.[243] Believers are therefore encouraged to claim these blessings including insulation from disease, poverty, enemies and sin by making positive confessions and sowing seeds of tithes and offerings in order profit more money, etc. This is an avenue which is leading some to practice of magic and witchcraft.

The emphasis on health, wealth, money, promotion, advance, privilege, and power in the gospel of prosperity necessarily implies that those who preach it have a weak theology or catechesis of hard-work, pain and suffering. Rather than address the systemic socio-economic failures brought on African countries and their people by greedy and corrupt leaders, pastors and people alike accept witches and demons as convenient causes of negative life experiences. Explaining poverty in terms of witch activities has led to a situation in which Pentecostal / charismatic healing camps receive not only people accused of witchcraft but also perceived victims looking for divine intervention in their plight. The accusers and the accused turn to the same well in seeking help.[244]

Evil Magic and Witchcraft as a Human Rights Issue

Many people who are accused of witchcraft are innocent, yet they are abused, isolated, tortured and murdered. International human rights activists have recently become interested in violence perpetrated against accused sorcerer and witches. The issue of evil magic and witchcraft as an issue of human rights and social justice has received attention from, among others, the United Nations (U.N.) Special Rapporteur on Violence Against Women (2002), the U.N. Special Rapporteur on Extra-Judicial Killings (United Nations High Commission on Refugees –

---

[243] A. Baudena, Nature and Supernatural Worldview of Magical Experiences, Harmondsworth: Penguin Books, 2010, 55-58.

[244] D. Macphearson, The Contemporary Understanding of Witchcraft and Sorcery, Manchester: Burns & Hills Publications, 2003. 29-22.

UNHCR, 2009), the U.N. High Commission on Refugees (Schnoebelen 2009; UNHCR 2004, 2009, 2011), UNICEF (Cimpric 2010), and the European Parliament (Hanson and Ruggiero 2013), as well as NGOs such as Save the Children (Molinar 2006), Help Age International (2011), and Stepping Stones (Foxcraft 2009). All these international bodies have renounced witchcraft because it eats the fiber of human rights and justice. Governments, Churches, religions, NGOs, institutions of learning, families and international community are challenged to have a holistic, credible and long-term strategy of addressing magic and witchcraft in global context.[245]

Many innocent accused witches have been executed by hanging, burying alive, drowning and burning with fire. The victims are often from vulnerable groups: the elderly, the disabled, those with albinism and, children (UNHCR & Fahamu Trust 2012). We should not be indifferent or silent about these abuses of human rights. We should not observe these unjust and criminal practices from a distance and do nothing about it. Doing nothing about witchcraft is to become part of the challenge. Many people who worry about magic or witchcraft see these phenomena as raising an important issue of justice and human rights, one that goes beyond the simple problem of false accusation and involves harm done by witches to their victims, or by people to innocent suspects. There is need to intensify holistic sensitization and teaching of human rights for all in our institutions of education, churches and societies.[246]

---

[245] Un Reports: The Whrin & Human Rights, Releases Latest Report 2017: Witch Hunts, October, 2017.

[246] R. Anderson,. Convergence and Divergence of Magic Today, London: Nelson Press, 2013, 78-79.

In Search of Ethical Mental Health and Psychosomatic Spiritual Counselling

Erick Erickson (1980) proposed a psycho-social developmental stage theory, based in part on the insights of depth psychology, biology, sociology and anthropology which was grounded in Sigmund Freud's theory of five stages of psychosexual development. If there is a gap in any of these stages, then fear and helplessness begin to develop in a person leading to psycho-spiritual deficiency, fear and sense of helplessness. These attitudes easily lead people to seek meaning and help in magic and witchcraft surety.[247]

Essentially witchcraft is distorts the mind, the inner self and is idolatry. It rejects God as the source of Wisdom, Truth and Meaning. Moreover, when God is rejected, the Truth is rejected also and all forms of egocentrism, evil and negativity like witchcraft infiltrates into human mind. When the superstitious ideas and witchcraft-thoughts saturate human mind, they confuse one's inner spirit, psychology and interior self. These in turn affect negatively the mental health and human body. Holistic healing or therapy comes with the needed help for such mental and socio-psycho-spiritual deficiency or illness.

Recommendations

(a). Develop societal and governmental measures that ensure that those suspected or accused or mistreated in the name of witchcraft are able to report and speak out of injustices to the judicial or legal structures, police, District Commissioners' or relevant NGOs for just action. (b). On-going campaign for a new revised legislation and Witchcraft Act which protects human rights by continuing to decriminalize witchcraft and criminalizes accusations from all corners of

---

[247] Stephanie Scheck, The Stages of Psychosocial Development According to Erick H. Erickson, Munster: GRIN Verlag, 2014, 55-58.

society. (c). Civic and religious strengthening policy and strategies of protecting and supporting victims of magical and witchcraft-based violence by building the capacity of other offices such as Social Welfare Offices, the police Victim Support Unit, the church or religious counselling services and relevant NGOs. (d). Provide on-going catechesis and train traditional, political, religious leaders, teachers and people at the grassroots and community levels in the truth about magic and witchcraft and holistic counselling. (e). The Ministry of Education ; Public research centres and institutions of higher learning to develop policies, curricular and systems of education which address this challenge of ignorance of magic and injustice of witchcraft, and continue embarking on relevant research investigations (f). Strategize long term on-going formation conversation and awareness-raising forum and education about alternative causes of explanation for poverty, fear, sickness, death and misfortune in society, as well as sensitization about the legal frameworks in place and human rights for all (g). Promotion of rigorous campaigns that injustices and violence of destructive magic, sorcery and witchcraft is now on the radar of national governments and international human rights bodies, and this should be used as a springboard to push forward the necessary societal reforms in the light of 2030 Developmental goals.

Conclusion

Historically, socio-religiously and philosophically, the reality of magic and witchcraft is real and even today forms a fundamental part of the world-view of society. Magical beliefs and witchcraft practices are difficult to destroy for they form a mystic system which can absorb and explain many challenges of life together with human failures and apparently contradictory evidences (Gluckman, 1965:89). These vices seem to suggest and provide means of addressing some fears, pain, evil and difficulties of life. The study revealed that these are serious socio-religious issues to be addresses strategically by the government, the Church, NGOs and other pertinent structures which champion social justice and integrated progress in society. There is urgent need for on-going dialogue and engagement by various stake-holders in Africa and beyond to review and map up transformative strategies of addressing this issue. The educational curriculum, policy and system should consider this issue in schools, colleges and universities. Church's and religious institutions should come up with Catechesis and moral instructions which teach about love, justice, peace, unity, progress, national building and transformation for all in society as a pastoral approach of addressing challenges of superstition, magic and witchcraft.

References

Alumbuwao, D. Evolution of the Wisdom of Magic and Its Contribution to Civilization, London: Panaf Books, 1998.

Anderson, R. Convergence and Divergence of Magic Today, London: Nelson Press, 2013

Baudena, A. *Nature and Supernatural Worldview of Magical Experiences*, Harmondsworth: Penguin Books, 2010.

Benedict XVI, *Africae Munus, Post-Synodal Apostolic Exhortation on the Church in Africa in Service to Reconciliation, Justice and Peace,* Vatican City: Libreria Editrice Vaticana, 2011.

Brooks, A. Witchcraft Goes Mainstream: Uncovering its Impact on You and Your Family, Eugene, OR: Harvest House Publishers, 2004.

Chikanga, N., *The Battle Against Witchcraft in Malawi,* Zomba: Kachere series 2003.

Compendium of the Catechism of the Catholic Church, Vatican: Libreria Editrice Vaticana, 2005.

Compendium of the Social Doctrine of the Church, Pontifical Council for Justice and Peace: Vatican: Libreria Editrice Vaticana, 2005.

David Parkin *The Anthropology of Evil,* Oxford Basil Blackwell Ltd. 1985.

Demos, J. P, *Entertaining Satan; Witchcraft and the Culture of Early New England,* London, 1982

Eastwood, B. Magic Impedes People's Transformation, New York: The Seabury Press, 1998.

Evans-Pritchard, E. E., *Witchcraft, Oracles and Magic Among the Azande,* Oxford: Clarendon Press, 1937, 1976.

Fazimaka, H., *Christianity and Witchcraft in Africa* London: Simpkin and Marshall Press, 2000.

Gibeni Alexander, *Fear of Witchcraft in the Church,* London: Sussex and Georges Publishers, 2004.

Jenkins, J. *Ethics and Religion*, Oxford: Heinemann, 1999.

Magesa, L. *African Religion: The Moral Tradition of Abundant Life*, New York: Orbis Book, 2002.

Majawa, C. *A Handbook on Borderline between Christianity and Witchcraft*, Book 1 (2017) and Book 2, Nairobi: Scroll Technologies, 2018.

Majawa, C. *The Holy Spirit and Charismatic Renewal in Africa and beyond,* Nairobi: Creations Enterprises, 2007.

MacLemon, C. Christianity and Occult Religions, New York: Exposition Press, 2008.

Macphearson, D. The Contemporary Understanding of Witchcraft and Sorcery, Manchester: Burns & Hills Publications, 2003.

Mbiti, J. S. *African Religious and Philosophy,* London: Heinemann Books, 1969.

Nock Judy, A. The Modern Witchcraft: Book of Natural Magick, New York: Adams Media Publishers, 2018.

Pfeiffer, A. Human Consideration of Magic, Boston: Beacon Press, 2010.

Robbins, R. H. *The Encyclopedia of Witchcraft and Demonology,* 1959

Robinson, P. *Natural and Supernatural Reality of the Invisible Powers*, New York: Guild Press, 1998.

Shaw, J. R. *Magicians, Sorcerers, Witches and Human Suffering,* New York: MacGraw Hill, 2010.

Shorter, A. *Jesus and the Witchdoctor: An Approach to Healing and Wholeness,* London: Cassell Ltd, 1985.

Weeds, R. *Wicca Magicians and Contemporary Scientists*, New York: Scribner Publications, 1976.

Williamson, G. Addressing the Vice of Superstition and Magic for World Transformation, Ontario: Prentice-Hall INC, 2003.

17

FACING THE CHALLENGES OF EDUCATION WITH A VISION: 100 YEARS BEYOND THE KENYA VISION 2030

Jude Likori Omukaga

Introduction

The Moral Impetus to Buoyant Education

The cross-road experience of the education system in Kenya today is arguably facilitated by the threats of irrelevance to societal needs, pragmatic alternative in talent and ability or cheaper avenues to wealth and honour.[248] Its grievous challenges are even more visible in the vanquished image of a scholar, rampant unethical approaches of its experts and by its own complicity in mediocrity and tendencies for the fix-it-quick approach to problems. While this catalogue represents real threat to education, every societal undertaking must face challenges that sustain its antithetical disposition towards creative tensions that attract its relevance to the needs of the time. Whilst appreciating their historical value, this paper will highlight both the antithetical value of these challenges and their role as a moral impetus. It will focus on sound vision as the link between the educational aspirations and the promise of the future. But what is the content of such a vision? This paper will

[248] Jude Likori Omukaga, Priest, Catholic Diocese of Bungoma, Kenya.

assess the dream of seasoned sociologists of education like John Dewy and Benjamin Bloom as reflected in the endeavours of renowned Kenyan patriots and scholar like Oginga Odinga and Wangari Mathai. It will also critique the ethics of vision in the relevant educational policy in order to clarify its role in these challenges. It will argue that a steady vision will buoy the system beyond the challenges of its time. The discussion will propose a moral-ethical matrix founded on a tri-partite educational creed comprising of a socio-cultural, economic, and science and technology pillars. The conclusion will recommend National Honorary Academic Chairs to preside over the three-party concerns and to facilitate a socially relevant and culturally buoyant educational system for the future.

Endangered Vision: Interrogating Attitudes to Education Today

Kenya's Educational Doom's Day

An expert educationist in Kenya was invited to deliver a key note address to stake holders gathered in one high school in a rural setting to mark their esteemed annual education day. Before the keynote address, the audience was treated to hilarious entertainment facilitated by a cocktail of selected creative presentations from talented students. This comprised of poems, choral verses, talk shows, climaxing in a vigorous traditional local dance generated from locally assembled instruments. The song lyrics of this captivating climax were not only familiar and wise, they were well chosen to communicate hearty pieces of advice, and character praises, powerful exhortations and hearty warnings against the perceived social dangers of the time. Furthermore, the tunes and choruses sang in response to the melody din of soloists made irresistible appeal to the audience, men and women, the young and the old, who responded through wonderfully telling body movement in ecstatic dance. The gifts offered to appreciate this rare show of talent further indicated the place it had won in the hearts of the audience. Finally, the education expert stood up to address the audience: "...Before I deliver my speech allow me to invite the following students to stand up. Meanwhile, I invite their respective lead class teachers to each stand and come to the podium in front..." Firstly, I invite the most improved student in form 3B class to stand up... the teacher representative of this class, kindly arise and come along to the podium." After about three minutes of waiting in silence, no one responded. The speaker proceeded and posed the same request randomly to three more cases: the student who scored the highest grade in Form 2 C, the student who scored the least grade in form 4A, and the student who is best talented in form 1 D. For the third time the speaker reminded the respective class teachers to arise and walk to the podium. After this final attempt, only one student and one teacher succeeded in this assignment: the last invitees. The teacher representative was then requested to introduce her student, she could not remember his names, but knew very well that the boy was the best talented in modern rap music dance. Lastly, the speaker invited the deputy head teacher to come to the podium and "kindly remind the audience, the school Moto and Vision." He fumbled but the Head teacher quickly came to his rescue when he requested the secretary to rush to the office and collect the inscriptions from his official file in the office cabinet. Meanwhile a number of students rushed to the gate to check school signpost on which the motto, Mission and Vision, and the cherished values of the school were inscribed in big Capital Letters. They all returned successfully and assisted the deputy Head Teacher to remind the audience that the School Moto was: "Today Better than before," the Vision being: "To Provide Quality Education For Success In Life." These, he explained, "were engendered by their cherished values of honesty, hard work and accountability.

Internal Challenges to Education

As the audience struggled to interpret the Guest Speaker's intention for this prelude, the speaker posed three questions that captured the mind-set of the audience thus: are students and teachers in this school aware of their core mission in education? Secondly, he turned to the audience comprising of distinguished dignitaries of different walks and asked a direct question, "what did you enjoy most, the sweet rhythm of the local drum in music or the hullabaloo of questions and assignments?" Thirdly, he turned to the teacher who walked to the podium and asked: What made you remember one student member of your class and why? The questions were rhetoric, meant to generate individual reflections as his speech was in progress. However, important observations can be made from the above prelude: firstly, that although the school had the requisite motivational instruments there was no spontaneous consciousness regarding their role in the routine service of education. When key educators are casual about key concerns of the learning institutions, overall commitment to strict goals of education is proportionately relaxed. Secondly, the commitment to the hard challenges of academic work represented by attention to the details such as setting targets, cultivating scholarly discipline, attention to individual learner needs, or improving score passes, seem to cede relevance to disproportionate attention to extracurricular talent, popular traditional pass-times like song, dance or entertainment. Thirdly, the prelude exposed the helpless attitude of stakeholders in education to insist on the essentials. The Parents, distinguished guests, community leadership appear easily carried by starling display of talent and entertainment but appear impatient even irritated by rigorous insistence on routine educational formalities. On the overall, emotive dance, frenzied cheers, and charismatic display of extraordinary talents easily inspire awesome followership and evoke passionate attraction as compared to rather cold rigid pursuits of formal education.

This day events exposed the attitudes that have entrenched a broader concern over challenges commonly associated with the internal operations in the learning institutions. Higher enrolments have not been marched by proportionate development of physical facilities and hiring of class room teachers. This has in turn destabilised the equilibrium in the student-teacher ratio whose impact reflect immediately in moral behaviour and academic performance. Furthermore, curriculum structure development, supervision and completion face perennial challenges that have led to exam cheating, mass exam failure, higher drop-out rates and overall low quality education in both primary and secondary school education. The sum of this internal hiccups result in the infamous 'half baked' graduates considered not prepared adequately to handle the jobs for which they were trained. As the teaching and training perform below expectation, research activity and innovation too lugs behind, remains unpopular and of little impact to the progress of society.

External and Real Challenges of Education in Kenya

Beyond the challenges arising from routine activities within the educational structures, we face even strong competing interest from the outside. These challenges are stronger in cases where many young people find alternative pursuits more attractive, easily attainable with a better promise than education system can offer. These pursuits include live television and radio talk shows, public joke-making, music and dance, and the exceptional abilities in athletics and sports. The mention of these pursuits and the names behind them in public rouses immediate interest. Add to this the high class of the distinguished wielders of power politics and ethnic chauvinism, the new tycoons of the betting industry and the corruption schemes, the drug marketers and the business moguls in parastatals and industry. These groups represent the definition of success in Kenya today, they wield power, own prime and superfluous property, are popular and famous, enjoy top of the range material luxury. They influence decisions in the job market, business enterprise, development projects, and in government policy. Their signature appendages sanction all undertaking, more effective than any research outcome. They generate protectorates and partition society into sections of influence. These personalities not only afford regular nationwide audience but attract fanatic followership and play role models as they maximise their economic earning to live high class luxury. On a larger scale these challenges not only provide easily coveted happiness and comfort, they, above all, offer promise of higher incomes leading to comfort and happiness long promised by education.

The flip side of this narrative contains the stack antithesis of performance in the formal educational expert arena. The medical doctors and nurses, the University lecturers, and teachers in the public institutions of learning have been in and out of national strikes for the last five consecutive years. This group represents Kenya's most learned cadre. Training for medical practitioners: specialised doctors, pharmacists, dentists, clinicians is not only the most expensive undertaking of the government on education, it is also the highest coveted professional training that attracts the highest cut off point entry. This means these areas absorb the best Kenyan brain and trained personnel. It goes without saying that their trainers couldn't go for anything less. The Professors, Lecturers and University staff workers are not only the highest trained but handle the highest level of academic training in the country. Their sustained strike for salary and benefit increase does not only obstruct the country's premier expert services, it also exposes the underlying social injustice and inequality in the distribution of the country's wealth. This is not to mention the insignificant social rating of the contribution of Kenya's renowned scholars. The recent demise of Prof. Ali Mazrui, William Ochieng, Henry Odera Oruka and Calestus Juma provided little to celebrate in terms of pomp and material honour; they passed on without ritual or notice. Their life was spent in serene reflection of hard realities, it lacked fun, pomp or popularity, and it wouldn't attract it at death. The remaining luminaries like Ngugi Wathiong'o, Bethwell Allan Ogot and others remain hardly noticeable in the public rating. Their names are mentioned in difficult assignments of publication, course undertaking or in international conference arenas accessed by a few of the same or higher academic standing. Thus, on the standard of visible material influence, returns and social regard, the local formal academia regrettably compares insignificantly to the above varied alternative avenues. While the strenuous and expensive formal education promised white colour status with its strappings, present talent oriented livelihood offers more by a lower cost within a shorter period with little requirement: luxury and comfort, fame and higher status, not to mention quick access to the country's premier resources. In the final analysis, easy talent oriented pursuits of the young people offers a competitive alternative to the otherwise demanding requirements of formal education.

Recovering the Vision of Education in Kenya

The False Hope

The litany of the ills that bedevil education in Kenya today is as discouraging as it beckons hope for a better tomorrow. But to discern the rays of hope in this situation, which is a necessary path at this point, forces us to identify the root causes of the current situation: Where and when did things go wrong? This situation can be traced to the evolution of society's understanding of the role of education. Education has long been associated with life process, never ends but continues with life as a spotlight to its dark portholes. Thus, while the effects of the old mind set in the education process still linger and influence its capacity to appreciate its current challenges, the onset of new mind set implies a disturbance with an equal potential for either destruction or construction. An honest reconstruction therefore, must consider the depths of the historical potholes of education. This reflection sees this pothole in society's long esteemed creed on the promise of education. It will unpack it within the framework of the *Idea of the University* as the ultimate dream for a formal educational process that dominated the mind set of academia of a long time.

The history of university education has oscillated between two visible poles. On one hand, university education sponsors critical mind development endeavour that emphasizes the development of the individual to full all-round personality with ability to solve his/her own or society's problems as they come. This perspective of university education sees a university as an *alma mater* commissioned to nurture individual potential to full maturity in a formational exercise. Envisioning this image in his work, *The Idea of the University*, Henry Newman saw a University as "a seat of truth," a place where one went to seek for the knowledge as a refinement of the self that leads to the uncompromising truth. The ultimate embrace of the truth was to him the entire end of a university education thus, the essence of a university lies in the teaching required to promote intellectual culture and the training of the mind, this is the ultimate, nothing less, nothing more: " A University… is a place of teaching universal knowledge its object being the diffusion and extension of knowledge rather than the advancement," (Newmann, 1996).

The emphasis on knowledge and formation was tailored to inculcate capacity and abilities that enable a trained person to fit and lead any circumstance of need. University graduates were trained leaders of any area of need in society. They were armed with skills of applying knowledge, interpret, and solve problems of any nature. Socially, a University graduate was considered all-round trained adult capable of undertaking any challenge, any assignment. The immediate circumstance of this understanding was reflected in top management positions of areas of service in private companies or public offices. Coincidentally, this position was white-colour, reserved for the highly learned, University graduates. They carried the highest salaries, many privileges and premier service conditions. This was also socially associated with successful life of dream, luxury, and comfort among other promises. This peak ultimate destination of the educated in society set the target for the ultimate hope for a happy life. In so far as education in Kenya was the promise of a better tomorrow, key to success or the highest earned prestige for a better life, its promise remained the one most coveted achievement in the life of everyone. But what better role does it still play where alternative achievements earn the same or even better returns?

The Promise of Modern Education

However, transitional experience of education in the history observes growing emphasis on research. The postmodern view of University education triumphs in specialization and vocational training, involving consultation, teamwork and reference over and above the 'banking' of knowledge to create an all mighty university intellectual giants. University systems are more driven by targets, focus is directed more on the measurable impact. Instead of entering higher education to become a "general scholar" immersed in becoming proficient in the entire curriculum, we now meet a type of scholar whose concern is relevance of university education to the needs of society. Crucial in this description is the demand that modern scholar engages in dialogue, beginning with the presumption that he or she may not know everything, and in fact, other people could know more. On this footing, Ultimate University degrees competes other talents particularly in the business fraternity. Organizations managed in post-modern principles are thus capable of producing individuals or corporate ventures that by far surpass the creativity of an ultimate University degree holder and therefore receive proportionately superior benefits. Likewise, respect for talent or other abilities falls under the realization that the University graduate is not the ultimate, but a team player who remains equally in need of supplementation for relevance in societal needs. Although the progressive expansion of enrolment in the university, admitting an ever wider number of students, requires keen appreciation of the need for balance between competition and formation, recent development in the structuring of the University education emphasize research oriented model globally. Comparing 'the *Magna Carta* of the European Universities' in the Bologna declaration, 1988, and the priorities of the Commission of University Education in Kenya, the thrust of University education today is three fold, namely: the interest in quality teaching, the central place of research and innovation and the imperative of extensions or community service. These three aspects today define the potential of a university institution with emphasis on the extension programmes.

Society: The Source and Destination

The Role of Pedagogy

A honest recourse to the vision of education in society is the most probable step to take at a crossroad where the educational role in society begins to fed as it is today in Kenya. The review of educational vision does not only clarify its role and place in society but also helps to put into perspective the competing interests often mistaken as its alternatives. Society, its circumstance and needs perhaps remain the best platform from which educational vision can be assessed. What therefore is the promise of a good education to our society today? The view and example of experts in the sociology of education gives a reliable guide as to the proper place of education in society. More specifically, the drafters of method or pedagogical approaches to education have particularly been careful about designing pedagogical methods that produce outcomes that are relevant to society's needs and progress. The success of a pedagogical method have always been by natural selection where good pedagogy is liked by the learners, bears visible fruits and lasts in honour. Bad pedagogy on the other hand burdens the attention of learners, attracts no response and naturally pales in the horizon with time. The assurance of this review lies in the fact that these experts often came up with alternatives that were directed towards solving the social problem of their time. Creative approaches to pedagogy by masters of education in history revealed a lot in terms of the role of education in society. This stream of concern was clearer in the life and profession of experts in the sociology of education like Maria Montesori, Benjamin Bloom, Paul Freire, and John Dewey. We will therefore consider their input in this subject.

Expert Contribution to Sociology of Education

Maria Montessori, a trained medical doctor, adjusted her profession to the service of the needs of disabled children. When it became clearer to her that the mentally disabled children needed education more than routine health care and sympathy, she changed her medical career to illustrious life of education by her advocacy for 'scientific pedagogy' suitable for the mentally handicapped at the time but later adapted to mainstream education through the famous 'Montessori Method' coveted around the world for childhood education. Her educational theory emphasized the pedagogy of sensory exploration and manipulatives that trained children in physical activities such as walking and the use of a spoon, training their senses by exposure to sights, smells, and tactile experiences, and introducing letters in tactile form. These activities developed into the Montessori "Sensorial" materials (1900-1901). This method gave ground to Montesori's "scientific pedagogy", in which she called for not just observation and measurement of students, but for the design and development of methods which would transform them. "Scientific education, therefore, was that which, while based on science, modified and improved the individual," (Montesori, 1920). Montesory believed that education itself needed to be transformed by science. In the final analysis Montesori advocated a transformative education system powered by methods tailored to transform individuals. This was backed by her elaborate theory of internal human development revealed by the children's spontaneous activity in their respective environment. The appropriate role of the educator, in this case, is to remove obstacles to this natural development and provide opportunities for it to proceed and flourish. Ultimately, the Montesory Method of education for young children stresses the cultivation, development and the flowering of a child's own initiative and natural abilities, as a child prepares to face the challenges of life. This in itself comprised of the vision of education for society: a truly transformative enterprise to prepare the individual for the challenges of society, to discover the treasures of nature and use it for holistic progress in society.

The famous American educational psychologist, Benjamin Samuel Bloom (February 21, 1913 – September 13, 1999), made even more strenuous effort in this direction of nurturing and cultivating individual abilities for progress. Through the instrumentality of scientifically structured goals and objectives of education, Bloom engineered 'mastery learning' as an instructional strategy directed towards the development of exceptional talent that could facilitate individual eminence, or exceptional achievement in society. In this strategy, students must achieve a level of mastery (e.g., 90% on a knowledge test) in prerequisite knowledge before moving forward to learn subsequent information. If a student does not achieve mastery on the test, they are given additional support in learning and reviewing the information and then tested again. This cycle continues until the learner accomplishes mastery, and they may then move on to the next stage, ((Benjamin S.

Bloom, 1981). The focus of instruction is the time required for different students to learn the same material and achieve the same level of mastery, in contrast with classic models of teaching, which focus more on differences in students' ability and where all students are given approximately the same amount of time to learn and the same set of instructions. In mastery learning, there is a shift in responsibilities, so that student's failure is more due to the instruction and not necessarily lack of ability on his or her part. The challenge in a mastery learning environment is providing enough time and employing instructional strategies so that all students can achieve the same level of learning albeit in different time duration.

Going beyond the individual cultivation, the Brazilian educator, Paul Freire (1921-1997), evaluated pedagogy within the context of the forces of oppression in society. The prevalence of oppression in society according to him is sustained by a process of mutual disregard for freedom by both the oppressor and the oppressed. While the powerful dread freedom of all, the powerless in society too can be frightened of freedom. Owing to his own experience in education, Freire considered the classical pedagogy of his time as an instrument of oppression through which the oppressed are trained to fear freedom. The traditional approach to education in his view entrenched what he called a 'banking approach' in which the student was viewed as an empty account to be filled by the teacher. He notes that "it transforms students into receiving objects. It attempts to control thinking and action, leads men and women to adjust to the world, and inhibits their creative power. This, in his opinion, results in the dehumanization of both the teachers and the students. The banking approach stimulates oppressive attitudes and practices in society. In this background, Freire advocated responsible pursuit of freedom as the indispensable condition for the quest for human completion." But this pursuit must engage an 'authentic approach' that is more world-mediated and facilitates mutual co-creation of knowledge, (Cf. *Freire, 1963*). In his opinion "authentic" approach to education allows people to be aware of their incompleteness and strive to be more fully human. In the place of the classical "banking" approach therefore, Freire introduced the concept of "Conscientization" to facilitate 'authentic approach' to education. This approach facilitates education as a means of consciously shaping the person and the society. Freedom as the immediate object of education therefore is a praxis of informed action only attained as a result of a balance between theory and practice.

In contrast to the oppressive traditional pedagogy, Freire entrenched the new 'pedagogy of the oppressed' into his final dialogic as liberating instruments against the colonizers. He proposes orderly patterns of dialogue as the instrument to free the colonized, through the use of cooperation, unity, organization and cultural synthesis. This is in contrast to the use of conquest; manipulation, cultural invasion, and the concept of divide and rule without appreciation of dialogue. This is Paul Freire's contribution to liberation of the oppressed in society through the use of constructive pedagogy. But perhaps the most comprehensive contribution to education as a tool of social progress was manifest in the work of the American functional psychologist and educational reformer, John Dewey, (Dewey, *The Scool and society*, 1936).

In his educational theory, Dewey argued that education and learning are social and interactive processes, and thus the school itself is a social institution through which social reform can and should take place. In his earliest reflection, Dewey traced the problems of society to the education curriculum and traditional training pedagogy that focus almost solely on the subject matter taught and entrench inactivity of the student where "the child is simply the immature being who is to be matured; he is the superficial being who is to be deepened," (Dewey, 1902). In response, Dewey crafted a theory of 'progressive learning' based on experience, (Dewey, 1889). A progressive learning theory conceptualizes the learner not just as a blank slate waiting to be filled with knowledge, but as subjects with capacity to organize fact-based comprehension through meta-cognition, or by building onto prior experiences, preconceptions, and knowledge. The educator's role here is in creating an educative experience, (Dewey -1938). According to Dewey education stifles individual autonomy when learners are taught that knowledge is transmitted in one direction, from the expert to the learner. To make education effective, content must be presented in a way that allows the student to relate the information to prior experiences, thus deepening the connection with this new knowledge, (Dewey, 1902). However, a balance must be maintained between the child's inactivity and overreliance on the child. "We must take our stand with the child and our departure from him". In order to rectify this dilemma, Dewey advocated for an educational structure that strikes a balance between delivering knowledge while also taking into account the interests and experiences of the student. Dewey's idea eventually influenced Problem-Based Learning (PBL), which precipitates today's method of learning through active inquiry

This elaborate science of educational formation was ostensibly tailored to nothing less than the progress of both the individual and society at large. Dewey viewed the mind and its formation as a communal process. The individual is a meaningful concept only when regarded as an inextricable part of his or her society, and the society has no meaning apart from its realization in the lives of its individual members. With this model, Dewey uniquely associates the growth and progress of the individual to the growth and progress of society, thus:

With the growth of civilization, the gap between the original capacities of the immature and the standards and customs of the elders increases. Mere physical growing up and mastery of the bare necessities of subsistence will not suffice to reproduce the life of the group. Deliberate effort and the taking of thoughtful pains are required. Beings that are born not only unaware of, but quite indifferent to, the aims and habits of the social group have to be rendered cognizant of them and actively interested. According to Dewey, education, and education alone, spans the gap, (Dewey, 1916).

Thus, in his theory of education, Dewey conceptualizes Schools which prepare citizens for ethical participation in society, preparing students to be reflective, autonomous and ethical beings capable of arriving at social truths through critical and inter-subjective discourse. He draws a pejorative contrast with schools which cultivate passive pupils via insistence upon mastery of facts and disciplining of bodies. Or those that prepare students for docile compliance with authoritarian work and political structures, discouraging the pursuit of individual and communal inquiry, those that perceive higher learning as a monopoly of the institution of education, (Dewey, 1899).

Kenyan Role Models

This instinctive desire to use education as an instrument for the progress of individual and the society at large has a wider appeal in the construction of every society's fabric. Remarkable contribution of renowned leaders in Kenya replicates the pattern of social involvement of the experts considered above from a totally different perspective. The founding father of the Kenyan Nation, Jomo Kenyatta, a graduate of the London school of economics, observed the dangers of European influence over a population of people whose entire lives are based on social customs and religious ideas. His great fear was that the idea of Christian education from the West (the Watch Tower Movement), was largely disrespectful of the local culture. He encouraged indigenous Africans to espouse the key tenets of the African culture. He therefore made a call for understanding of Gikuyu customs and laws whilst urging for all who seek to help the Gikuyu to first learn their culture, history, and social customs in an effort to allow for progress without a loss of individuality and cultural identity. The relevance of education therefore, depended on the extent to which it addressed the realities of the culture, customs or the lifestyle of a people in society, (Kenyatta, Facing Mt. Kenya). Like Jomo Kenyatta, Jaramogi Oginga Odinga received western education very early in Kenyan history. Jaramogi's 'Not yet Uhuru' highlighted the role of missionary schooling in developing intellectual elite, divorced from, and hostile to, its African upbringing. This inspired him to fight a continual battle to assert the right of Africans to equal education against the colonial schooling for subservience, and at the same time for the right of Africans to maintain their national identities against colonial assimilation. It was not until Jaramogi discovered it was impossible to change the educational system without changing the governing authority that he got actively involved in power politics for independence. In the final analysis, the two leaders made use of their earlier education as a tool to guide the progress of their people. In areas where progress was not forthcoming, the two used their learning to point out at what was not going on right. Here education was clearly a tool of social analysis and social progress.

The preference for education for the progress of the individual and society as contrasted to education for subservience, fear or indifference was even more manifest in the life of the expert award winning Kenyan environmentalist, Prof. Wangari Mathai. Despite her superior credentials in Veterinary anatomy, she understood her education as a stepping stone to service of core interest in society. She actively campaigned for equal benefits for all gender through the Kenya Association of University women due to what she saw as unequal regard of the staff based on gender. She became involved in a number of civic organizations such as the Kenya Red cross Society, Environment Liaison Centre where she promoted the participation of non-governmental organizations in the work of the UNEP. Through her work at these various volunteer associations, it became evident to Maathai that the root of most of the problems facing the Kenyan society was environmental degradation.

The Nature of Educational Vision

The above reflection confirms that education consists in the cultivation of individual human potential for holistic self-understanding in view of one's full participation in the progress of society. Consequently, the School is the social institution that facilitates progressive change both in the individual and in society. The educated in society therefore are beacons of hope not necessary for the immediate material benefits they obtain but the active role they play in the general progress of society. From the Kenyan example the educated suffered instead but kept focus of their vision not because of the personal benefit but in anticipation of the general good of the society. Society today still needs honest people, living models whose life radiates values that last and spur society's concern across the ages. When society appears complacent with temporary material comfort, there must be a call beckoning society towards hard work and commitment to knowing the world around it for its betterment, and towards lasting values as a heritage for the next generations. Most of the items in the catalogue of the challenges to education in Kenya today indeed reflect a false hope for ultimate happiness in riches, luxury honour and power. On the contrary, education is not just about going to school, getting a degree and accumulating material wealth in consequence, "It's about widening your knowledge and absorbing the truth about life," (Shakuntala Devi, 2012).

Sage philosophy confirms that "if you sawed wealth you will reap burdens…if you sawed education you will reap the wealth of generations." In other words, material wealth or its corollary attracts burdens, more than they solve individual problems. On the other hand, the serene struggle and sacrifices individuals invest in excavating the treasure of creation in a honest education beget inexhaustible heritage of value for the future generations. The testimony of sage philosophy enhanced by a life experience of reflective thinkers on strategic pedagogy based on sound sociology of education attest to education as an instrument of progress in society, or as experts put it, "the ability to expose and endure the challenges of society and the courage and the patience to experiment important alternative solutions," to society's problems, (Oruka, 1994). It is far more than the material benefits it promises. This is the basis of the need for continuous review of our education system for relevance. Therefore, the challenges that abound on education are not huddles on the way of good education, rather they are beacons of moral impetus that facilitate continuous review of the role of education in society. In this context, educational goals for society are wider in scope, lengthy in span and indeed deeper than any of its individual manifestations in raw talent or academia. A sound educational vision, therefore, should target the cultivation of the individual, invigorate the institution and spur holistic progress of society for an overall betterment of humanity. As to whether or not education is still relevant in the midst of so many challenges, the answer is like that of the expert physicist who, when asked to express in a sentence her most exciting regard of Physics in our times, replied: "I am amazed by the consideration of the fact that, in the entire created universe, all we have managed to know of …the sum total of mass and energy tangible and visible to us in the created biosphere…so far is only 4 per cent. "My wonder, like many of you is.." she posed, "what is the content of the remaining 96 per cent?" This response captures the nature of a vision whose horizon is as open ended as infinity *ad infinitum* but whose influence fills every member of society with the aroma of confident wholeness.

The social strategy of The Kenya Vision 2030 which largely envisions a high quality life in a prosperous nation, projects the goals of education and training that remain limited to concrete, physical structure oriented establishments and administrative models that still remain far short of the span of sound educational vision. Although this limitation is understandable in the background of the time limit of the Kenya Vision 2030, it should never limit the overall educational vision to little lopsided apparent successes registered in talent vending or the idle betting exercise rife in Kenya today no matter the size of the economic return they promise. To be specific, the nature of sound educational vision should build a stronger individual and a social brain power to discover the 96% of the unknown world mass and make use of the mystery of creation to advance human welfare furthest possible, targets the maturation of individual talent and consolidation of natural public goods and invigorates the school as a social institution to champion the revolution needed in society for the ultimate betterment of humanity.

Preserving our Educational Vision

Tri-partite Educational Creed: The Honorary Academic Chairs

The Nature of the Creed

This reflection suggests a structural intervention in a tri-partite educational creed founded on the moral integrity. This creed roots for the education system that cultivates and integrates human potential on the basis of three complementary sources: The Socio-cultural, Economic and scientific-technological spheres. These three bases are understood to be at the root of all gifts, talent or all potential abilities capable of cultivation in a good education system. The creed will be nurtured in a developmental milieu which spans between the immature ignorance at birth and the mature wisdom of the adult members. The ignorant, immature new-born members of the group in society (its future sole representatives) are not to be merely physically preserved in adequate numbers for political, cultural or economic purpose but must be initiated into the interests, purposes, information, skill, and practices of the adult mature members who possess the knowledge and the customs of the group, (Dewey, *Democracy and Education*, 1916). This continuity to must be inculcated into society by an effective education system and should also constitute the central vigour of society, all to be the core concern of the Creed. The Socio-cultural Chair superintends human potential in fine, creative and liberal art structured carefully within the formal education curricular. It will likewise tap, consolidate and wisely deploy raw talent and sage (informal) philosophy. The Economics Chair will superintend progress of potential in all Business, commerce, economics and the related disciplines as judged by its experts. Finally the Science and Technology Chair will oversee the progress, the use and the integration of science and technology in society. The three chairs will be coordinated in the Council of the Wise (COW).

The Honorary Academic Chair

The structure shall commission each section under a Honorary Academic Chair (HAC) which will define, monitor and evaluate the operations of each sphere in accordance with the expectations of society. The core role of the individual HAC is to tap, guide and superintend the progress and integration of the available human potential as a natural resource to be guarded as a social value and legitimate heritage of the country. HAC shall endeavour to facilitate education more as a cultural value and legitimate heritage of a people. It shall be the heart and heritage of Human resource in the country that facilitates and fosters a holistic development of individuals born of society, nurtured in society and integrated as treasured resource for progress in society. Through the instrumentality of the education system HAC will monitor the progress of human potential both on individual and community level. Individual progress can be traced through the respective stages of formal education, whereas community progress is traced through cooperate with regional political administration to direct informal talent in order to entrench the tri-partite creed as society's cultural value through its learning institutions (school, colleges, Universities).

The Honorary Chair Holders

An honorary chair is bestowed upon people of great achievement either from the formal education section, informal sector of talent or unique unprecedented sage achievement in society. This is bestowed upon them after their ordinary period of service as professional or, in the latter case, at a ripe age of visible talent maturity. They lead the Chairs with the council of equally acclaimed individuals of achievements. Every Chair will attract a group of highest achievers in the respective abilities around the country and they will form the respective Chair Council which, with highest wisdom, will oversee the overall formation and integration of human resource in society through the best education system of the time. The chair will rotate among the council members in A term of given duration.

The Council of the Wise – COW

The Council of the Wise (COW) shall be the supreme organ, the climax of the wisdom necessary to guide the moral and cultural dimensions of education in society. It will comprise of a select number of representatives from each of the three academic-moral spheres acclaimed in the creed, that is, Socio-cultural, economic and scientific spheres. The primary goal of this Wise Council is to operationalize respect for education as a means of progress for both the individual and society. They will oversee education both as a cultural value and a promise for a better future of every person in society, and as a heritage received and passed on jealously. The COW will meet from time to time, sponsor national and international symposiums to deliberate on issues of education. In consultation with the ministry of education and other experts, the COW will champion regular review of the national goals of education in tune with the aspirations of each sphere of the Creed for relevance and effectiveness. It will be the highest independent moral authority behind Kenya's education and its benevolent sponsor. It will advise the relevant government ministries on suitable steps towards improving education. While the government ministries will be the formal organizers, planners and educational service providers, the COW will represent the moral force of education as a cultural value which should resonate with societal demands of the time. It will decide on issues across the three spheres of the Creed and such other issues that shall be deemed necessary in the pursuit of holistic education.

Conclusion

This reflection on the vision of education in Kenya unfolded in three sections. The first section exposed the dangers facing education. In its prologue this section highlighted a practical case sampling the attitudes that ail education. The assessment of the case sited revealed the casual attitude of the education managers which did not only induce careless attitudes in teachers and students, but that gradually influenced the stakeholders' attention more on extracurricular events. With this finding, it was clear that any serious random case analysis of the performance of education sampled from any part of Kenya is most likely to show a rather confused regard for educational priorities. Over and above localised case studies, the sad regard for education was made clearer on a wider national scale when one goes deeper to assess and appreciate real challenges posed by competing alternatives that promise far better returns in comparison to education. Once considered the key to happiness in society, educational promise appears subdued by other competing endeavours in society.

The second section traced the root cause of educational decadence to false hope planted by the older aspirations of higher learning. The older school model targeted to cultivate the highest best of the individual academic potential and the return of which was also proportionately high. Consequently, both the journey to the highest level of education and the general social conscience was conditioned to expect the highest material reward. In the advent of alternative pursuits that promised the same or better end, and visible negligible relevance of those well-endowed with education, society has gradually relegated education to a lower position of its priorities and celebrates achievers in this alternative means at a regrettable expense of education. This reflection restores the holistic image of the role of education in a modern model whose ultimate aspiration incorporates learning alongside competitive interdisciplinary research and extension in relevant service to the community. The vigour of this complete image prevailed as indeed the core intention of school education through the work of famous sociologists of education like Maria Montesori, Paul Freire, Benjamin Bloom and John Dewey. The consideration of these roots not only supported the holistic image of education but refocused the vision of education as the binding imperative which must be kept ever in focus as both the source and ultimate end of a relevant education system. Honest consideration of educational vision in this background does not glory in the promise of material luxury, power or fame but in the zeal to cultivate and deploy genuine human potential for the general wellbeing of humanity and entire creation. Furthermore, an honest vision casts the aspirations of society far beyond the temporal material concerns of restructuring management models or improving institutional physical infrastructure as envisioned in the Kenya Vision 2030. The reflection eventually appraised educational vision as an open ended aspiration toward the highest possible wellbeing which at the same time animates all endeavours for full-some cultivation of individual and common potential for highest well-being.

The third section traces the logical highlights of this reflection to four areas: the competing means to higher life, the inordinate quest for material success, the failure of education to serve the needs of society, and, above all, also the crucial role of research, innovation and extension. These four aspects capture the key concerns that define the weaknesses and the strengths of education in Kenya today. This assessment attracted an actionable proposal for a moral-ethical matrix in a Tri-partite Creed to oversee the development, integration and entrenchment of a holistic education as a cultural value in society. The creed will guide society's human resource in all its expression through the Socio-cultural, Economics and the Science and technology matrices. The reflection recommends the founding of Honorary Academic Chairs supported by respective Chair Councils to oversee holistic education as a value in society. At the top of the three Honorary Chairs is the great Council of The Wise charged with the ultimate moral duty of oversight on the entire education system to ensure comprehensive approach targeted at integrating all individual potential into the general progress in society.

In conclusion, this reflection observes that education is the key value that gives expression to people's regard for meaningful life and value in society. In order to keep focus of the important role of education in society, it is important to be true to the vision of education set by society's tradition of civilization and its experts for holistic progress of the individual and society. Though competing interest and forces in society pose constant challenges to education system, steadfast focus on its vision must be jealously guarded by regular reviews and insights by the concerned experts. In this background, such a review has yielded a proposal to reinvigorate the education system by the moral input of the wise in society. Though the dynamics of their contribution have been well structured in an orderly moral matrix, they are not meant to replace but complement and reinforce the work of government experts on routine paid duty. Education oversight provided by an independent group of honorary men and women of experience is not only long overdue in Kenya, it is an imperative required to superintend a holistic education system that must remain a cultural value in the years to come.

References

Dewey, John, *The School and Society: Being Three Lectures*, University of Chicago, Chicago, 1932.. *The Child and the Curriculum: Including the School and Society*, Casino Classics, 1902., *Democracy and Education: An introduction to the Philosophy of Education*, CreateSpace Independent Publishing Platform, on-line, 1916, (2016). . *Experience and Education*, Kapa Delta Pi, Illinois, 1938, retrieved in 1998

Freire. Paul, *Pedagogy of the Oppressed (30th anniversary ed.)*. New York: Bloomsbury. 2000.

Kenya Vision 2030, http://vision2030.go.ke/ (Accessed 28th. March 2018).

Montesori, Maria, *The Montessori Method: Scientific pedagogy as applied to child education in "the children's houses" with additions and revisions by the author. New York: Frederick A. Stokes Company.*

Mwaka, Marcella, The National Goals of Education in Kenya: Interrogating the Achievement of National Unity, in the Journal of Education and Practice, Vol.4, No.4, 2013, www.iiste.org ISSN 2222-1735

Newmann, John Henry, *The Idea of the University*, Frank M. Turner Editor , Yale university Press, New York, 1996.

18

ETHICS IN COMMERCIAL ENTREPRENEURSHIP

Joseph F. Ntale, Kate O. Litondo

Introduction

The concept of ethics in entrepreneurship is growing as a business area of concern and study. [249,250] A case in point is the universal move to deal with corruption in the world of entrepreneurship. Entrepreneurship is an application of economics whereby the entrepreneurs provide services to society. Generating new ideas and converting them into reality for the good of society is the whole mark of ethical entrepreneurship. However, this is not always the case because some of the innovations of entrepreneurs are not good for the society. The concern of ethics in entrepreneurship is to ensure that entrepreneurial venture is sustainable and not injurious to society. Without a clear and organized universality of ethical guidelines, this leaves policy makers, scholars, students, and practitioners of entrepreneurship at a loss. The purpose of this paper is to provide framework within which one can judge what is right and wrong in entrepreneurial activities. This desk research informs, forms, and transforms commercial entrepreneurship from the unified field of ethics. Based on eclectic theory of entrepreneurship, indicators of ethical entrepreneurship were identified.

---

[249] Clement Majawa, Professor,Catholic University of Eastern Africa.
[250] Kate O. Litondo, Dr, University of Nairobi - School of Business.

This paper established that ethical commercial entrepreneurship leads to economic growth, wealth creation, job creation, human dignity, sustainable development and international competitiveness. Furthermore, the study acknowledges that being an ethical entrepreneur not only requires a creative idea and a superior work ethic, but it is also manifested in practice of morality, corporate social responsibility, ethical business, and running business in a way that minimizes harm to people and the general environment. Therefore, an entrepreneurship code of conduct was proposed.

The world of business is appalled by the rapid disappearance of the sense of moral and ethics consciousness. At the same time, anti-moral ways of thinking in business are on rise even if it is acceptable to think that people are free to do what they want, it is not right to be unethical in your thinking (Ackoff, 1987). As a result, various kinds of social and economic crimes of the confusion of profiteering are on the rise. One of the causes of the confusion is that human pattern of thinking has fallen into materialism, violation of traditional values and norms of ethical behaviour. In order to solve this problem of social and economic chaos and build social order, we must establish a new perspective of ethics in the world of entrepreneurship (Anokhin & Schulze, 2009).

The discipline of entrepreneurship is relatively young as compared to other disciplines of social sciences. The last three decades has given rise to a number of research, policy and practitioner practices concerned with understanding or nurturing ethical entrepreneurial attitudes, behaviours, processes, structures, discourses, actions and contexts (Bruton, Ahlstrom & Obloj, 2008). Reflecting the energy and enthusiasm of a flourishing field, scholarly interest in entrepreneurial endeavours has not only embraced theories from the core disciplines of economics, psychology as well as sociology (albeit to a lesser extent), it has expanded to related fields (i.e. management studies, strategic management marketing management, finance management and international business) which are also appreciating the contemporary meaning and relevance of entrepreneurial activities (Acs, Braunerhjelm, Audretsch & Carlsson, 2009; Aldrich & Martinez, 2001). As a result, some new academic sub-fields of inquiry have emerged within main the discipline of entrepreneurship (such as corporate entrepreneurship, international entrepreneurship, minority entrepreneurship, social technological entrepreneurship, agricultural entrepreneurship, entrepreneurship and family entrepreneurship) (Brenkert, 2002).

The main issue of concern is that there is no universally accepted code of conduct for entrepreneurs to regulate their activities. In commercial entrepreneurship one is often forced to find out the boundaries of ethical entrepreneurial behaviour. How much profit one can make before one feels like an extortionist? How many people should an entrepreneur email before it becomes spam? Just like doctors, entrepreneurs are faced with difficult questions every day. Maybe an entrepreneurial code of conduct would stop the unethical entrepreneurs from exploiting the people. Things would work differently if young entrepreneurs are introduced to entrepreneurial code of conduct in their formative early stage. The main objective of this paper is to provide a framework for entrepreneurs, policymakers and scholars to appreciate ethical entrepreneurship in the world of business.

Entrepreneurship

Entrepreneurship is the process of designing, launching and running an enterprise offering a product, process or service for sale or hire. This reality is growing, both as a business phenomenon and as a specialized area of study (Werhane, Kelley, Hartman & Moberg, 2009). This development of entrepreneurship into the mainstream of study coincides with an economic need to deal with high unemployment in our environment, but it is also the result of encouragement by our leaders on both sides of the spectrum as well as the increasingly high profile of a new breed of celebrity entrepreneurs, such as Allan sugar, Mark Zuckberg, Oprah Winfrey, Steve Jobs, Billy Gates, and Richard Branson, Jack Ma, Prof. Yunus Mohammed (Ziegler, 2009). Entrepreneurial Typologies, investigating which sorts of business enterprise are the most successful; Business Leaders, asking who the entrepreneurs are and where they come from; and entrepreneurial Culture or Institutions, considering what has the most effect on the abundance and quality of entrepreneurship in any given country (Wood & Lodgson, 2002).

It is also becoming apparent that many theories are emerging specifically from within the research field of entrepreneurship. Some of the theories focus on identifying unique concepts, theories, terminologies and analytical categories that capture what is unique about entrepreneurial phenomena (that is, entrepreneurial heuristics, opportunity discovery, design thinking, effectuation, arbitrage, creative destruction, uncertainty bearing or creative imagination) (Sarasvathy, 2004). Domain-specific studies centre on identifying the multiple variables or inter-related factors that come together in the shaping of entrepreneurial endeavours (i.e. individual-opportunity nexus, multi factorial structure-agency relationships and process models). Sometimes these are examined from the point of view of complexity, hierarchy or systemic models which take account of evolutionary dynamics such as adaptive tension, opportunity tension, degrees of emergence, Campbellian antimonies, dynamic creation and multi-level complexity. In other cases, studies draw attention to the contextualized, dynamic and processual nature of entrepreneurial activity through notions such as effectuation, design thinking, action-interaction nexus, artefact-making, entrepreneurial transformation, idea-opportunity development, entrepreneurial enactment entrepreneurial script duality and entrepreneurial ethics (Sarasvathy, 2001).

Eclectic Theory

According to Verheul, Wennekers, Audretsch and Thurik (2001), Eclectic Theory provides a unified framework for understanding and analysing the indicators of entrepreneurship. They argued that Eclectic Theory of entrepreneurship integrates the different strands from relevant fields into a unifying, coherent framework. Integration of factors shaping the demand for commercial entrepreneurship and those influencing the formation of entrepreneurs are at the centre of the Eclectic Theory. The understanding of the role of entrepreneurial public policy is through identifying those channels shifting either the demand for or the supply of entrepreneurship by policy instruments.

Lopes (2010) stressed that, by utilizing the framework provided by the Eclectic Theory of Entrepreneurship indicated in Figure 1. The policymakers are able to regulate commercial entrepreneurship in a particular country setting at a particular point in time. This will be essential in formulating new public policies to promote ethical commercial entrepreneurship. These types of government intervention correspond with the dotted arrows in Figure 1 and represent the influence of government policy on entrepreneurial activity through the different indicators of entrepreneurship. This study discusses these five types of government intervention and thereby creating better insight into the processes by which the government can have impact on the rate of ethical entrepreneurial activities.

Figure 1: Framework of Indicators of Commercial Entrepreneurship

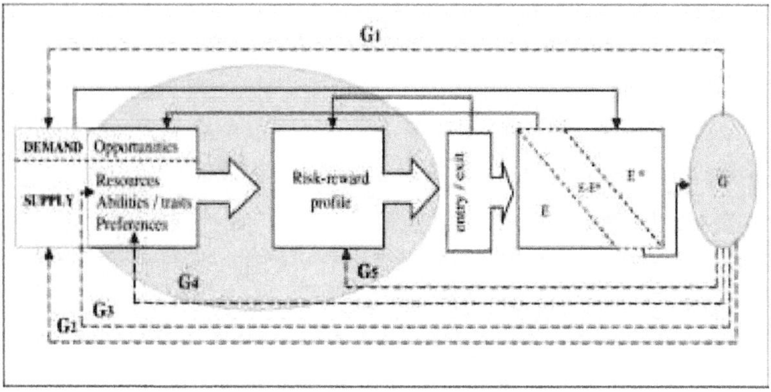

Source: Adopted from Verheul, Wennekers, Audretsch & Thurik (2001)

Based on the model, it is argued that the government is able to influence the rate of ethical entrepreneurship through the five different groups of indicators of entrepreneurship as represented in the framework. For this purpose a distinction is made between five types of policy measures that influence ethical entrepreneurship:

G1 - Government intervention on the demand side of entrepreneurship; influencing the number and type of entrepreneurial opportunities. G2 - Government intervention on the supply side of entrepreneurship; influencing the number and type of potential entrepreneurs. G3 - Government policies aimed at influencing the availability of resources, skills and knowledge of individuals. These policies generally deal with the input factors of entrepreneurship, i.e., labour, finance and information. G4 - Government policies aimed at influencing the preferences, i.e., values and attitudes, of individuals. G5 - Government policies (directly) aimed at the decision-making process of individuals. Given certain opportunities and individual characteristics, this type of government intervention directly influences the risk-reward profile of entrepreneurship (Verheul, Wennekers, Audretsch & Thurik, 2001).

Ethics

Lutz (2017) describes ethics as a body of principles that people use to decide what is right and what is wrong in society. Society gives ideas about the best way to live a human life, even though not many people think much about these ideas. Ethics entails thinking about the best way to live a human life. For example, many people assume, without thinking about it, that the best way to live a human life is to make as much money as possible. But ethics asks whether this is really the best way to live our lives. There is one thing that all human persons, without exception, try to attain happiness. The way to be truly happy is to be ethical. Therefore, ethics may also be defined as the study of how to be truly happy in life. This is not true, because many things that make us feel good do not make us truly happy. Ethics can be addressed to a certain extent by the policy, but it is a high call which goes beyond policy as some ethical issues are not regulated.

Ethics at the Personal Level

People perform actions with the objective of attaining happiness. But you probably want to be successful in business, not for its own sake, but in order to improve your personal financial situation and happiness. Ethical actions are actions that lead to true happiness. Unethical actions are actions that we believe will make us happier, but that will not. For example, earning money by working hard can help us buy the necessities of a good life, and can make us truly happier. Stealing money, on the other hand, does not lead to true happiness. Many people spend their entire lives pursuing happiness in wrong directions, where it cannot be found (Wempe, 2005). Some people attempt to distinguish between ethics and morality. *Morality* relates to a system of principles of right and wrong behaviour that is acceptable in a particular society. Therefore, the only significant difference between the two terms is that "ethics" is a Greek word and "morality" is a Latin word. So, the two terms can be used interchangeably (Werhane, 2000).

Ethical Rules and Regulations

The most common ethical rules and regulations include: tell the truth, do not kill, love your neighbour, be fair to others, and do not pay bribes among many others. The basis of all correct ethical rules is the natural law. The *natural law* is an unwritten moral law that is binding for all members of the human race, regardless of the culture to which they belong. It is different from civil law, which is written by governments and varies from one country to another. The natural law is "natural" for two reasons. First, it is based on human nature and it is a law for everyone who shares in human nature. Since all members of the human race share a common nature, it is a law for all human beings. Second, it is natural because we know it through natural reasoning, apart from divine revelation. One does not need to read holy papers to know the obligations of the natural law (Hannafey, 2003; Surie & Ashley, 2008; Teal & Carroll, 1999; Shane & Venkataraman, 2000; Anderson & Smith, 2007).

Discussion

Eclectic theory of entrepreneurship informs this discussion and was used to illustrate the government role in unified field of ethics to regulate the demand and supply of entrepreneurship in any given country for the common good. Based on the eclectic theory of entrepreneurship, the government is morally obliged to regulate entrepreneurial behaviour over and above everything else. A broad range of indicators explains the level of entrepreneurship, including economic and social factors. Moreover, it is generally accepted that policy measures can influence the level of ethical entrepreneurship. The government can exert influence on entrepreneurship in different ways;

directly through specific measures and indirectly through generic measures.

Indictors of commercial entrepreneurship can be studied from different perspectives, as indicated in the eclectic theory which is framework explaining the role of the government in ethical entrepreneurship. The government institutes different disciplinary approaches, levels of analysis, a distinction between the demand and supply side and a distinction between the actual and "equilibrium" level of entrepreneurship. The framework refers to both the decisions of individuals to start up an enterprise and the decisions of owner manager to remain in business or to quit.

Type 1: Enterprise Enablers

"Type 1" government intervention, as represented by arrow "G1" in Figure 1, involves government intervention on the demand side of entrepreneurship. This is the government intervention that (in)-directly impacts the type, number and accessibility of entrepreneurial opportunities. Some of these policies help to create demand for entrepreneurship whereas others enable small enterprises to make use of the room that is created by market demand. Policies stimulating technological developments and income policy belong to the first category of policies, whereas competition policy and establishment legislation pertain to the latter category of policies.

Technological advancements create opportunities for entrepreneurial ventures through new ideas or new application processes. These advancements can be stimulated by the government through (subsidizing) expenditures on R&D. Income policy can create opportunities for entrepreneurship through higher wealth or income disparity, inducing demand for tailor-made products and services and thereby stimulating demand for entrepreneurship. Competition policy improves the accessibility of markets through reducing market power of large enterprises and lowering barriers to entry for small businesses. Moreover, establishment legislation tends to negatively influence the access to markets, through the implementation of business licensing requirements.

When comparing the elements of "type 1" intervention with traditional perspectives on government intervention as distinguished in the previous section, there is little similarity. Income policy is generic, focusing on all households within the economy, whereas other policies, in particular R&D subsidies, are more specific. However, competition policy and establishment legislation can both be related to deregulation and simplification, influencing the access to the market.

Type 2: Population Policies

"Type 2" government intervention, as represented by arrow "G2" in Figure 1, involves government intervention to affect the pool or supply of potential entrepreneurs at the aggregate level. These policies can take the form of influencing the characteristics or the number of people within the population. Policies that pertain to "type 2" intervention include immigration policy and regional development policy (dealing with (sub)- urbanization processes), influencing the composition and the dispersion of the population, respectively. Moreover, the fiscal treatment of families with children, including family allowances, may influence the age composition of the population, rural development policies, and immigration policies.

Type 3: Predisposing Factors

"Type 3" government intervention, as represented by arrow "G3" in Figure 1, impacts the availability of resources, skills and knowledge of potential entrepreneurs. Resources, skills and knowledge are all internal individual characteristics that can be acquired or further developed through training or education. Inborn characteristics, such as learning capacity and personality traits, are far less likely, if not impossible, to be developed through education and training. Government policy will have to focus on, for instance, overcoming the finance and knowledge gap through increasing the availability of financial and informational resources, respectively. For example, policies aimed at the (development of the) venture capital market can help improving the access of (small) business owners to financial capital needed to start or expand a business.

Direct financial support, i.e., subsidies, grants and loan guarantees, can also increase the availability of resources of (potential) entrepreneurs. The knowledge base, consisting of both skills and knowledge, of the (potential) entrepreneur can be influenced through the direct provision of relevant 'business' information, i.e., advice and counselling, or through the educational system. "Type 3" policies can be typified as input-related policies, since they refer to both material, i.e., financial capital, and immaterial, i.e., knowledge, inputs in the entrepreneurial process.

Type 4: Role Models

"Type 4" government intervention, as represented by arrow "G4" in Figure 1, works through the preferences of individuals to become an entrepreneur. Preferences of people, as expressed through values and attitudes, are developed during upbringing. Although preferences are culturally determined, the government can play a role, albeit small, in shaping entrepreneurial values and attitudes by introducing entrepreneurial elements in the educational system and by paying attention to entrepreneurship in the media. "Type 4" policies are characterized by the assumed broadness of the concept of government policy, including the educational system and overlapping, to some extent, with culture. The relationships between culture, institutions and entrepreneurship are the subject of the next section.

Type 5: Legal-Political Factors

"Type 5" government intervention, as represented by arrow "G5" in Figure 1, is directed at the decision-making process of individuals, i.e., potential entrepreneurs. Given opportunities, resources, ability, personality traits and preferences, the risk-reward profile of entrepreneurship can be influenced by this type of government intervention. Policies that are relevant in this respect, are taxation, influencing business earnings, social security arrangements, influencing the willingness of people to give up their present state of (un)employment to become an entrepreneur, and labour market legislation regarding hiring and firing, thereby determining the flexibility of the business and the attractiveness to start or continue a business. Bankruptcy policy can also influence the risk-reward profile. For example, when legal consequences of bankruptcy are severe, this may lead people to shy away from self-employment. Note that "type 5" policies are generic macro-economic policies, as they apply to all economic actors.

Type 6: Unified Field of Ethics

Eclectic theory illustrates that the government operates in a universal field of ethics. The policies are informed above everything else by ethics. We can say that ethics is the prime mover of policies to regulate the commercial entrepreneurship. The government has moral obligation above, anything else to ensure ethical entrepreneurship place takes at individual, organizational/institutional, national, international levels. The government is morally obliged to provide an enabling environment for ethical commercial entrepreneurship to take place.

Social Responsibility of Individuals and Enterprises

Social responsibility is a concept based on ethical theory, in which individuals are responsible for fulfilling their civic duty; the actions of an individual must benefit the whole of society. In this way, there must be a balance between social-economic growth and the welfare of society. If this equilibrium is maintained, then social responsibility is accomplished. The theory of social responsibility is built on a system of ethics, in which decisions and actions must be ethically validated before proceeding. If the action or decision causes harm to society or the environment then it would be considered to be socially irresponsible and unethical.

Moral values that are inherent in society create a distinction between right and wrong. In this way, social fairness is generally believed to be in the "right", but more frequently than not this "fairness" is absent. Every individual has a responsibility to act in manner that is beneficial to society and not solely for him/her. The theory of social responsibility and ethics applies to both individual and groups. It should be incorporated into daily actions/decisions, particularly ones that will have an effect on other persons and/or the environment. In the larger, group capacity, a code of social responsibility and ethics is applied within said group as well as during interactions with another group or an individual.

Businesses have developed a system of social responsibility that is tailored to their business environment. If social responsibility is maintained within an enterprise than the employees and the environment are held equal to the enterprise's economics. Maintaining social responsibility within a enterprise ensures the integrity of society and the environment are protected. Often, the ethical implications of a decision/action are overlooked for personal gain and the benefits are usually material. This frequently manifests itself in enterprises that attempt to compromise environmental regulations. When this happens, government interference is necessary as she has the moral obligation to protect the public from harm.

Conclusion

It can be established that ethical commercial entrepreneurship leads to economic growth, wealth creation, job creation, human dignity, sustainable development and international competitiveness. Furthermore, the study acknowledges that being an ethical entrepreneur not only requires a creative idea and a superior work ethic, but it is also manifested in practice of morality, corporate social responsibility, ethical business, and running business in a way that minimizes harm to people and the general environment. The level of ethical entrepreneurship differs considerably across countries and periods. Ethical entrepreneurship is a multidimensional concept, the definition of which depends largely on the focus of the research undertaken. This study deals with the factors determining the level of ethical entrepreneurship. A broad range of indicators explains the level of ethical entrepreneurship, including economic and social factors. Moreover, it is generally accepted that policy measures can influence the level of ethical entrepreneurship. The government can exert influence on ethical entrepreneurship in different ways; directly through specific measures and indirectly through generic measures. For example, when stipulating a competition policy, the government can influence the market structure and (indirectly) the number and type of entrepreneurial opportunities.

The goal of this paper is threefold. *First*, it attempts to integrate different perspectives of the indicators of ethical entrepreneurship. *Second*, an extensive description of the role of government is provided in an endeavour to answer the question of how policy measures may influence ethical entrepreneurship. *Third*, our model may serve as means for explaining temporal en cross-sectional differences in the rate of ethical entrepreneurship. The paper is motivated by the recent increase in corruption plus in many modern economies, by the considerable occurrences of malpractice across countries and the importance of ethical entrepreneurship for growth.

The level of ethical entrepreneurship in a particular country can be explained making a distinction between the supply side (labour market perspective) and the demand side (product market perspective; carrying capacity of the market) of ethical entrepreneurship. This distinction is sometimes referred to as that between push and pull factors of entrepreneurship. The indicators of ethical entrepreneurship can be studied according to micro, medium and macro level of ethical entrepreneurship. Studies at the micro level focus on the decision-making process by individuals and the motives of people to become self-employed. Research into the decisions of individuals to become either wage or entrepreneurs focuses primarily on personal factors, such as psychological traits, role models, formal education and other skills, financial assets, family background and previous work experience. Studies at the medium level of ethical entrepreneurship often focus on market-specific indicators of ethical entrepreneurship, such as profit opportunities and opportunities for entry and exit. The macro perspective focuses on a range of environmental factors, such as technological, geographical, economic and cultural variables as well as government regulation.

This paper has tried to build on the positive challenges of ethical entrepreneurship research by drawing on the rich traditions and findings spanning a broad spectrum of academic disciplines to develop an integrated eclectic theory of ethical entrepreneurship. This eclectic theory incorporates multi-level units of analysis – micro (individuals) as well as macro (countries). In addition, it draws on the perspectives and traditions of a number of disciplines, including sociology, management, psychology, social science, and economics. The improved eclectic theory provide a unified field of ethics as part of conceptual framework for analysing both the indicators of ethical entrepreneurship as well as the consequences or impact of commercial entrepreneurship across a broad array of industry, national, spatial and temporal settings. The improved eclectic ethical entrepreneurship theory can serve as a link across the broad array of academic disciplines, reflecting the rich diversity of settings in which ethical entrepreneurship takes place.

Recommendation

This paper proposes an Entrepreneurship Code of Conduct to give a sense of directions to the call of ethical commercial entrepreneurship by the public and governments in the world of business. The Entrepreneurs Oath suggested by this paper is a replica of Hippocratic Oath of medical doctors rewrote to fit ethical commercial entrepreneurship.

Every commercial entrepreneur should promise to fulfil, to the best of his/her ability and judgment, this covenant that they should:

- Give value for money
- Respect the creative and innovation of those entrepreneurs in whose steps you follow, and gladly share such business knowledge with others.
- Apply, all means required in my business for the benefit of my customers, shareholders and partners.
- Avoid excessive self enrichment by all means
- Acknowledge that there is art to entrepreneurial activities as well as science, and that warmth, sympathy, and understanding may outweigh the entrepreneurial skills and experience
- Not be ashamed to say "I know not," nor will I fail to call in my colleagues when the entrepreneurial skills of another are needed for project success.
- Respect the privacy of my customers, partners and shareholders, for their information is not to be disclosed to the world. Most especially must I tread with care in matters of profit and loss? If

it is given me to make profit, all thanks. But it may also be within my power to lose my shareholders money; this awesome responsibility must be faced with great humility and awareness of my own weakness. Above all, I must not play at God.

- Acknowledge that he/she does not serve an anonymous person, but a human being, whose needs may affect the person's family, business and economic stability. My responsibility includes these related problems, if I am to care adequately for the customer and everybody affected by my actions as an entrepreneur.
- Prevent problems caused by my business whenever I can, for the social impact of my enterprise is as important as its goal of turning a profit.
- Acknowledge that he/she and his/her business remain a member of society, with special obligations to all my fellow human beings, those sound of mind and body, rich and poor, ignorant and knowledgeable, men and women, weak and strong, young and old etc.
- If the entrepreneur does not violate this oath, may he/she enjoy long life, friendship, revenues and respected while he/she lives and be remembered with affection thereafter. May he/she always act so as to preserve the finest traditions of his/her calling and may he/she long experience the joy of serving those who seek to acquire his/her products, services or enterprise.

References

Ackoff, R. L. 1987. Business Ethics and the Entrepreneur. Journal of Business Venturing, 2: 185-191.

Acs, Z. J., Braunerhjelm, P., Audretsch, D. B., & Carlsson, B. 2009. The Knowledge Spillover Theory of

Entrepreneurship. Small Business Economics, 32(1): 15-30.

Aldrich, H., & Martinez, M. 2001. Many Are Called, but Few Are Chosen: An Evolutionary Perspective for the Study of Entrepreneurship. Entrepreneurship Theory and Practice, 25(4): 41-56.

Anderson, A. R., & Smith, R. 2007. The Moral Space in Entrepreneurship: An Exploration of Ethical Imperatives and The Moral Legitimacy of Being Enterprising. Entrepreneurship and Regional Development, 19(6): 479-497.

Anokhin, S., & Schulze, W. S. 2009. Entrepreneurship, Innovation, and Corruption. Journal of Business Venturing, in press (in press): tbd.

Brenkert, G. 2002. Entrepreneurship, Ethics, and the Good Society. The Ruffin Series, 3: 5-43. Brenkert, G. 2009. Innovation, Rule Breaking and the Ethics of Entrepreneurship. Journal of Business Venturing, in press(in press): tbd.

Bruton, G. D., Ahlstrom, D., & Obloj, K. 2008. Entrepreneurship in Emerging Economies: Where We Are Today and Where Should the Research Go in the Future. Entrepreneurship Theory and Practice, 32(1): 1-14.

Lopes, T. S. (2010). The Entrepreneur, Ownership Advantages and the Eclectic Paradigm, Multinational Business Review, 18(2), 71 – 88.

Lutz, D. (2017). Business Ethics in Ntale, F. J. (ed.) Small Business Management Training Manual. Lap Lambert, Germany.

Sarasvathy, S. 2001. Causation and Effectuation: Toward a Theoretical Shift from Economic Inevitablility to Entrepreneurial Contingency. Academy of Management Review, 26(2): 243-263.

Sarasvathy, S. 2004. Making It Happen: Beyond Theories of the Enterprise to Theories of Enterprise Design. Entrepreneurship Theory and Practice, 28(6): 519-531.

Shane, S., & Venkataraman, S. 2000. The Promise of Entrepreneurship as a Field of Research. Academy of Management Review, 25(1): 217-226.

Surie, G., & Ashley, A. 2008. Integrating Pragmatism and Ethics in Entrepreneurial Leadership for Sustainable Value Creation. Journal of Business Ethics, 81(1): 235-246.

Teal, E. J., & Carroll, A. B. 1999. Moral Reasoning Skills: Are Entrepreneurs Different? Journal of Business Ethics, 19: 229-240.

Verheul, I., Wennekers, S., Audretsch, D. & Thurik, R. (2001). An eclectic theory of entrepreneurship: policies, institutions and culture. Discussion Paper, Tinbergen Institute

Wempe, J. 2005. Ethical Entrepreneurship and Fair Trade. Journal of Business Ethics, 60(3): 211-220.

Werhane, P. H. 2000. Business Ethics and the Origins of Contemporary Capitalism: Economics and Ethics in the Works of Adam Smith. Journal of Business Ethics, 24(3): 185-198.

Werhane, P. H., Kelley, S. P., Hartman, L., & Moberg, D. J. (2009). Alleviating Poverty through Profitable Partnerships: Globalization, Markets, and Economic Well-Being. London: Routledge.

Wood, D. J., & Lodgson, J. M. (2002). Business Citizenship: From Individuals to Organizations. The Ruffin Series, 3: 59-94.

Ziegler, R. (2009). An Introduction to Social Entrepreneurship: Voices, Preconditions, Contexts. Cheltenham, U.K.: Edward Elgar

CONTRIBUTORS

Catacutan, Maria Rosario holds an undergraduate degree in Accountancy from the University of the Philippines, a Master's degree in Corporate Governance from the University of Navarre, Spain, and a PhD in Education from the Pontifical University of Santo Tomas, Manila Philippines. She is a senior lecturer in Business Ethics at Strathmore University, Kenya. Her research interests are in the areas of accounting ethics, business ethics education, and corporate social responsibility.

Haaz, Ignace is the Publications Manager at Globethics.net and the Online Ethics Library Programme Executive. Ignace was awarded a Doctorate of Letters from the University of Geneva and taught ethics and political philosophy at the University of Fribourg's Philosophy Department. He did a five years habilitation research focusing on applied ethics. His latest work can be downloaded for free on: https://repository.globethics.net/p/author/Haaz_Ignace

Ike, Obiora is the Executive Director of Globethics.net, but he is also a human rights activist, development practitioner, public speaker, author, teacher, and pastor across continents. Dr Ike studied in Nigeria, Austria, Germany, France and UK, and holds degrees in philosophy, theology, economics, journalism and political science, gaining his doctorate in Bonn, Germany, with a specialisation in Christian Social Principles in 1986. He founded a number of development organisations in Nigeria, including the Catholic Institute for Development Justice Peace and Caritas (CIDJAP) and the Umuchinemere Procredit Microfinance Bank. His author page on Globethics.net Library: https://repository.globethics.net/p/author/Obiora_Ike

Isaboke, Crispin Ong'era is currently a member of Academic Staff at Chuka University, Kenya, where he teaches Philosophy. He holds an M.A. and a B.A. in Philosophy from The Catholic University of Eastern Africa (Nairobi) where he is pursuing his Ph.D in Moral Philosophy (Ethics). Earlier on, he studied Philosophy and Religious Studies at the Spiritan Missionary Seminary, Arusha.

Katundano, Theonestina Senior Lecturer of Educational Administration, Catholic University of Eastern Africa

*Kemboi, Benjamin O.*is Library Assistant, Technical University of Kenya. His contribution to this book was presented at the Globethics.net East African Interdisciplinary workshop in May 2016, at the Catholic University of Eastern Africa.

Kibugi, Sarah W. is Director of the Library and Learning Resources service at the Technical University of Kenya. Her contribution to this book was presented at the Globethics.net East African Interdisciplinary workshop in May 2016, at the Catholic University of Eastern Africa.

Lilian, Linda has recently concluded her PhD in Philosophy and holds a Masters Degree in Ethics and Public Management from Makerere University. She has worked as a Lecturer, Mentor, Researcher and Communication Specialist in her career. She currently works with the Uganda Industrial Research Institute, a government parastatal whose mandate is to promote industry in Uganda. She is also the representative for Uganda on the Globethics.net East Africa Board.

Litondo, Kate Oyiela. Associate Professor at the Department of Management Science University of Nairobi, School of Business. Chair Department of Management Science. ICT Coordinator Department of Management Science.

Majawa, Clement is part of the Steering Committee for Research, Conferences and Publication for Dogmatic and Spiritual Theology at the Catholic University of Eastern Af rica.

Makinda, Herbert is currently the Programme Executive, Globethics.net East Africa Programme. He holds a Master of Education degree in Educational Research and Evaluation and is also a PhD candidate in the same field.

Mbae, Justus is the immediate former Vice Chancellor of The Catholic University of Eastern Africa where he served as Deputy Vice Chancellor, Academics Affairs and Director of the Institute for Regional Integration and Development (IRID). Prof. Mbae also worked in the U.S. Embassy, Department of State, and Cultural Affairs Section as the Cultural Affairs Specialist from 1993 to 2009. Prior to that Prof. Mbae worked in Kenyatta University as a Lecturer, Senior Lecturer and Head of Department-Department of Educational Foundations from 1982 to 1993.

Msafiri, Aidan G. is Globethics.net. East Africa (Tanzania) Advisory Board Member and Lecturer at St. Augustine University of Tanzania.

*Nganga, Francis G.*is Assistant Counselor in the Student Support Services department at the the Technical University of Kenya.His contribution to this book was presented at the Globethics.net East African Interdisciplinary workshop in May 2016, at the Catholic University of Eastern Africa.

Njihia, Rose Wambui graduated with a PhD in Educational Planning and Administration from the The Catholic University of Eastern Africa. She rendered service as an assistant director in an Australian charity foundation known as Women for Women Africa based in Nairobi 2013 to 2016 and as an Adjunct Lecturer between 2016 and 2017 at Moi University. She currently teaches at the Catholic University of Eastern Africa her Alma Mater.

Ntale, Joseph F. Senior Lecturer Business and Administration, The Catholic University of Eastern Africa. Initiator of a business incubation center for the Catholic University of Eastern Africa.

Nwankwo, Samuel C. Department of Theology at Wesley University, Ondo, Nigeria.

Oketch, Selline is a Senior lecturer in the Department of Languages, Literature and Communication at the Catholic University of Eastern Africa, Kenya, where she teaches Literature. She holds a doctorate from Nelson Mandela University, Port Elizabeth, South Africa. Dr. Oketch's main research interest is in gender issues in African literature, focusing specifically on the juxtaposition of context and fictional characters. Her current research explores literary possibilities that allow each gender to affirm the other's humanity. Her publications are in the areas of Literature and Gender, Literature and Ethics, Gender and Indigenous Knowledge, as well as the Teaching of English and Literature in the Kenyan secondary school curriculum.

Ogbuehi, Mary Rose-Claret is a Lecturer at the Department of Foreign Languages and Literary Studies, Faculty of Arts, University of Nigeria. Founder and Facilitator for Women Empowerment Through Education, a leading Human Development NGO, she is a member of the Immaculate Heart Congregation with

Mother House at Onitsha and currently conducting a Fellowship and Research Program at the University of Bonn, Germany.

Okutu, Aggrey Asitiba Lecturer of Educational Administration and Planning, Kisii University - Kenya

Omukaga, Jude Likori Rev. Dr., is a priest of the Catholic Diocese of Bungoma, Kenya. He holds a PhD in theological ethics from the Katholieke Universiteit Leuven, Belgium. Among other duties, he serves as an external examiner in the Centre for Social Justice and Ethics as well as the Faculty of Moral Theology, in the Catholic University of Eastern Africa, Nairobi.

Onyia, Chidiebere is Senior Advisor, Globethics.net Geneva and CEO of OrgLearning Consult and a member of the Governing Council at Chrisland University, Nigeria. Additionally, he served as visiting professor at the University of Nigeria

Permata, Alviani is currently a faculty member of the Humanities Department of Duta Wacana Christian University in Yogyakarta, Indonesia. Her background is Linguistic and Anthropology. She teaches Civics and some other subjects in Humanity fields.

Globethics.net Publications

The list below is only a selection of our publications. To view the full collection, please visit our website.

All products are provided free of charge and can be downloaded in PDF form from the Globethics.net library and at www.globethics.net/publications. Bulk print copies can be ordered from *publictions@globethics.net* at special rates for those from the Global South.
Paid products not provided free of charge are indicated*.
The Editor of the different Series of Globethics.net Publications is Prof. Dr Obiora Ike, Executive Director of Globethics.net in Geneva and Professor of Ethics at the Godfrey Okoye University Enugu/Nigeria.

Contact for manuscripts and suggestions: *publications@globethics.net*

Global Series

Christoph Stückelberger / Jesse N.K. Mugambi (eds.), *Responsible Leadership. Global and Contextual Perspectives*, 2007, 376pp. ISBN: 978–2–8254–1516–0

Heidi Hadsell / Christoph Stückelberger (eds.), *Overcoming Fundamentalism. Ethical Responses from Five Continents*, 2009, 212pp.
ISBN: 978–2–940428–00–7

Christoph Stückelberger / Reinhold Bernhardt (eds.): *Calvin Global. How Faith Influences Societies*, 2009, 258pp. ISBN: 978–2–940428–05–2.

Ariane Hentsch Cisneros / Shanta Premawardhana (eds.), *Sharing Values. A Hermeneutics for Global Ethics*, 2010, 418pp.
ISBN: 978–2–940428–25–0.

Deon Rossouw / Christoph Stückelberger (eds.), *Global Survey of Business Ethics in Training, Teaching and Research*, 2012, 404pp.
ISBN: 978–2–940428–39–7

Carol Cosgrove Sacks/ Paul H. Dembinski (eds.), *Trust and Ethics in Finance. Innovative Ideas from the Robin Cosgrove Prize*, 2012, 380pp.
ISBN: 978–2–940428–41–0

Jean-Claude Bastos de Morais / Christoph Stückelberger (eds.), *Innovation Ethics. African and Global Perspectives*, 2014, 233pp.
ISBN: 978–2–88931–003–6

Nicolae Irina / Christoph Stückelberger (eds.), *Mining, Ethics and Sustainability*, 2014, 198pp. ISBN: 978–2–88931–020–3

Philip Lee and Dafne Sabanes Plou (eds), *More or Less Equal: How Digital Platforms Can Help Advance Communication Rights*, 2014, 158pp. ISBN 978–2–88931–009–8

Sanjoy Mukherjee and Christoph Stückelberger (eds.) *Sustainability Ethics. Ecology, Economy, Ethics. International Conference SusCon III, Shillong/India*, 2015, 353pp. ISBN: 978–2–88931–068–5

Amélie Vallotton Preisig / Hermann Rösch / Christoph Stückelberger (eds.) *Ethical Dilemmas in the Information Society. Codes of Ethics for Librarians and Archivists*, 2014, 224pp. ISBN: 978–288931–024–1.

Prospects and Challenges for the Ecumenical Movement in the 21st Century. Insights from the Global Ecumenical Theological Institute, David Field / Jutta Koslowski, 256pp. 2016, ISBN: 978–2–88931–097–5

Christoph Stückelberger, Walter Fust, Obiora Ike (eds.), *Global Ethics for Leadership. Values and Virtues for Life,* 2016, 444pp. ISBN: 978–2–88931–123–1

Dietrich Werner / Elisabeth Jeglitzka (eds.), *Eco-Theology, Climate Justice and Food Security: Theological Education and Christian Leadership Development*, 316pp. 2016, ISBN 978–2–88931–145–3

Obiora Ike, Andrea Grieder and Ignace Haaz (Eds.), *Poetry and Ethics: Inventing Possibilities in Which We Are Moved to Action and How We Live Together*, 271pp. 2018, ISBN 978–2–88931–242–9

Christoph Stückelberger / Pavan Duggal (Eds.), *Cyber Ethics 4.0: Serving Humanity with Values*, 503pp. 2018, ISBN 978–2–88931–264-1

Texts Series

Principles on Sharing Values across Cultures and Religions, 2012, 20pp. Available in English, French, Spanish, German and Chinese. Other languages in preparation. ISBN: 978–2–940428–09–0

Ethics in Politics. Why it Matters More than Ever and How it Can Make a Difference. A Declaration, 8pp, 2012. Available in English and French. ISBN: 978–2–940428–35–9

Religions for Climate Justice: International Interfaith Statements 2008–2014, 2014, 45pp. Available in English. ISBN 978–2–88931–006–7

Ethics in the Information Society: The Nine 'P's. A Discussion Paper for the WSIS+10 Process 2013–2015, 2013, 32pp. ISBN: 978–2–940428–063–2

Principles on Equality and Inequality for a Sustainable Economy. Endorsed by the Global Ethics Forum 2014 with Results from Ben Africa Conference 2014, 2015, 41pp. ISBN: 978–2–88931–025–8

Water Ethics: Principles and Guidelines, 2019, 41pp. ISBN 978–2–88931-313-6, available in three languages.

Praxis Series

Christoph Stückelberger, *Responsible Leadership Handbook : For Staff and Boards*, 2014, 116pp. ISBN :978-2-88931-019-7 (Available in Russian)

Christoph Stückelberger, *Weg-Zeichen: 100 Denkanstösse für Ethik im Alltag*, 2013, 100pp SBN: 978-2-940428-77-9

—, *Way-Markers: 100 Reflections Exploring Ethics in Everyday Life*, 2014, 100pp. ISBN 978-2-940428-74-0

Angèle Kolouchè Biao, Aurélien Atidegla (éds.,) *Proverbes du Bénin. Sagesse éthique appliquée de proverbes africains*, 2015, 132pp. ISBN 978-2-88931-068-5

Nina Mariani Noor (ed.) *Manual Etika Lintas Agama Untuk Indonesia*, 2015, 93pp. ISBN 978-2-940428-84-7

Christoph Stückelberger, *Weg-Zeichen II: 111 Denkanstösse für Ethik im Alltag*, 2016, 111pp. ISBN: 978-2-88931-147-7 (Available in German and English)

Elly K. Kansiime, *In the Shadows of Truth: The Polarized Family*, 2017, 172pp. ISBN 978-2-88931-203-0

Christopher Byaruhanga, *Essential Approaches to Christian Religious Education: Learning and Teaching in Uganda*, 2018, 286pp. ISBN: 978-2-88931-235-1

Christoph Stückelberger / William Otiende Ogara / Bright Mawudor, *African Church Assets Handbook*, 2018, 291pp. ISBN: 978-2-88931-252-8

Oscar Brenifier, *Day After Day 365 Aphorisms*, 2019, 395pp. ISBN 978-2-88931-272-6

Christoph Stückelberger, *365 Way-Markers*, 2019, 416pp. ISBN: 978-2-88931-282-5 (available in English and German).

Benoît Girardin / Evelyne Fiechter-Widemann (Eds.), *Blue Ethics: Ethical Perspectives on Sustainable, Fair Water Resources Use and Management*, forthcoming 2019, 265pp. ISBN 978-2-88931-308-2

Theses Series

Kitoka Moke Mutondo, *Église, protection des droits de l'homme et refondation de l'État en République Démocratique du Congo*, 2012, 412pp. ISBN: 978–2–940428–31–1

Ange Sankieme Lusanga, *Éthique de la migration. La valeur de la justice comme base pour une migration dans l'Union Européenne et la Suisse*, 2012, 358pp. ISBN: 978–2–940428–49–6

Kahwa Njojo, *Éthique de la non-violence*, 2013, 596pp. ISBN: 978–2–940428–61–8

Carlos Alberto Sintado, *Social Ecology, Ecojustice and the New Testament: Liberating Readings*, 2015, 379pp. ISBN: 978-2–940428–99–1

Symphorien Ntibagirirwa, *Philosophical Premises for African Economic Development: Sen's Capability Approach*, 2014, 384pp. ISBN: 978–2–88931–001–2

Jude Likori Omukaga, *Right to Food Ethics: Theological Approaches of Asbjørn Eide*, 2015, 609pp. ISBN: 978–2–88931–047–0

Jörg F. W. Bürgi, *Improving Sustainable Performance of SME's, The Dynamic Interplay of Morality and Management Systems*, 2014, 528pp. ISBN: 978–2–88931–015–9

Jun Yan, *Local Culture and Early Parenting in China: A Case Study on Chinese Christian Mothers' Childrearing Experiences,* 2015, 190pp. ISBN 978–2–88931–065–4

Frédéric-Paul Piguet, *Justice climatique et interdiction de nuire*, 2014, 559 pp. ISBN 978–2–88931–005–0

Mulolwa Kashindi, *Appellations johanniques de Jésus dans l'Apocalypse: une lecture Bafuliiru des titres christologiques*, 2015, 577pp. ISBN 978–2–88931–040–1

Naupess K. Kibiswa, *Ethnonationalism and Conflict Resolution: The Armed Group Bany2 in DR Congo.* 2015, 528pp. ISBN: 978–2–88931–032–6

Kilongo Fatuma Ngongo, *Les héroïnes sans couronne. Leadership des femmes dans les Églises de Pentecôte en Afrique Centrale,* 2015, 489pp. ISBN 978–2–88931–038–8

Bosela E. Eale, *Justice and Poverty as Challenges for Churches: with a Case Study of the Democratic Republic of Congo*, 2015, 335pp, ISBN: 978–2–88931–078–4

Andrea Grieder, *Collines des mille souvenirs. Vivre* après *et* avec *le génocide perpétré contre les Tutsi du Rwanda,* 2016, 403pp. ISBN 978–2–88931–101–9

Monica Emmanuel, *Federalism in Nigeria: Between Divisions in Conflict and Stability in Diversity*, 2016, 522pp. ISBN: 978–2–88931–106–4

John Kasuku, *Intelligence Reform in the Post-Dictatorial Democratic Republic of Congo*, 2016, 355pp. ISBN 978–2–88931–121–7

Fifamè Fidèle Houssou Gandonour, *Les fondements éthiques du féminisme. Réflexions à partir du contexte africain*, 2016, 430pp. ISBN 978–2–88931–138–5

Nicoleta Acatrinei, *Work Motivation and Pro-Social Behaviour in the Delivery of Public Services Theoretical and Empirical Insights*, 2016, 387pp. ISBN 978–2–88931–150–7

Timothee B. Mushagalusa, *John of Damascus and Heresy. A Basis for Understanding Modern Heresy*, 2017, 556pp. ISBN: 978-2-88931-205-4

Nina, Mariani Noor, *Ahmadi Women Resisting Fundamentalist Persecution. A Case Study on Active Group Resistance in Indonesia*, 2018, 221pp. ISBN: 978-2-88931-222-1

Ernest Obodo, Christian *Education in Nigeria and Ethical Challenges. Context of Enugu Diocese*, 2018, 612pp. ISBN: 978-2-88931-256-6

Fransiska Widyawati, *Catholics in Manggarai, Flores, Eastern Indonesia,* 2018, 284pp. ISBN: 978-2-88931-268-9

A. Halil Thahir, *Ijtihād Maqāṣidi: The Interconnected Maṣlaḥah-Based Reconstruction of Islamic Laws,* 2019, 200pp. ISBN 978-2-88931-220-7*10*

Tibor Héjj, *Human Dignity in Managing Employees. A performative approach, based on the Catholic Social Teaching (CST),* 2019, 320pp. ISBN: 978-2-88931-280-1

Sabina Kavutha Mutisya, *The Experience of Being a Divorced or Separated Single Mother: A Phenomenological Study,* 2019, 168pp. ISBN: 978-2-88931-274-0

Florence Muia, *Sustainable Peacebuilding Strategies. Sustainable Peacebuilding Operations in Nakuru County, Kenya: Contribution to the Catholic Justice and Peace Commission (CJPC),* 2020, 195pp. ISBN: 978-2-88931-331-0

Mary Rose-Claret Ogbuehi, *The Struggle for Women Empowerment Through Education,* 2020, 410pp. ISBN: 978-2-88931-363-1

Education Ethics Series

Divya Singh / Christoph Stückelberger (Eds.), *Ethics in Higher Education Values-driven Leaders for the Future,* 2017, 367pp. ISBN: 978–2–88931–165–1

Obiora Ike / Chidiebere Onyia (Eds.) *Ethics in Higher Education, Foundation for Sustainable Development*, 2018, 645pp. IBSN: 978-2-88931-217-7

Obiora Ike / Chidiebere Onyia (Eds.) *Ethics in Higher Education, Religions and Traditions in Nigeria* 2018, 198pp. IBSN: 978-2-88931-219-1

Obiora F. Ike, Justus Mbae, Chidiebere Onyia (Eds.), *Mainstreaming Ethics in Higher Education: Research Ethics in Administration, Finance, Education, Environment and Law Vol. 1*, 2019, 779pp. ISBN 978-2-88931-300-6

Ikechukwu J. Ani/Obiora F. Ike (Eds.), *Higher Education in Crisis Sustaining Quality Assurance and Innovation in Research through Applied Ethics*, 2019, 214pp. ISBN 978-2-88931-323-5

Ethical Sieve Series

Paul Dembinski, Josina Kamerling and Virgile Perret (Eds.), *Changing Frontiers of Ethics in Finance*, 2019, 511pp. ISBN 978-2-88931-317-4

This is only selection of our latest publications, to view our full collection please visit:

www.globethics.net/publications

Printed by Amazon Italia Logistica S.r.l.
Torrazza Piemonte (TO), Italy

37686100R00238